The life and rhymes of

KEVIN BLOODY WILSON

DILLIGAF

Kevin Bloody Wilson and Gavin Miller

ALLEN&UNWIN

First published in Australia in 2010

Allen & Unwin
83 Alexander Street
Crows Nest NSW 2065
Australia
Phone: (61 2) 8425 0100
Fax: (61 2) 9906 2218
Email: info@allenandunwin.com
Web: www.allenandunwin.com

Cataloguing-in-Publication details are available from the National Library of Australia
www.trove.nla.gov.au

ISBN 978 1 74237 520 5

Typeset in 11.5/15.5 pt Sabon by Midland Typesetters, Australia
Printed and bound in Australia by Griffin Press

10 9 8 7 6 5 4 3 2 1

MIX
Paper from
responsible sources
FSC
www.fsc.org   FSC® C009448

The paper in this book is FSC certified. FSC promotes environmentally responsible, socially beneficial and economically viable management of the world's forests.

Contents

Foreword   vii

Introduction   xi

1   Let's call him . . . Kev!   1
2   Let the music begin   10
3   Discovering Australia   21
4   Kalgoorlie gold   32
5   When Kevvy met Betty   41
6   This song is suitable for miners   53
7   Radio days   68
8   Mr Dennis the music teacher   79
9   Your average Australian yobbo   89
10   Cock on the block   99
11   The boardroom barndance   116
12   Kev's back   127
13   How lucky can you get?   149
14   Ground zero   156
15   Long service leave   169
16   What happens on the road   180
17   Buddy Holly Airlines   190
18   And the show goes on   201
19   Takin' it to the world   211
20   What Kev does GAF about   216
21   The kid in Kev   230
22   Disgraceland   248

23   Ups and downs and demons   259
24   Mates and fans   273

Kev's discography   293
Jenny Talia's discography   305

Foreword

I remember once reading that 'Anyone with half a brain can write a book . . . and most do.' Given this, I figure that if *two* people, each with half a brain, hooked up, perhaps they could come up with a book that would be a *half-pie* decent read.

This presented me with my first challenge in what was going to be my (hopefully short) quest to become a Whurlitzer Prize winner . . . Whoops, make that *Pulitzer* Prize and add another challenge, *fuckin' research*!

For years my mates have been urging me to write a book. In much the same way, back in 1984 they were responsible for nudging me into the recording studio to put together my first collection of self-penned songs on a cassette album called *Your Average Australian Yobbo*. The songs on this recording were no more than stories about these very same mates of mine, and about situations that either they or myself had been involved in. To put it simply, I was writing songs for my mates, about my mates.

In over twenty-five years of songwriting this has not changed one bit: I continue to write songs for and about my mates. So then, which one of these mates with half a brain could I call on to help me with my bloody book? For that matter, who else did I know who could both read *and* write, let alone fuckin' grammerise propper?

Enter Gavin Miller. Gav and I have been staunch friends for over fifteen years. We first eyeballed each other as interviewer (Gav) and interviewee (*moi*) on radio Kick AM (formerly 2SM) in Sydney. I remember that interview well because I knew that 2SM was a Catholic-owned station and that the SM in their call sign stood for Saint Mary, so when Sony Music told me that they'd lined up an interview through the station's program manager, I had visions I'd be talking to a fuckin' priest, and that he'd be grilling me big time about my ten years of Catholic school education versus my adult career path of writing and performing bawdy ballads.

Armed with this misconception of the station's agenda, and with my finger wrapped firmly around the trigger of a loaded 'Go and get fucked', I was escorted into the Kick AM studio. To my surprise, the interview couldn't have gone better. There was none of the conservative attitude or pompous presenters I'd expected ('Keep it clean, Kev'), nor was it contrived ('Hey folks, you'll never believe who just wandered into the studio') or even scripted ('Hey Kev, what's your favourite colour?'), because unlike most other interviews, when I sat with Gavin it was casual to the point that it just felt like two good mates having a bit of a chat.

I found out that day that the recently rebranded Kick AM was Australia's only capital city commercial radio station that included country music in its format, and Gavin Miller was one of the station's most popular present-ers. I soon discovered why. Not only did Gav possess a great radio voice and on-air personality, but it was instantly apparent that he had studied his craft with a passion that enabled him to talk on just about any subject, and his thirst for knowledge about almost every musical genre was second to none.

Years later, when Gav and I sat down and started talking about writing this book, we both agreed that it should contain three prime elements: truth, humour and motivation. However, I would like to make one small amendment to one of those elements, and that is 'truth . . . as I remember it'.

For those of you who aren't yet familiar with the term DILLIGAF, let me explain. DILLIGAF is an acronym for *Do I look like I give a fuck?* I'd love to lay claim to that term but it's not mine. DILLIGAF belongs to all of us. It was brought back to Australia by our troops after the Second World War. There is an American version which contains two Fs, DILLIGAFF, but *flying fuck* seems a bit of an overkill, so let's K.I.S.S.

Our navy also brought back their own acronym, BOHICA, which means *Bend over, here it comes again.* While this may seem appropriate for the navy, BOHICA has almost the direct opposite meaning to DILLIGAF: it's a little like yin and yang. Given their meanings, would you prefer to have a DILLIGAF or a BOHICA day? I have a DILLIGAF tattoo on the inside of my left wrist, a gift from my wife Betty, as a reminder that most things just aren't worth stressing over.

DILLIGAF

I'm the sorta bloke that'd like to think
That if I could go back in time
Banjo, Henry and even Ned Kelly
Would all be good mates of mine
'Cos they're pisspots, poets and outlaws
And I can relate to that
And I can relate to their attitude too
In a word, DILLIGAF!

DILLIGAF

That's spelt D-I-L-L-I-G-A-F, DILLIGAF.

Which means, do I look like I give a fuck? DILLIGAF!
Am I being direct enough? DILLIGAF!
It's just another way of sayin'
I couldn't give a fuckin' rat's arse, mate
And do I look like I give a fuck? DILLIGAF!

It's stress relief made easy
It's simple and it works
Just say DILLIGAF next time you've gotta deal
With dickheads, wankers and jerks
And when you go out, stick a DILLIGAF
On your T-shirt or your hat
And when some cunt's givin' you the shits
Just say, 'Mate, read that!'

That spells D-I-L-L-I-G-A-F, DILLIGAF.

Which means, do I look like I give a fuck? DILLIGAF!
Am I being direct enough? DILLIGAF!
It's just another way of sayin'
I couldn't give a rodent's rectum, mate
And do I look like I give a fuck? DILLIGAF!

Kevin Bloody Wilson
May 2010

INTRODUCTION

It's the middle of winter, 1986. I'm in Year 8 at Bathurst High School and there's a banned substance being passed around in the playground at recess. It's a cassette copy of Kevin Bloody Wilson's album *Kev's Back (The Return of the Yobbo)*.

I check to see no teachers are watching, then take the cassette from my friend and quickly slip it into my pocket. I need to make sure I'm not sprung with this tape, or it will ruin everyone's fun. There's this really rude song about Santa Claus on the end of side B that has been making us all laugh until our sides ache.

The fact that we're not supposed to be listening to this stuff only serves to make it funnier. The fact that it is illegal to take this cassette home and make my own copy of it means that I probably owe Kev an apology. Sorry, Kev.

Ten years later I'm working on the radio in Sydney and Kevin Bloody Wilson is booked as a guest live on my drive program. I'm excited about meeting him but have no idea what he will be like as an interview subject, so I double-check that the studio's delay system is working. I'm playing a Dwight Yoakam track. My hands are sweaty. The studio door opens and this friendly looking bearded bloke walks in, grins broadly and sticks his hand out. 'G'day, mate, I'm Kev. How the fuck are ya?'

The first thing I notice about Kevin Bloody Wilson is that he is not eight feet tall, as he appears to be on stage. (I have since learned that this is a really common reaction when you meet famous people. They are almost always shorter in real life. Shania Twain is a *pixie*.)

The next thing I notice is that Kev speaks very softly when he is not on stage. To this day I sometimes have to lean forward to catch what he is saying. He chooses his words carefully and enunciates them perfectly, making him sound almost posh in an ocker kind of way.

The third thing I notice is that Kev is a true country music enthusiast, sharing with me a bunch of information I didn't know about Dwight Yoakam as the song starts fading out.

I don't remember exactly what was said in that interview; all I know is that Kev didn't swear and I got to keep my job. What I do remember is that Kev was the textbook definition of a great radio guest. He was friendly, he was funny, he told great stories, he played a couple of songs live to air, and above all he was gracious enough to tone his act down just enough to keep us both out of trouble.

It's an odd thing ending up friends with someone you started out as a fan of, but that's what happened between myself and Kevin Bloody Wilson. I'm *still* a fan of Kevin Bloody Wilson's incomparable body of work, and of Kev as a bloke. I'm excited about helping Kev tell his story in this book, not only because it's such a great yarn, but also for the inspiration Kev's story will no doubt give young performers currently clawing their way up the entertainment or corporate ladder, all the while being told by people far less creative than themselves, 'You can't do that!'

Most Australians can quote lines from at least one of his colourful and explicit songs, but not too many people know what really makes Kevin Bloody Wilson tick, and where he *really* came from, as opposed to the Kev mythology of the guy who was born in Kalgoorlie. Sure, the Kevin Bloody Wilson character was born in Kalgoorlie, but there's a much bigger backstory to the man himself.

One of the things that makes the Kevin Bloody Wilson story so inspiring is that Kev didn't even exist until his creator, a bloke by the name of Dennis Bryant, was thirty-seven years of age—so much for having to figure out in high school what you want to do with your life. Kevin Bloody Wilson is living proof that it's never too late to have your million-dollar idea.

Having said that, it's a lot easier to have a million-dollar idea than it is to actually put in the work and follow through on it, and Kevin Bloody Wilson is the master of the follow-through. (Just ask his wife Betty—she's the one who washes his undies.)

Kevin Bloody Wilson followed through on his success at home in Australia by making his indelible mark around the world, particularly in the UK where his unique brand of Aussie humour has propelled him into a long and successful career as a touring artist.

Now, with the help of his family and friends, his former and current business associates, his fellow performers and above all Kev himself, the time has finally come to tell the full story of the man Billy Connolly calls 'the world's funniest Australian', Kevin Bloody Wilson.

CHAPTER 1

Let's call him . . . Kev!

'Kevin is just Dennis with a beer, a guitar, and a fuckin' microphone.'
Kevin Bloody Wilson

The story of Western Australian comedy legend Kevin Bloody Wilson begins in another state, and under another name.

On 13 February 1947, Dennis Vincent Bryant was born in Royal Prince Alfred Hospital in the Sydney suburb of Camperdown. He was one of six children Cecil Joseph Bryant and Hazel Margaret Bryant (nee Tanner) brought into the world during their sixty-plus years of marriage. They had married when Hazel was just fifteen, and pregnant. This was back when, as Kevin Bloody Wilson recalls, 'You either got married or went to jail, I believe.'

Their first baby, Barry, fell victim to diphtheria at eighteen months. They soon had Paul, followed by Maureen, Terry, Dennis and Kay. When Kay was about nine years old, Cecil and Hazel decided to adopt two little boys, Kevin and Stephen. Now with seven kids, it was a full house in the Sydney suburb of Berala.

Hazel did shift work in a cotton factory in Flemington and spent every other available minute looking after her brood. Cecil had several jobs, including driving ambulances, making gas meters and working on the railway, providing young Dennis with a few memorable moments.

'When I was a young kid I remember Dad was with the tramways in New South Wales, 'cos I remember they used to have the big tramways Christmas parties. One year the party was at Sydney Stadium in Rushcutters Bay; Santa was in the boxing ring and he called out your name and you went up to get your pressie. That was my earliest memory of what my dad did. I believe he was an ambulance officer during the war—he used to tell us he fought with the 25th Chairborne Pencil Sharpeners.

'He was also with the railways for a long time until he got his foot crushed when a fuckin' safe fell on it while he was assistant station master at Sydney's Flemington station. It wasn't like he was doing a Ronnie Biggs or anything like that. He was just doing his job wheeling the safe off the train for delivery to the Flemington abattoirs. That was the first time I ever saw my dad cry. He was bedridden for months in unbearable pain, and there was fuck-all any of us, including Mum, could do to help. The NSW railways looked after him but he didn't go back to the railways after that.'

Cecil's sense of humour was something he couldn't help but pass on to his kids, as Dennis's brother Terry explains. 'One day I walked into the bathroom and saw Dad standing there naked, shaving. I pointed at Dad's tackle and said, "Look at all the wrinkles on that!" to which Dad replied, without pausing the shaving process, "Each wrinkle represents one inch, son!" I said, "That can't be true, Dad. Your cock isn't a hundred and six inches long!"

'The old man was a good fella. He very seldom hit us with anything other than his hands, and those times were few and far between. But he knew how to put the fear of the Lord into you. He'd give you that stare. His old favourite was, "If I have to talk to you again . . ." and you knew what was going to happen. We took more notice of our father than we did of Mother even though she punished us the most.'

According to Terry, Hazel could be a little heavy-handed when it came to dealing out punishment. 'She'd go crazy with the ironing cord and flog us. You'd come up with welts and everything, all over you—she didn't care where she hit you, either. The old man never liked it. I know they clashed a few times over what she did to us. She had five young kids, I s'pose. I mean, in those days every kid got hit. We weren't the only kids in the area who got hit with ironing cords, I know that for a fact. I always used to say to her, "When I get big enough I'm gonna get an ironing cord and give *you* a flogging."

'One time Kev threatened Mum with a pitchfork. Half our backyard was a vegetable garden; we had to dig it up and everything else. Mum came down and admonished us about something and Kev had the pitchfork in his hand. She was gonna take a whack at him so he bailed her up: "Don't come near me or you're gonna cop it!" I knew who was gonna cop it when the old man got home.

'Mum retreated into the house, but Kev knew his punishment was coming. That was probably one of the few times the old man ever laid into him.'

Young Dennis did what he could to get some extra cash, not all of it legal. He would occasionally 'find' a pushbike, then disassemble it to sell off as spare parts. His entrepreneurial skills were evident even back then, as he took orders and delivered within twenty-four hours. In his own small way, Dennis owned and operated one of Australia's first custom chop shops; bike bells, handlebars and seats were his specialty. His tool of trade was a spanner that he kept in his schoolbag.

He also used to collect bottles, which he would cash in at the local grocery store for thruppence (three pence) each. This was pretty standard for kids of that era, but again Dennis added a twist: ably assisted by his brother and accomplice Terry, he would wait a while, jump the fence and pinch those same bottles from behind the store, then take them back around to the front, approach a different shop assistant and redeem them all over again.

Indeed, for those who knew him—or who had something of theirs taken by him—the larrikin streak which would become the backbone of Kevin Bloody Wilson's persona was already well and truly at work before young Dennis had even turned ten.

Before continuing with Kev's story, I need to address the matter of what to call him. When Dennis Bryant was first involved in show business he adopted the name Bryan Dennis, and then of course he became Kevin Bloody Wilson—more on that later. From now on, though, for the sake of simplicity we'll just use the name everyone calls him by. It also happens to be the title of one of his albums: *Let's Call Him . . . Kev!*

The first school young Kev attended was St Columbus Primary School in Leichhardt: 'The smell of plasticine still reminds me of that school.' Then he and his siblings were enrolled at another convent school where Kev went on to win a state bursary that paid for the first three years of his secondary-school education. It was during these formative years at St Peter Chanel that Kev first became acquainted with the hypocrisies of religion, specifically Catholicism.

'In my last year at St Peter Chanel the nun was a fuckin' psychopath. She was from the order of the Little Sisters of Absolutely No Fuckin' Mercy. She taught by the Marquess of Queensberry rules, the same rules that govern boxing. Terry and I still refer to her as Attila the Nun and we both still have flashbacks of her every time we watch cagefighting on telly. Fuckin' violent Irish bitch. She would literally beat the shit out of you.

'She used to punch kids right in the face or use whatever weapon she could get her hands on to inflict the most violent punishment imaginable. There was never any recourse to home at all—according to Mum, "You must have deserved it."

'I saw some weird things with nuns and priests. Shit that made me think, "Well, that's not fuckin' right." Real people don't act like that. Sure, we copped it at home, but Attila was permanently premenstrual. I remember one time she dragged me out the front of the class for whatever reason, probably for using my rosary beads as a calculator, and she was holding me by the ears and slamming my head against the fuckin' blackboard. It was one of those double-sided ones on a central swivel; as she slammed my head against it, the blackboard did a half rotation and the heavy wooden frame came down and clouted her on the fuckin' noggin with the full force of the Lord Jesus Christ himself. She went down like a bag of shit, and the rest of my classmates pissed 'emselves laughin' as I looked towards heaven and whispered, "Thank you Baby Jesus!"'

Terry also shudders when he tells stories about Attila the Nun. 'She caned the whole class one day. Somebody didn't own up to something so she just caned every single one of us. She should have been in jail. I'd piss on her grave if I ever found it. That's how much I detested her.'

Time has given Kev some perspective on these events. 'I just remember thinking, "Why do you have to do that? Why are you so fuckin' violent? What is it that's got you so fucked up?" Now it has become glaringly obvious to me that it was fuckin' religion with its guilt and repression that had damaged those poor cunts.'

By now Kev knew better than to mess with the nuns at his school, but he would still push the boundaries at home if he thought there was a chance he'd get away with it, as his brother Terry recalls. 'In those days everyone in Sydney had iron roofs, which had to be painted. Every school holidays—usually around Christmas time, the hottest time of the year—the old man made us paint the roof. It was stinkin' hot, and we hated being up there, especially Kev.'

On one occasion, Kev decided to make a statement. 'I painted HELP on the roof in huge letters. Back in those days you had those Tiger Moth planes that people used to practise flying in; at one stage there were about three of them circling the house 'cos they'd seen HELP written on the roof. Dad wasn't terribly impressed when he found out.'

Terry suspects it was the neighbours who dobbed the pair in. 'Dad never used to get up there and inspect it, but when he heard about it he got up there pretty quickly and we got down pretty quickly. I don't think he ever flogged us for it, though.'

Kev wasn't the tallest kid in his class, nor was he the best fighter, but he knew how to talk his way into—and out of—trouble, and his quick wit often saved the day. Says Kev, 'I had a fight with this kid in school once and I said to him,

"Instead of using our fists we get three free kicks at each other's balls." Once he agreed to that I said, "I'll go first."' Kev managed to walk away from that fight with no injuries apart from a slightly sore foot.

A Catholic school in central Sydney played host to Kev's first three years of high school. Kev explains, 'It was a technical school and included subjects like woodwork, metalwork and technical drawing along with the usual maths and English, et cetera. I struggled with shit like algebra— what was the point of learning algebra when I was never likely to visit the fuckin' country anyway? I wasn't a fuckin' idiot, I just wasn't fuckin' interested. DILLIGAF!'

The discipline under the brothers was similar to his old school. Kev comments philosophically, 'In hindsight, if they weren't belting you they were probably fucking you. With that mob you never knew what to expect when you were told to bend over.'

It is hardly surprising to learn that Kev was conflicted in his religious beliefs by the time he was in his early teens. 'Confession? Fuckin' confession?! Goin' into a little dark room by yourself then tellin' some bastard who's never had a root in his life all about your impure thoughts while he's jackin' off into his fuckin' cassock?'

Kev often wagged mass, which was considered a mortal sin on a par with murder and masturbation. When he did show up he tended to ask some tricky theological questions, more often than not just to test his teacher's beliefs. 'I remember asking, "If God knows everything, why did he bother putting us here?" The answer was: "It's up to you to make the choices." I said, "But God already knows what choices I'm going to make, so why bother?" There was never an answer to that.

'At this stage I had well and truly discovered mastur-bation, so my other concern was how priests, nuns and the brothers dealt with celibacy. Fancy givin' up rootin' and wankin' for your invisible and imaginary friend! After all, the Catholic Church is run from Rome, so it's not like the fuckin' Pope is ever gonna be peekin' through the curtains when you're stabbin' the rabbit. I wouldn't mind betting the circle-wank was invented in a monastery.

'Being a recovering Catholic is almost as intense as being a recovering alcoholic in as much as it's always around you trying to tempt you back into your old ways and totally fucking up your life in the process. I still regard the Catholic Church as travel agents for guilt trips.'

Aside from questioning his religion, there was a recurring event in Kev's childhood that raised many questions in his fertile young mind about the possibility of an afterlife.

Kev never got to meet his eldest brother Barry, who was claimed by diphtheria before Kev was born. If he'd survived, Barry would be in his seventies by now. To ensure that Barry was not forgotten, his only baby picture was framed and hung on a nail above the fireplace of the Bryant family's Berala home.

'There were about four times I can recall that Barry's picture fell,' explains Kev. 'It used to fall in the middle of the night. Sometimes the chain on the photo frame would snap. Sometimes the chain would just come off the nail in the wall. Spooky shit. Every time Barry's photo fell, someone in our circle of friends or immediate family would snuff it. We used to shit ourselves every time Barry's photo fell down.' Not surprisingly, when they moved house years later Kev's mum didn't put Barry's photo back up on display.

As an adult, Kev has his own theory on life after death: he has christened the first and most often the brightest star of the evening 'the Mates Star' and says this is where all his family, mates and other good people (and even their pets) hang out when they check out from down here. As he explains, this star turns up each night right on time for first drinks; Kev's first drink is always dedicated as a toast to those who have made it to the Mates Star.

At school it was getting harder and harder for Kev to believe in this cruel and judgemental God he was hearing so much about. 'I still couldn't get past things like wankin'. I'm thinking, "If this is so fuckin' wrong then why does it feel so fuckin' right?" If God didn't want you to play with your cock then he'd have stuck it in the middle of your fuckin' back. Adam and Eve's two sons, Cane and Abel, would also have become the world's first motherfuckers.'

This contact with Catholicism lasted until Kev finished his intermediate certificate, which meant his third year of high school. He passed four out of a possible nine subjects: woodwork, metalwork, English and, ironically, religion. The fact that he failed everything else was of no concern to Kev ('DILLIGAF'), but there was one subject he would have got straight As in which was not on the school curriculum, and that was music.

CHAPTER 2

Let the music begin

'We'd just grab a handful of chords and someone would yell "Ready! Set! Go!"'

Kevin Bloody Wilson

There were no musical instruments in the home when Kev was growing up. 'My first "guitar" I made out of an old ham tin with fishin' wire strings. I played it like a guitar but because it couldn't be tuned, it sounded like a percussive instrument. Interestingly enough, I used this method when teaching the kids on School of the Air many years later.

'In the late 1950s my family finally got a radiogram and whenever Mum saved up enough money she used to buy 45 rpm records and 33 rpm vinyl albums. From memory, the first of these was the Coasters' "Charlie Brown" backed with "Gonna Find Her". I also remember a Johnny Cash four-track vinyl extended play featuring "Ballad of a Teenage Queen", "The Ways of a Women in Love", "Hey Porter" and "Give My Love to Rose". I used to flog them constantly on this radiogram and I loved it. It was a huge thing to have music in the house.

'Then for my thirteenth birthday I got *my* first-ever record. It was a 78 rpm record of "Rock Around the Clock" by Bill Haley and the Comets. It was a present from my Aunty Merle and Uncle Doug. I remember the B-side too, a song called "Thirteen Women". I must have played it a thousand times.'

Black and white television had recently made its way to Australia and young Kev got to see his musical heroes in action on shows like *Tex Ritter's Ranch Party*, *The Perry Como Show* and *Six O'Clock Rock* hosted by Australia's pioneer rock legend, Johnny O'Keefe. Says Kev, 'While all my mates were talking about buying their first cars, my focus was on another area altogether. I had to have a guitar. I begged, borrowed and washed shop windows till I could afford to buy my own. I knew that most of my heroes were playing Maton guitars but Maton didn't make a ten quid model so I couldn't afford one.

'The first time I was ever shown how to play anything on guitar was by a bloke called Warren. His sister Del Reynolds owned the local shop where I was washing windows, and he played guitar, and he ended up giving my brother Terry and me some informal guitar lessons. He showed us a few chords and stuff. I don't know what standard he was but to us he was a fuckin' genius 'cos he could play guitar and sing at the same time. Not only did he sing the old country songs, but he was also getting into this rock and roll stuff, which got my attention as well. Because I knew through Mum's collection that country—or country and western as it was called back then—and rock and roll were the styles of music I was interested in. Warren also taught us the traditional twelve-bar blues pattern which is the staple diet for all wannabe guitarists.'

Kev was never particularly into the theory of it all, prefer-
ring to learn guitar the way he would learn most things—by
jumping in and having a go. As he explains, 'Warren didn't
know any real guitar theory, yet he sounded good to our ears
so we figured maybe all this theory bullshit wasn't necessary.
We just wrote down the words of a song then put the chord
changes in over the top of the lyrics. Fuckin' simple, just like
it's supposed to be.

'Back then we didn't give a shit if it was actually in
tune or not. We preferred bashing out a tune by ear rather
than the drudgery of learning scales, reading sheet music or
taking formal guitar lessons. On telly none of our heroes ever
looked down at their sheet music, they were all looking at
their audience, and to me that made sense.'

To this day, despite the fact that he went on to teach
guitar and vocals with the Western Australian Department
of Education for four years, Kev still hasn't bothered to
learn to read and write music. 'I'm having too good a time
without it!'

Kev writes left-handed—'Just to fuck the nuns up, they
called it the devil's hand'—and yet he plays guitar and does
everything else (including the obvious—I asked) with his
right hand. So that makes him ambidextrous, which Kev
reckons means he can live on land or in water.

Along with the chords he was learning, young Kev soon
discovered a talent for deconstructing other people's songs.
These early attempts, which predate the invention of Kevin
Bloody Wilson by about twenty-five years, give a few clues
as to where young Dennis Bryant's creativity was leading
him. Remember Bobby Vinton's 'Roses are Red'? Here's
what young Kev turned that into:

Roses are dead my love,

Violets are too,
Sugar is cheap, my love,
But not as cheap as you.

The first song Kev can remember writing from scratch was written with his brother Paul:

I Like Girls

I like girls, 'cos girls are lots of fun
I like girls, I like to see 'em run
I like girls, but I could never tame 'em
Girls like me, and I can't say I blame 'em.

I went down to my Sheila's place
She cried, 'Oh dear, oh dear,
While you were away a burglar got in here!'
I asked, 'Did he get anything before he shot through?'
She cried, 'He got the lot, 'cos I thought he was you!'

My secretary said to me this mornin'
'I know it'll be a loss
but as from tomorrow you'll no longer be my boss
I've got my resignation all I've gotta do is type it
I've found a new position.'
I said, 'Well, shut the door and we'll try it!'

Kev would play these songs for his brothers; they were impressed enough that when his cousins and young mates came around, they would demand that he get his guitar out and 'play one of those funny songs you wrote!' Kev knew he was hardly an accomplished musician at this point, but it didn't matter. He was experiencing for the first time the thrill

13

of performing in front of a live audience, even if they were mostly related to him. He wanted more.

It was the early sixties, and surf music and the Stomp were huge, with the likes of the Beach Boys and Jan and Dean climbing pop charts all over the globe. In Australia the charge was being led by Billy Thorpe and the Aztecs, the Atlantics and Little Pattie, and venues all over Sydney were full of young people dancing around like they were attempting to extinguish cigarettes with their feet. At fourteen years of age Kev had acquired enough confidence in his playing to appoint himself the rhythm guitarist in a makeshift Stomp band he formed with brother Terry.

'We were called the Bruvvers, 'cos it was my brother Terry and me, and there was already an English band around called Joe Brown and the Bruvvers. I've since met *the* Joe Brown and told him the name of our band and how bad we were and he pissed himself laughin'. I don't think Joe had too much to worry about. I knew about three chords in those days, and I remember one night busting an A string at the beginning of a gig and I didn't have any spare strings so I just kept fuckin' ploughing on.

'I wasn't playing lead guitar, I was playing rhythm and like my homemade ham-tin guitar it was more percussive than melodic. And I still maintain that as far as guitar players are concerned I'm a percussionist who just happens to be holding a fuckin' guitar.'

Looking back on his time in the Bruvvers a few decades on, Kev is blunt. 'We were fuckin' awful. We didn't play the hits of the day 'cos we couldn't, we weren't that good. We'd just grab a handful of chords and go for it. Most tunes start with a "One . . . two . . . three . . . four!" but our fuckin' racket started when one of us would yell, "Ready . . . Set. . . Go!"

'It was just fuckin' noise. It was what you would expect to hear from a garage band that was about three weeks old. Actually, you couldn't even call us a garage band. We didn't even have a fuckin' garage to practise in. We were a back verandah band, and a pretty ordinary one at that. Less than ordinary actually, but we still had fun, and we packed 'em in at two bob a head.'

After leaving school Kev worked around Sydney doing various odd jobs; by the time he turned eighteen he'd had a crack at everything from making gas meters in the same building his father used to work in, to working in a dry cleaners and being an inspector's clerk at the Parramatta police station running papers to and from court. He loved that job but was soon transferred against his wishes to the local government department in downtown Sydney as a mail boy. 'That was the final job I had before leaving home, and it was really the job that helped me in my decision to leave Sydney. It was such a boring bloody job.'

However, sitting next to a bloke in the mailroom who constantly had seizures provided some light entertainment. 'The entire staff would take bets on when he would have his next seizure and then sit there watching him like a hawk. This guy represented all the things you didn't want to be when you grew up. He was probably only about twenty-five, half bald with the comb-over, and right before he had a seizure he'd dribble. That was good. He sat facing me so I'd always be on the lookout for that little hint of dribble. "Here it comes! It's coming . . . it's coming . . . there it is! I win!"'

Another distraction from the monotony of his office job came in the unlikely form of magic tricks. 'I was taking the mail up to the GPO from the office in Bridge Street, and there was this bloke out the front of Coles demonstrating a magic kit. These magic kits were on sale for anywhere between five bob and five quid [five shillings and five pounds], so I probably got the two-quid version. From then on that's how I used to occupy at least half of my day. I would hide in my little booth in the corner of the mailroom practising magic tricks. No cunt knew what I was doing because I was hiding behind my desk, but I could still keep an eye on Seizure Guy.

'One of the first tricks I learned was the little cup trick, a little urn type thing with a red ball inside it that disappears and keeps coming back and you can make it appear to pop out of your ear or your arse or whatever. Great for the kids, and my brother Terry loved that one too. He could never work it out . . . still can't!'

Kev's first real gig as a musician was as a support act to the LeGarde Twins—known behind their backs as Le Garbage Bins—who had been in America for many years and were now trying to get an Australian version of Nashville's Grand Ole Opry off the ground. They gigged regularly at a theatre called Five Ways in Paddington. Kev played there on Thursday and Friday nights as one of many support acts, to a mostly indifferent and slightly intoxicated crowd.

He remembers, 'It was good 'cos I was getting paid the same rate as the top artists were getting paid, which was fuck-all. Nobody got paid and if I had signed the contract those pair of wankers offered, I'd still be payin' the shifty bastards on my earnings today. It was a good early lesson in dealing with sharks and shysters and there's any amount of those cunts in the entertainment industry. But, more importantly, there are always positives that come out of these situations and there are more good people than bad—it was on this show where I met one of my lifelong muso mates, Wayne Pride.'

Wayne Pride—who Kev calls Jock—recalls hearing Kev sing for the first time in 1964: 'I was the head lackey for those two crooks and Kev came and auditioned. We first got to know each other on that show. It was the greatest rip-off in the history of the world but it was also an education you couldn't knock back. You learn so much from shifty people like that.

'Kev got up and did a Roger Miller song—he did Roger Miller better than Roger Miller, that's what I thought at the time. I'm a Roger Miller fanatic and I was a bit pissed off. I thought, "How can you do that? Roger Miller is my hero, not yours!" But he's always liked Roger as well and we became instant mates.'

Just as it does now, the music that most spoke to Kev during these early days was country music. 'My whole family loved country music. Reg Lindsay used to host a show on 2KY in Sydney on a Wednesday night and we all used to listen to it. Then, as a teenager I got the courage to ring him up and go in and meet him. He was there with his missus, Heather McKean, the sister and singing partner of Slim Dusty's wife Joy McKean, and what surprised me was that the joint was absolutely fucking empty. Everybody had gone home because it was on at half past six in the evening. I'd have thought there'd still be people hanging around 'cos you got to hear a lot of the latest country music on that show.'

The experience of sitting quietly in the corner of the 2KY studio immediately sparked Kev's interest in radio, an interest that would play a big part in the years ahead. It was also through this connection with Reg Lindsay that Kev got his long-awaited ticket out of Sydney.

Buddy Williams is considered by many to be Australia's original country music star. He toured outback Australia almost non-stop for nearly fifty years before his death from lung cancer in 1986. He was renowned for being a tough old bugger, having served as a Bren gunner in the 2/31st Battalion in the Second World War. He was very nearly killed while serving in Borneo, and was only rescued from the heap of dead when a passing doctor heard his cry for water. The doctor saved him, but the scars and some of the shrapnel remained for the rest of his life. Kev recalls that Buddy used to say things like, 'When you shake someone's hand, do it firmly, and look them in the eye,' and 'Say what you mean, and mean what you say.' Over the years many of Australia's finest performers, people like Frank Ifield, Kev's mate Wayne Pride and Tommy and Phil Emmanuel, all got their start in show business by touring with the Buddy Williams show.

One night Buddy was a guest on Reg Lindsay's radio show, and he got chatting to the softly spoken boy who was sitting in the corner. Upon learning that young Kev had been playing guitar and singing for a few years, Buddy took his family along to watch Kev's performance with Le Garbage Bins. After the show, Buddy went backstage and invited Kev to join him on his next tour around Australia.

Says Kev, 'I figured I must have been OK with a guitar to be offered a job with a travelling show, but the truth was I was only armed with about half a dozen chords.' Kev's initial answer was a polite 'No thanks, Mr Williams', but over the weeks that followed he started to rethink his decision. He hated his day job, he'd already learned all the magic tricks in his kit, and Seizure Guy had started taking medication to control his fits. Kev was also well and truly over being a support act for Le Garbage Bins.

Kev recalls the moment he finally decided to get out of town. He was just eighteen. 'It was about three weeks after Buddy had made that initial offer. I'd become friends with his daughter Kaye, so I wrote to her and asked her where her dad was. She told me he was currently touring Queensland. I had a mate who was about to leave Sydney to head to Proserpine in north Queensland, so I knew I could get a lift up there with him. I asked Kaye if her dad was going anywhere near Proserpine and she said he would be there in six weeks. So that's when I decided to leave Sydney and take on a bit of fuckin' adventure.'

There was another factor Kev had to take into account when making his decision to leave Sydney. 'The most difficult part of the decision was that I had a girlfriend, and her brother was a muso who used to teach me different riffs and chords and stuff like that. I was getting guitar lessons from him, and then when he left for a gig I'd pork his sister.'

Kev's girlfriend, who I will call Karen (I won't mention her surname in case I embarrass the whole Howard family), had no hesitation in supporting him as he embarked on his big adventure, however, their plan to have a long-distance relationship soon hit the skids. It was Kev's first experience of how hard it can be to attempt to keep a relationship going while on the road, and it would not be his last. 'Pretty much as soon as I left town one of my mates started porking her, which is fair game I suppose. I doubt very much if anyone has satisfied her since, but there you go. Her loss. DILLIGAF.'

There was another woman in Kev's life who would find it a bit harder to embrace the idea of him leaving home.

'If my mum had her way right now I'd be the manager at Brite Nu Dry Cleaners in Auburn and speakin' fuckin' Arabic. How would that have turned out? She said to me, "You could be the manager there by the time you're twenty-one." As it happened, by the time I was twenty-one I'd done three laps of the country and settled into a really good life-style in Kalgoorlie.

'I remember Mum giving me ten bob out of her house-keeping budget as I was packing my guitar in the boot of my mate's car and she said, "Dennis, I wish you well, but you won't make any money playing guitar." I kissed Mum goodbye, turned the corner, and all I saw in front of me was adventure.'

CHAPTER 3

Discovering Australia

'Aussie Aussie Aussie . . . you fuckin' beauty!'

Kevin Bloody Wilson

Proserpine is about a thousand kilometres north of Brisbane on Queensland's famous Bruce Highway. It is famous for both its sugar production and its proximity to one of the world's greatest tourist destinations, the Whitsunday Islands. In march 1965 Kev arrived in Proserpine with about a month to fill before Buddy Williams rolled into town. He very quickly lined up a gig playing country music in a little pub for thirty shillings a night.

For Kev, it was the right gig at the right time as it gave him some much-needed guitar practice and a bit of play money. But as luck would have it, he couldn't have a drink after the show. At the time the legal drinking age in Queensland was twenty-one, so Kev decided to find a sober activity to pass the time while he waited for the Buddy Williams show to roll into town—he got his driver's licence.

The test Kevin Bloody Wilson passed in order to receive his first driver's licence was slightly unusual, at least by today's standards. He had to drive the police sergeant from the police station around the corner to the bottle shop, buy him two King Browns of XXXX beer, and return him to the station. That was it. The policeman, now filled with confidence in young Kev's driving ability, filled out all the appropriate forms and Kev was licensed to drive anywhere in Australia for the next five years. Dennis Bryant, the lad who was still about twenty years away from becoming Kevin Bloody Wilson, had learned to drive the same way he learned how to play guitar: bugger the technicalities of it all, just jump in and have a go.

This turned out to be a good philosophy, given that within a week Kev was driving a four-ton truck with a thirty-six-foot-long caravan behind it. Driving wasn't the only task Kev had to perform as part of his apprenticeship with Buddy Williams. He was also required to keep Buddy's trucks maintained, and he had to help put up the show's backdrop, then set up the sound system and the seating before each show. It was not unusual for Kev to be found washing the truck or even lying under it doing running repairs an hour before he was due on stage.

Buddy's wife, Grace, had a fairy floss machine, a crude but effective device made from the spin dryer of an old Hoover twin-tub washing machine, and getting it working each night was another job on Kev's list—at least this job came with the benefit of a free sugar rush.

Working on the Buddy Williams tour taught Kev a lot about the backstage elements that go towards putting on a show, and it also gave him the opportunity to get on stage. It was a steep learning curve. 'The first night I played with Buddy I was informed that I also had to play bass guitar in his backing band with him. I'd never played fuckin' bass in my life. I figured if I could play six strings on a normal guitar then four on the bass would be a fuckin' breeze.'

Buddy had a nickname for Kev: Pringle. For the record, it had nothing to do with potato chips, as Kev explains. 'I used to play Hank Williams's song "Jambalaya" in my set and it has a line about a pirogue, a small rowboat, and Buddy thought I was singing "pringle", so from then on he called me Pringle. I wasn't gonna fuckin' argue with him.'

There was no room on Buddy's show for any bugger-ising around. Kev would play his ten-minute set of straight country songs, run backstage to change and paint himself up as a clown for a comedy skit, and then leave the stage after playing a barber skit covered in coloured dishwashing foam to check that the fairy floss machine was still running. Then he'd quickly clean himself up and return to the stage to play bass in Buddy's backing band. Straight after the last song the banners would be taken down, the fairy floss machine packed away, the trucks loaded up, and after a few hours' sleep they'd all be off to the next town.

That tour took almost a year and travelled all over Australia, including some spots so remote that the local Aborigines had never seen a white man before. Says Kev, 'You should have seen the looks on their faces when they first saw us white fellas with electricity and guitars. They couldn't speak English, but their kids could because they were being taught it in their remote community schools. These Aborigines were the real deal, and they loved the music even though they didn't really understand it. And farting jokes. They loved those too.'

Kev—now going by the stage name Bryan Dennis—was fascinated by Aboriginal culture. As a young entertainer he noted that while his Indigenous audience loved the music and flashy outfits, they only partly related to the musical acts. That was when he decided to inject some comedy into his act, something that he knew would relate directly to his target audience. 'I picked up a couple of Aboriginal swear words like *goona* [shit], *todoi* [cock] and *budju* [cunt], and I'd drop one or two of these in every now and then and the mob'd go off like a frog in a sock. Buddy and the missionaries who ran most of these communities had no idea what I was up to, but me and the audience fuckin' loved it.'

This experience of Indigenous Australia sparked an interest in the Aboriginal culture and way of life that remains with Kev to this day. His respect for Aboriginal culture is reflected in the lyrics of one of three songs that he penned many years later for Slim Dusty. Slim recorded the song Kev wrote for him and included this and 'A Bad Day's Fishing' on his hundredth album.

Rainbow Over The Rock

There's a rainbow over the rock
And the sun has started shinin'
And I've just seen a flock of cockatoos fly by
And I see a silver linin'
On the clouds as they roll on
Bringin' life to the desert and stock
And you've gotta believe in a god
When there's a rainbow over the rock.

Call it Ayers Rock or Uluru
They both mean much the same
Named after our ancestors
From both our yesterdays

Now here we stand on common ground
Still drenched from the desert rain
In awe of what's before us
And breathing in being Australian
. . . and just look at that!

There's a rainbow over the rock
And the sun has started shinin'
And I've just seen a flock of cockatoos fly by
And I see a silver linin'
On the clouds as they roll on
Bringin' life to the desert and stock
And you've gotta believe in Dreamtime
When there's a rainbow over the rock.

There stands that magic majestic rock
The rain has washed her clean
Dressed in the colours of the rainbow
As if for a new beginning
And there's a brand new day on the horizon
And there's a brand new feelin' in the air
And now that the dust has settled
Advance Australia fair.

There's a rainbow over the rock
And the sun has started shinin'
And I've just seen a flock of cockatoos fly by
And I see a silver linin'
On the clouds as they roll on
Bringin' life to the desert and stock
And you've gotta believe in a god
When there's a rainbow over the rock

And you've gotta believe in Dreamtime
When there's a rainbow over the rock
And we've gotta believe together
When there's a rainbow over the rock.

'Going straight out of Sydney to the outback was completely mindblowing. It was a world I never knew existed. You learned about Aboriginal people in their own environment. I fuckin' loved it!'

Kev recalls another defining moment from his first tour of outback Australia. 'Buddy's entourage consisted of five or six trucks, each towing a caravan. We were travelling in convoy through the vast and empty Gulf of Carpentaria, and because of the dust being thrown up by each of the vehicles we spaced ourselves about a kilometre apart. It was fuckin' hot and I was sweatin' like a paedophile at a Wiggles concert. The dust, mixed with sweat, was turning into mud on my face and clothes, so I decided to stop till the dust had settled. I climbed onto the cabin roof to catch whatever breeze was blowing when I spotted another, even bigger dust cloud coming towards me from the north. As this huge red cloud got closer I became aware that this dust cloud was in fact being created by a mob of kangaroos . . . fuckin' thousands of the bastards!

'It took at least ten minutes for them all to pass by my truck, and as I stood there covered in even more dust and mud I realised that what I was seeing and experiencing could only ever happen in Australia. Here I was, a thousand miles from anywhere, and in the middle of nowhere. For the first time in my life, I felt I was part of the mob, I felt Australian.'

His first lap of Australia with the Buddy Williams show took Kev to parts of Australia that most Australians never get to see. 'We went from Proserpine to Cairns, Cape York to Mossman, Cooktown across to Burketown, to Mount Isa, Alice Springs, Darwin, then down to Perth, then across the Nullarbor Plain to South Australia. While it was great seeing places I'd only ever read about, it was the places we visited that I'd *not* read or heard of that impressed me the most.'

Kev was having a great time seeing his country, and his comedy was going down well with the indigenous audiences, but Buddy Williams eventually ran out of patience with his young recruit. 'Buddy sacked me in Meningie in South Australia. I was bucking this fuckin' work system. I was going, "Fuck it, I'm not a mechanic. I can't do that. I don't want to be drivin' a fuckin' truck all fuckin' day then lying under the bastard till seven o'clock at night and then expected to go and wash the grease off and get on stage and play guitar." I was also quick to realise that guitar players get more roots than truck drivers.'

Buddy Williams replaced Kev with his mate Wayne Pride, and in October 1965 Kev hitchhiked his way back to Whyalla, where he'd heard work would be plentiful. He quickly found himself employed as a plant operator with Quarry Industries. There was an upside: 'Even plant operators get more fucks than truck drivers.'

The plant was situated not far out of Whyalla on the western side of Mount Laura; being the highest point close to town, Mount Laura was chosen as the site for the TV tower to receive this new and exciting medium from across the Spencer Gulf in Adelaide and into the homes of the Whyalla locals. Kev loved the work and outdoors lifestyle and was soon selected by the site manager, Jon Jonkers, to sit for his explosives operator ticket. That's right: Kev is a fully qualified powder monkey . . . Scary, huh?

The combination of Kev and explosives was a disaster waiting to happen. Sure enough, on his first attempt at stoking the 'shot' into the predrilled shot-holes Kev over-compensated with the ampho (which is really just a fancy way of saying he used too much explosive), setting off a charge that shook the newly constructed TV tower from its foundations.

Kev watched the tower rolling down the side of Mount Laura in a tangled mess of twisted and buckled steel, stopping within metres of the site office. He knew what he needed to do next. 'I hit the road to Port Augusta before that fuckin' tower hit the ground.'

All in all, Whyalla had still been good for Kev. It bank-rolled his next adventure and paid for his first Maton guitar, a custom twelve-string acoustic finished with burnt gum on-body trimming. His stage name—*Bryan Dennis*—was etched onto the twin scratch-plates.

These days Kev is Maton Guitars' 'favourite Australian' and most successful overseas ambassador. It was during a night on the singin' syrup with the CEO of Maton, Neville Kitchener, and Maton's head luthier and Kev's close friend Andy Allen that Kev coined his personal endorsement: 'Maton Guitars . . .? I fuckin' swear by 'em!' (A slightly amended version of this slogan has since been approved and used by Maton.)

But back then, once he had the guitar he'd always been after, Kev just wanted to get paid to play it. Now aged eighteen, Kev was off again on another lap of the world's biggest island, this time for two years, with the Rick and Thel Carey show. Says Kev, 'I loved Rick and Thel. They were good people. For a start, if Buddy was paying you ten quid a week they were paying you twenty, and you didn't have to wash trucks and shit like that.'

It was during this time that Kev started meeting some of the big wheels in Australian country music who were part of Rick and Thel's roadshow. People like Rex Dallas, Eddy Tapp and Chad Morgan. Kev was particularly taken with the audience response to some of Chad's bawdier work. Offstage, however, Kev couldn't help but notice that Chad was not the friendliest bloke he'd ever come across. Says Kev, 'I've seen him recently and he's got his shit together now, I guess by virtue of his old lady who got him off the piss, and he's turned into quite a nice old man.'

Kev tried hard to get on with Chad Morgan, even offering up some of his early songwriting attempts for Chad to use. 'I had my first songs published and recorded by Chad Morgan, and in the process learned a very important lesson about the music business. One of my songs was called "Problem Child"; the other was called "One, Too, Free for Marriage", and the idea for that one came from Roger Miller. I was a big Roger Miller fan, still am, 'cos I like the way he plays with words, and in this song I played a similar game with the numbers one, two and three.'

I'm one too free for marriage
I'm not looking for a wife
I ain't about to make the vow
That'll tie me down for life
I'm free to wander where I want
And do just what I like
I'm one two free for marriage
I'm not looking for a wife.

'However, both those songs turned up on Chad's album *The Artistry of Chad Morgan* as "written by Chad Morgan and Bryan Dennis", and the fact is Chad had fuck-all to do with them. I've never given him a song since.'

In whatever spare time Kev could make for himself he was quietly perfecting the art of 'decomposing'. That is, taking an existing song and changing the words to make it completely wrong and/or hilarious, just as he'd been doing since he was a kid. It was the response of his brothers and mates to these songs that had engaged Kev's imagination, and he kept on coming up with new ones whenever the mood struck him. Unfortunately for Kev, though, he couldn't road-test these new decompositions on a family variety show like the Rick and Thel show. Kev had to keep things fairly tame or else he would suddenly find himself unemployed. Again.

In mid 1967 the Rick and Thel show arrived in the Western Australian mining town of Kalgoorlie. It was an event that turned out to be life-changing for Kev.

'My first impression of Kal was that it was fuckin' cold. It was right in the middle of winter. And as I ended up finding out, Kalgoorlie winters are as cold as their summers are fuckin' hot. In summer, the whole town swelters until between four and six pm when those scorchin' hot summer days are cooled by the Esperance Doctor, which is what they call the soothing southerlies blowin' in from the coast some three hundred kilometres away. But in winter the cold winds blow in from the northern desert and it's not uncommon to have your household water pipes burst from the below-freezing overnight temperatures. Those northerly winter winds are known as the Leonora Undertaker.

'Other than the weather, the one thing that did strike me on my first visit to Kalgoorlie was the number of people who offered to do things for me. Like on that first night a bloke named Freddy Watson, who I had never met before, said, "Do you wanna come around for a beer at my place?" and I said, "Fuck yeah" and took the guitar around and had a party.'

There was a musician at that party, piano player Clarrie Hall, who made Kev a tantalising offer. 'He offered me a job in his fuckin' band. He said, "We're only a two piece at the moment, just me and the drummer Graham Bignell. If you can come back for the Kalgoorlie Race Round in early September there's a job there for you for a week or so."'

Kev thanked Clarrie for the offer and told him he'd give it some thought. At the time he still had a tour to finish with the Rick and Thel show. However, at the end of the Rick and Thel Carey tour a few weeks later, Kev contacted Clarrie Hall and asked whether the job in his band was still vacant. It was, and Kev lobbed into Kalgoorlie for what he thought would probably be about ten days. Fourteen years later he would leave Kalgoorlie with a wife, two kids, and the beginnings of an idea that would make him an international comedy legend.

CHAPTER 4

Kalgoorlie gold

'There are two types of Australians. Those that live in the outback and those that wish they could.'

Kevin Bloody Wilson

To an outsider, Kalgoorlie may not seem like the world's most liveable city. It's a long way from anywhere, but on closer inspection it is a picturesque place full of friendly, down-to-earth people and it also holds the dubious honour of having more pubs per square metre than any other city on earth. As Kev points out, 'We have so many drunks in Kalgoorlie we hire 'em out to towns that can't grow their own.'

At any time of the day or night these pubs are brimful of young men with grand plans of heading elsewhere once they've spent a couple of years getting cashed up working in the mines, and the older men who never quite saw that plan through and are still there twenty years on.

Kalgoorlie is in many ways a man's town, and the women you meet there tend to be just a little sharper and tougher than their suburban sisters. In Kalgoorlie, topless barmaids—known throughout Australia as Skimpies—are the norm. Then there's the infamous Hay Street brothels, which Kev pointed out to me as we drove around Kalgoorlie together. 'The hookers of Hay Street turned up the same day that the Irish prospector Paddy Hannan stubbed his toe on a nugget of gold way back in 1893.'

There are several local bylaws pertaining to the brothels; Kev is particularly amused by the one which states that a brothel can't be situated within a hundred metres of a church. 'Back then they had a lot of trouble moving some of them fuckin' churches.'

Right next door to Kalgoorlie is the town of Boulder. The area is officially known as the city of Kalgoorlie-Boulder, but Kalgoorlie people have always enjoyed a friendly rivalry with the residents of Boulder, something that Kev cottoned onto pretty quickly. 'Did you know that the toothbrush was invented in Boulder? If it had been invented in Kalgoorlie they'd have called it a teethbrush.'

After Kev's return to Kalgoorlie in 1967, Clarrie Hall, the musician who had offered him a spot in his band, was impressed enough to extend the job offer beyond the initial ten-day run. 'He said, "Do you wanna stay on?" I said, "Fuck yeah!" Kalgoorlie was an active place. There was a lot going on.'

The nickel boom was just beginning, and there were also vast quantities of gold that were still hidden below the ground waiting to be mined. 'I remember Clarrie saying to me once, "If gold gets to two hundred dollars an ounce, I'm staying in this town!" Now it's around six times that price.'

To help supplement his income as a musician Kev tried out a number of day jobs including sales ('Fuckin' hated that . . .'), working as a storeman ('Fuckin' hated that . . .'), and clerical work ('Fuckin' hated that . . .'), before finding a position at Musgroves, a shop that sold everything from musical instruments, records and hi-fi equipment to stoves and fridges.

'I fuckin' loved it,' says Kev. 'When I wasn't talking about musical instruments I was listening to music. The thing that became difficult for them was that the annual audit always necessitated at least a day or two at my place so as to include the stock I'd taken out on loan. It was a great arrangement: they'd take away the shit I'd borrowed to try out over the previous twelve months, then over the next couple of weeks I'd replenish my personal inventory with the latest state-of-the-art gear. Come stocktake time they'd always ask me, "What have you got at home?" and I'd tell 'em, "Whatever you don't have left in the fuckin' shop!"

'I was there for the advent of eight-track tape, and its demise as well. I had an eight-track radio in my car; it was the same shape as the eight-track cartridge with a radio inside it. You'd stick that inside the slot instead of the eight-track tape. That was pretty impressive in the old AP5 Valiant station wagon.'

One person who remembers that AP5 Valiant well is Kev's bandmate from his days in Kalgoorlie, guitarist Tex Curran, who first met Kev in 1968. Tex describes their meeting. 'I was walking along the Boulder road there in Kalgoorlie one day and this car pulled up, a white Valiant station wagon, and the bloke inside said, "Are you Tex?" I said, "Yeah," and he introduced himself to me and made arrangements to come along that night and have a bit of a jam and a practice with us, and it just went on from there.'

Kev soon became the lead singer and bass player of Tex's band Alley Katz. Terry Carlsson played piano-organ and Graham Bignell the drums. According to Tex, Kev fitted in right away. 'We had a pretty good recipe: anything that was a hit we played, so people could relate to the music. But also in our musical arsenal was the strict-time dance music, the old barn dances, maxinas, tangos, quicksteps and waltzes. Because our parents had danced to this type of music, we were all familiar with it and had all learned to play it at some stage. This proved invaluable a little later on when we cut back on the pub work and moved into the cabaret circuit, which paid much better.'

During this time Tex noticed that young Kev was starting to hone one of the most important skills of live performance: the ability to read the audience and adapt the show accordingly, to give them exactly what they wanted. For the little bloke who would one day become Kevin Bloody Wilson, the central element in his stage persona—even at this early stage—was that great Australian tradition of taking the piss. On many occasions, Kev's random on-stage shenanigans would make it hard for Tex to concentrate on his playing.

'We used to mess around a lot on stage. The crowd would have a good time because they could see us having a good time, and Kev was exceptionally skilled when it came to reading the crowd. Sometimes we'd be playing a flat-out rock song and then we'd throw in a waltz because it was needed, and it always worked.'

As a result of his years of practice and on-the-job training with Buddy Williams and Rick and Thel Carey, Kev also had the chops required to impress Tex and his other bandmates with his musicianship. 'I think Kev's a really good bass player,' says Tex. 'He always played it in a way that wasn't overpowering, where you only missed it if it wasn't there, which to me is what a bass should be. These days the bass is often so loud that the other sound gets lost around it. He plays bass as it should be played.'

Tex developed a friendship with Kev during those early years in Kalgoorlie that lasts until this day. 'We had a good time without even trying. Every night was a different show and there was always a lot of humour, spontaneous humour. We never planned a thing, it just happened. Setting farts on fire, putting prawns in the pockets of coats and jackets in the cloakroom, that kind of thing.

'In those days you still had deep mining going as well as the open-pit mine. Four kilometres out of Kalgoorlie you had Boulder, and all the mines were situated in Boulder, so come four o'clock on a Friday you had about four thousand blokes who would knock off and go straight to the pubs. And every second Friday they'd get paid, so they'd have a pocketful of cash and so you had that whole feel-good feeling about the town. In those days working on the mines was pretty big money, so even if they weren't pissing it up they were used to that level of income. That's why they used to say, "Once you get in the mines you can't get out."'

With their unscripted antics, their impressively large and hit-laden set list, and the frontman's curious habit of changing the words to other people's songs to turn an ordinary lyric into something hilariously wrong, Alley Katz were fast becoming the number one party band in Kalgoorlie, as Tex recalls. 'People would come up, particularly guys, and tell us that they were coming because they wanted to see what we would do that night. It was very unpredictable, even to me. Sometimes a funny situation would start and then it would snowball during the gig.'

Kev has a favourite story from that era which he recalls over lunch with Tex at one of his favourite haunts, the Marmion Angling and Aquatic Club, which is nestled on the beach a couple of blocks away from Kev's Perth home.

'It was the night of the Mayoral Ball. Tex was full-on fully pissed backstage messing with the left-to-right pan on the PA system. While the mayor was up there giving his speech, Tex began panning His Worship's voice from left to right, and unconsciously the mayor began leaning from side to side, following his voice from speaker to speaker. It became even better when the crowd of five hundred-plus pissed punters standing on the dance floor also started swaying from left to right in time to the mayor's speech. I wish we had a fuckin' video of that one!'

Tex chimes in with a favourite story of his own. 'We used to do quite a few of the Catholic church balls, and there was a lady by the name of Shirley who was very staid and quite high up in the church, and at these debutante balls they'd usually have a bishop or some other high holy roller come and introduce the girls. Of course, we're playing all these different songs and you could see that Shirley was on edge all night, wondering what we were going to do. So the bishop was standing at a table right in front of the stage and we were playing a quickstep and singing "If You Knew Susie". And of course Kev starts singing, "We went riding so I took a punt, I said Susie my God you have a lovely . . .", and an ashen-faced Shirley started to run towards the stage, screaming, "No! No!" just as Kev finished the line with "dress!" I think both Shirley and the bishop shit 'emselves that night.'

Lunch has arrived, and Kev's got another story. 'One time the mayor was about to make his speech and just for the fun of it we started throwing tin chairs one at a time down the concrete stairwell backstage at the Kalgoorlie Town Hall just to see whose chair would make the most noise on its journey down to the dressing rooms. "And now, ladies and gentlemen, the mayor of Kalgoorlie," and he came out and started addressing the crowd, and just as he got into the most poignant part of his speech suddenly the whole town hall was filled with a deafening, thunderous, fuckin' *bang! Crash! Fuckin' wallop! Boom!* The band had obviously discovered an entire fuckin' stack of metal chairs to play with.'

At this point Tex takes over the story from his old mate, who is laughing so hard that tears are rolling down his cheeks. 'Kev was standing side of stage, pretending he had nothing to do with it. He was looking off to the side of the stage while the mayor was giving his speech and mouthing the words, "You stupid cunts" and pretending to be outraged. He fuckin' started it!'

Kalgoorlie is a tough town and Kev watched his fair share of brawls break out while Alley Katz were on stage. 'People used to go to the Foundry Hotel on a Saturday night to watch the fights and occasionally a gig would break out, but it seemed we were a protected species. We were the band, so it didn't matter what we did. If anybody got their nose out of shape over what we may have said or done and then complained about us, then they would have gone home with their nose out of shape, literally!'

The heavies of Kalgoorlie were a relatively friendly lot, and thankfully they were also big fans of the band. Tex knew better than to go against the flow. 'Every town has its tough guys, the sort of blokes who would pick their teeth on a rusty nail and wipe their arse with broken glass. Then there were others who were *really* tough, but fortunately they loved us and always followed the band around from venue to venue. If anyone started to give us shit, as drunks sometimes do, well, they would be unceremoniously ejected from the gig by our own personal, hairy, scary security. I mean, these guys were rough bastards. Not evil blokes or criminals, just good brawlers and essentially good blokes.

'We were playing at Paddy's Parlour Nightclub, which was about a kilometre and a half away from the other nightclub up the top of Hannan Street, and a couple of our hairy, scary best friends got themselves full of piss. So we're playing on stage and they just grabbed Kev and his guitar, bundled both over their shoulders, gently deposited them both in the car then drove to the opposition nightclub where they propped him up on stage with the other band. Then they grabbed Kev's opposite number from that band and brought him down to our club venue, and as the night wore on they gradually went through the whole band. They finished up with the two bands almost completely swapped. It just happened, and there was no use fighting it.'

Some people can get away with saying whatever is on their mind, while other people end up getting punched in the face. Tex was relieved to discover that Kev belonged to the first category. 'I always felt really good about it because he just had that natural gift. If we were at a gig somewhere he could utterly insult some poor bastard and get away with it, and he'd have them laughing as well. But if I'd said the same thing I probably would have got smacked in the mouth. It is a gift to be able to do that.'

Alley Katz had become a staple of Kalgoorlie's live music scene, and there was always plenty of work around. Kev found himself playing nearly every night of the week, at everything from twenty-first birthday parties to balls as well as the occasional fundraiser. 'The better Miss Australia entrants, the ones with a bit of nous, used to throw a cabaret and raffle a car or something. There was a lot of money in Kalgoorlie.'

One of Kev's favourite party tricks was to sneak backstage and stretch the wires on the bingo cage so that when the hapless Miss Australia contestant spun the cage to determine the winner of the raffle, the little white balls would fly all over the room. The crowd loved that one, and the band would be standing backstage doubled over in laughter. If a Miss Australia entrant could survive a night in Kalgoorlie with Kevin Bloody Wilson and the rest of the pranksters in Alley Katz, chances are she was capable of just about anything.

Apart from the steady income, as a single bloke the other advantage for Kev of being in a band was that there was always a group of girls hanging around after the show who seemed keen to show their appreciation to the band's members, as it were. According to Tex, it was Kev who usually got the first offer. 'He didn't have to try.'

As Kev clumsily attempts to explain, 'I'd just be sitting there being inconspicuous, yep, just sitting in the corner licking my eyebrows. But I'm not a ladies man any more. I'm a lady man now. No, wait up . . . That doesn't sound right, does it?'

Kev soon started to feel right at home in Kalgoorlie, much more so than he'd ever felt in Sydney. He still missed his family, but what Kev had no way of knowing at that point was that he was about to start one of his own.

CHAPTER 5

When Kevvy met Betty

'She was as hot as a stolen Commodore . . .'

Kevin Bloody Wilson

The event that would in many ways shape and define Kev's life was the 1969 Kalgoorlie Easter Racing Carnival. Racing and gambling are extremely popular pastimes in the goldfields, and the annual Kalgoorlie Race Round in late August/ early September is much more than just a series of horse races: to people who live in the area it is the biggest social event of the year, and half of Kalgoorlie takes the entire week off work to enjoy the festivities.

At the Easter carnival that year the band was playing at the Foundry Hotel when Kev spotted a young lady on the dance floor. For Kev, it was love at first sight. 'She had the most magnificent smile I had ever seen.' Her name was Betty Pascoe. Although she had been born in Kalgoorlie, her family had left the goldfields for Perth when she was just a toddler.

Kev didn't realise it at the time, but Betty already knew

exactly who he was. 'I'd already seen him before in Kalgoorlie,' she reveals. 'He was in the band. I used to go to the pub with my cousin whenever we were in town, so I knew who he was but I didn't know he was interested.'

Kev couldn't keep his eyes off her. 'When she sat down with her friends she always seemed to be laughing. I thought, "Well, it's way too early to be pissed, so she must just be a naturally happy person!" The trouble was, she was there with a bloke I knew. So I let it go and then I saw her again at the races the next day.'

As Betty recalls, 'My brother has always been involved with horses so each year we went to the Easter carnival and the race round with my mum and dad and my aunty and cousin. It was the only place to go in Kalgoorlie where you could get dressed up. Back then you used to get *really* dressed up. The hat, the gloves, the shoes . . . the whole bit.

'There was a fashions on the field competition, where they just kinda drag you up on stage and make you stand there to be judged like a bloody horse. Kalgoorlie's like that.'

In his mind, Kev had already placed his bet. 'I said to my mate Leon "Fleabags" O'Donahue, "I reckon the sheila in the blue is gonna win the next one. She's got great fetlocks!"'

Kev continued admiring Betty as she was presented with the sash for best-dressed lady on the field. 'I said to Fleabags, "I'm gonna marry that sheila, she's fuckin' beautiful!" But of course Betty was there with Cousin Colin, who I thought was her boyfriend. He came over to say g'day to me and I said, "G'day Col, your new girlfriend is a bloody stunner," and he said, "That's not my girlfriend. She's my cousin and she wants to meet you." I immediately thought, "You fuckin' beauty, I'm in!"'

Sparks could be seen flying as far away as Esperance

when Kev and Betty got chatting to each other at the races that day. If this meeting had happened in the current millennium the two of them would have simply swapped mobile phone numbers. No such technology existed at the time, but Betty explains that people are never too hard to track down in a country town.

'We always used to go to the Foundry Hotel, 'cos that was the place to go, and my cousin and all my friends were going there, so I knew that I was gonna see him, and because I'd met him I thought he might talk to me. I thought, "If all the other sheilas would just piss off for a while I'd be right." There were always girls around him, groupies I guess you'd call them, but I wasn't gonna be one of those. I thought I'd sit back and he might come to me, and he did. He had a little chat to me.'

Later that night, Kev and Betty were seen disappearing together from the pub and heading in the direction of Betty's aunt's house, where legend has it Betty sat on Kev's knee for the first time, right there in her Aunty Pat's kitchen.

The boundaries of Kev and Betty's young love were being tested right from the start, as they would be again in the years to come. 'That was the first time we chatted and spent any amount of time together and then I went straight back to Perth,' says Betty. 'We didn't really have phones. I had to use a public phone box to call him. We both went to a bit of effort. We wrote letters. Because he worked in music he was always busy weekends. The odd time he would drive to Perth during the week and see me.'

At this early stage the relationship had not been consummated, but Betty reveals that Kev was giving it a serious crack. 'He was trying really hard. He was coming down to Perth as often as he could.'

As Kev so delicately puts it, 'She was as hot as a stolen Commodore and I wanted a quick test drive.' At twenty-two, Kev was by far the more experienced of the two. 'I'd knocked around a bit, but I was surprised at how naïve Betty was.'

Still, whatever Betty needed to know, she knew she could ask Kev and he'd not only give her a straight answer, he'd even offer to perform a demonstration. 'I think that was part of the attraction. I knew I could talk to him about anything and he never ever didn't give me an answer. He was very worldly compared to me because he'd been around Australia so many times and met so many people.

'At that stage we both knew it was getting serious but I thought it wouldn't work because of what he was doing, which was music. When other people got time off that's when he was at his busiest, so he really didn't have spare time to be coming to Perth all the time. I was playing sport on weekends as well, so I didn't always get up to Kalgoorlie either, it was just every now and again.'

Before too long Kev and Betty decided that what was happening between them was indeed the real deal, and the whole living-in-separate-cities thing had to stop. 'He couldn't move to Perth, that was never gonna happen. I still had my Aunty Pat and some other distant family up there so I said I'd go back to Kal, and I did, much to my parents' surprise at the time. My dad said he'd worked his whole life to get us out of that town. I said, "Yeah, well, Dad, things have changed," and it worked out all right, didn't it?'

Betty moved in with her Aunty Pat, while Kev had a little rented room at the back of Kalgoorlie's Foundry Hotel. 'Occasionally he would come to my aunt's for dinner but most of the time he'd just pick me up and we'd go up to the Golden Mile dining room. It was this old-fashioned dining room, upstairs. You could get a roast dinner for about four bucks, so we'd eat there a lot of nights.'

By now there was no doubt in Kev's mind that this was the woman he wanted to marry. 'It's not what I wanted, it's what I needed, a proper girlfriend. Someone to deliver me from temptation and help keep me off the piss every night.'

He had already sneaked into Smales Jewellers on Hannan Street and bought the ring; now he needed to think about the venue for the proposal. The two most readily available places were his beloved AP5 Valiant, where many key moments of Kev and Betty's courtship had already taken place, or Aunty Pat's kitchen. The kitchen won out, and with Kev on bended knee Betty had no hesitation in saying yes.

'I was really impressed. It was romantic and wonderful. I mean, it wasn't a really big ring, but to me it was huge. There wasn't a lot of money around for either of us back then.

'We had already organised to go to Perth in October that year for my twenty-first birthday, so we had a party in Kalgoorlie with a few friends and then we went to Perth. We had my twenty-first at the back of my parents' house in Morley, and we announced our engagement at that party. He'd already proposed and I was wearing the ring, so everyone was all excited.'

A photographer was hired to take photos of the engagement, but every single one of his photos ended up being horribly underexposed; instead of getting upset about it, Kev turned it into an opportunity to have some fun.

'In the photos Betty came out looking quite dark so I told my mum and dad back in Sydney that Betty was black, and I sent the photos over with a note saying she was a topless dancer with the South African Ballet, who were touring

Australia at the time. My dad simply asked, "Are you happy, son?" I said, "Yes, Dad," and he said, "Well, that's OK with us."'

The next logical step was to choose a wedding date, although the timing of that turned out to be beyond Kev's control. 'The doctor sort of did it for me.'

Betty, who it is safe to say was no longer a virgin by this point in the story, was walking home from work for lunch one day when, out of nowhere, she started throwing up. 'I really was very naïve, and you didn't speak much about the birds and the bees back then. You didn't ask a lot of questions, so I was in the position where I didn't know how far I could go without getting pregnant, if you know what I mean. I really didn't know what it was all about.

'I had no idea about the pill. I had been to the doctor, who was a strict Catholic, and he wasn't very forthcoming. He didn't explain anything to me at all. I just said to him, "I'd like to go on the pill now," and he got all huffy and puffy. I just couldn't believe it. He wrote the prescription out and threw it at me. I was too scared and embarrassed to ask any questions so I just grabbed it and took off.

'You had to take one pill every day for the whole month—I don't know if some of them were sugar or whatever, and when you had your period you were supposed to take these other ones. Well, it seems that I took the bloody things back to front.'

In the late sixties falling pregnant before marriage was still something of a social taboo, especially in a country town where everybody knew everybody else's business, but Kev never regretted his and Betty's happy little accident. 'It was at the tail end of the whole stigma thing, but there was never a stigma as far as I was concerned. We were both arse over head in love, Betty was pregnant, and we were having a baby. Fan-fuckin'-tastic!'

The next step was to inform Betty's father that he was about to become a grandfather. This was not an easy call for Betty to make, as she recalls. 'We went to the phone box that was near the Kalgoorlie Car Barn, and I rang and I was starting to speak to my dad, and I couldn't tell him. I started crying and Kev said, "Do you want me to talk to him?" and I said, "Yes please."

'Kev got on the phone and told Dad. He just said, "This is the way it is. As you know we are engaged and we plan to get married, well, now we just have to put it a little sooner. We should probably have it around the January coming up."'

Both of Betty's parents offered their full support, as did Kev's, but just in case they didn't Betty had a backup plan in mind, even if it was a slightly sketchy one. 'I was heading straight east. Even as silly and naïve as I was, I thought, "I can't go home." I don't know what I was gonna do but I was going east. I was twenty-one.'

Betty's parents quickly adapted to the news, but not without quizzing their daughter about whether or not this was definitely the man she wanted to marry. Says Betty, 'I never really had any doubts that he truly loved me, but almost in spite of myself I did say to Kev, "If you're doing this just because I'm pregnant then don't be doing it. I can't have you marry me just because I'm having a baby." I knew the sort of life that he had had up until then, and I knew there were a lot of women in Kalgoorlie who had been rather close to him and were still hanging around, so to speak. That's why I said, "Don't be feeling sorry for me or anything." He didn't shy away from it at all. That's one of the qualities I continue to find in him. He was very open and always positive.'

For Kev, there was only ever one course of action he was

going to take when it came to his freshly knocked up fiancée. 'There was never any doubt in my mind that we should get married. We loved each other, simple.'

Kev, who has described himself as a recovering Catholic, and Betty, who cheerfully admits to being a 'bush Baptist', were married at St Mary's Church in Kalgoorlie on 10 January 1970. Some of their friends and family may have been surprised to see them having a big church wedding, but Kev and Betty chose to do this for their parents' benefit.

The reception was a fairly low-key affair at the Kalgoorlie RSL. Alley Katz guitarist Tex Curran was among the guests, and he recalls the effect on some of the locals of the marriage of one of Kalgoorlie's most eligible bachelors. 'The town was abuzz. To be honest, there were so many other chicks who were always hanging around Kev, but until that day I wasn't sure if Kev thought that Betty was just another one. There were chicks hanging around outside the church too.'

Tex and his wife Carol could not afford a wedding present, not that that bothered Kev or Betty one bit. Says Kev, 'I remember that Tex and Carol's wedding present to us was to invite us around for a barbecue the weekend after the wedding. That was the scene, everybody was struggling, and he told me quite openly that he couldn't afford a wedding present but he'd love to have us round for a family barbecue. We understood, because financially we were in the exact same position. Of all the wedding presents we were given, Tex and Carol's family barbecue was the one we both treasure and remember most.'

Betty and Kev moved into their new home straight away. It was, Betty recalls, 'this tiny little apartment at a place called Fordville Flats, and they were primitive to say the least, with wooden verandahs, corrugated iron roof, lino on the floors, wood stove and a chip heater for the bathwater. We didn't even have a shower.'

The newlyweds could not afford a honeymoon, nor could they afford to take any time off. On Sunday, the night after the wedding, Kev did a gig with Alley Katz at the Foundry Hotel. 'At that stage too we were playing Thursday, Friday and Saturday, as well as two gigs every Sunday. We had two nights off and on one of those nights we practised. Everyone had jobs during the day, too. Tex was a barber, Terry was an underground surveyor and Graham was working with WD & HO Wills as a cigarette distributor.' It would be another seven years before Kev and Betty would finally go on what they describe as their honeymoon, when they had the first of many overseas adventures together in Japan.

News travels fast in a country town, especially something as deliciously scandalous as a shotgun wedding, and Betty knew people were talking about it behind her back. 'Up until we got married he was a bit of a local playboy, so when we got married so quickly of course the first thing people said was, "She's gotta be pregnant." But I did have them thinking a bit because I never showed until right before I went into hospital.'

The other thing which probably threw some of the locals off the scent was the fact that Betty continued playing hockey for Kalgoorlie Police and Citizens, or KPC, until she was six months pregnant. 'Nearing the end of my pregnancy I was starting to feel quite tired and when I got to around seven months I stopped work. I got really lazy, which isn't like me at all. So Kev would get up to go to work and I'd have breakfast with him and then I'd go back to bed. Some nights he'd come home and I'd still be asleep. I always think, "How did I do that?" because I'm nothing like that now.'

Like pregnancy itself the process of labour was still a bit of a mystery to Betty, even while it was happening to her. 'The night before Travis was born I was getting backaches. I hadn't any books on the subject, and I didn't want to go back to that pompous doctor, so I had no idea what was going on. I had a really restless night, but I still didn't realise I was in labour. Then I got up and told Kev I felt a bit yucky. He said he'd take me to hospital and I said I didn't want to go. I wasn't ready.'

Kev thought that Betty was very ready indeed, but instead of pushing the issue he enlisted an older widowed neighbour to keep an eye on Betty while he went to work. He told Betty he'd be back at lunchtime to check on her, and at the exact moment he kissed her goodbye Betty's waters broke. 'He said, "That's it, you're going!" and I was pleading, "No! I'm not ready!" I was really quite upset because I was scared.'

It was around eight am on 3 July 1970. This was an era when fathers were not encouraged to stay with their wives during childbirth. Kev explains: 'My mates told me that watching your wife giving birth is like watching your favourite pub burn down.' In fact, they were actively discouraged from being involved. Says Betty, 'The new dads can be there now and I so wish Kev could have been there back then because he would have loved it. He wanted to be there but the tough-titties matron wouldn't let him.'

It's fair to say that Kev has always had a problem dealing with bureaucracy, and it certainly showed on this all-important day. 'I took Betty to the hospital, then they just told me to fuck off so I went to work. Then at about eleven in the morning I snuck back to check on her. When I got there she was being prepped, that involved shaving and everything in those days. So I bent over to give her a kiss and she fuckin'' spewed all over me. I thought, "Fuck! It's not just the cranky old matron! Betty hates me too! I'm outta here!"'

Betty explains, 'I'd had some cereal in the morning, which I probably shouldn't have, but I was hungry and I didn't know you weren't supposed to eat.'

Kev had kissed Betty twice that day and was starting to become concerned with the pattern that seemed to be emerging. 'The first time I kissed her, her waters broke. The second time, she fuckin' spewed all over me. I wasn't fuckin' game to kiss her again in case she pulled out a knife and cut me knackers off.'

Thankfully, Kev's fears were unfounded and from then on it was a relatively quick and uneventful labour. Travis Ronald Bryant was born around lunchtime while his father paced the corridors of Kalgoorlie Regional Hospital waiting to meet his firstborn. Betty also had to wait a while to do some mother–son bonding. 'Back then they'd take the baby from you and they'd do the weighing and everything, and Kev was desperate to see me and his son but they wouldn't let him. Eventually they took the baby down to the nursery, so Kev saw him quickly as he came out before they took him away for all of his tests.'

For Kev, laying eyes on his infant son for the first time was nothing short of monumental. 'I didn't realise it at the time, but without doubt it is the most life-changing event in your entire existence. Your life is just stopped at that point, then instantly rearranged. It now spins around this little infant who is totally and forever the hub of the wheel. Everything you do from now on in is done with them in mind, and it still is, thirty-plus years later.'

When it came to choosing a name for their son, there had been two front-runners: Travis and Benjamin. Kev had always thought that Benjamin Bryant had a ring to it, but Betty wasn't so sure. 'It didn't sit with me, so I told him he could call our recently acquired dog Benjamin instead, which he did. I'd never heard the name Travis. I thought it was really different.'

Kev explains, 'Merle Travis is a country guitar player. I'd never heard Travis used as a Christian name, and I just liked the sound of it; it's a strong-sounding name. It means one who travels, which turned out to be very prophetic considering he's now a pilot. Travis was about three months old when I found out that Glen Campbell also had a baby son named Travis. That was the first time I'd ever heard somebody else use the name.'

While Betty was still in hospital with Travis, Kev was determined to be with his wife and his newborn baby boy as much as he could or, more to the point, for as long as the matron would allow. It didn't take Kev long to bend the rules, as Betty recalls. 'All the other dads would come during the regimented visiting hours but Kev would come and see me before work and then he'd come again in the middle of the day while he was out on a delivery from Musgroves. He loved just being there watching me as I adjusted to being a new mum.

'I remember the cranky old matron shaking her finger at him, threatening, "You're going to have to pay for another bed if you keep coming in here all the time!" She waved her finger towards the door—"Out!"—and I remember he came straight back at her and said, "Listen here, vinegar tits, that's my wife, and that's my son, so *you* do the fuckin' off," so she did, and I sat back laughing, thinking, "That's fair enough." After that old vinegar tits was a whole lot more gracious.'

Just over a week later Betty was sent home with Travis. 'I thought, "How am I going to be a mother?" I'm sure that goes through most new mums' minds. It seems that certain instincts just kick in, because we all survived.'

CHAPTER 6

This song is suitable for miners

'I think there's a certain respect for electricians 'cos unlike plumbers you're working with shit you can't see.'

Kevin Bloody Wilson

In the early 1970s, Kalgoorlie was experiencing the beginning of a massive nickel boom which continues to this day. Kev, performing four nights a week with Alley Katz, applied for an apprenticeship as an electrician at the nickel smelter; he became the first adult apprentice to be employed by Western Mining Corp. He recalls, 'They were hiring school leavers, so I simply asked them to consider me. I was married and settled so I managed to sell them on the idea. We'd both live to regret that one.'

It was a five-year apprenticeship that would finish when Kev was thirty-one and give him another profession to fall back on as he struggled to provide for his young family. 'In

Kalgoorlie if you had a trade you had it made,' says Kev. 'I thought being a sparky was something that would engage me. I didn't particularly fancy building stuff or being a boilermaker.'

One of the first friends Kev made when he started his apprenticeship was leading-hand instrument technician John Merry. 'John went on to tutor me in electronics. It was fairly early days in the industry. I remember learning the difference between electrics and electronics: with electrics, you burn things down; with electronics, you blow things up.'

John had seen Kev on stage and had an idea of the sort of character he was dealing with. 'Kev used to play at the Exchange Hotel and someone would make a request or something and he'd just make up a song about it. He made up songs about me—there was one time years later when he came back to Kalgoorlie as Kevin Bloody Wilson and was doing a big function at the Kalgoorlie-Boulder racecourse, and I walked in a bit late. He spotted my bald head, stopped what he was doing and he said, "Look, there's a bloke here who's forgotten to take his fuckin' hard hat off!" Everyone looked around and saw me straight away. It was just unbelievably embarrassing, and then of course he continued to pick me out for the rest of the evening. But it was all good fun. Kev was very much his own man, even back then. Once he was in full flight you had no hope.

'He wasn't afraid of anything. He just said what he felt at the time and that was it. I think he did a very brave thing by taking on the adult apprenticeship. Most of the others were fifteen or sixteen and he would have been in his mid-twenties. I remember having a chat one day and I said, "When you get your electrician's ticket you'll be right, you'll be set for life," and he said, "I'm not gonna be an electrician. I'm gonna be a performer."'

The seven am starts soon began to take their toll on Kev, who was tired from gigging at night. John Merry would occasionally find him passed out in a quiet corner somewhere. 'That was one of Kev's problems: he couldn't make the early morning starts too well 'cos he'd be up all night playing with his band. At the smelter, there were a few places where he could go and have a sleep for half an hour during the day. It wasn't only Kevin; if we'd go out on a job all of us would put a pile of sacks in a corner and have a rest, then you'd go back to work and you'd be fine.'

John was impressed with Kev's determination. 'Doing what he was doing with the band and starting early in the morning you're bound to be a bit weary at times. But his drive was absolutely amazing. He wasn't gonna be an electrician for the rest of his life, it was just a thing he could do if everything went belly-up. But it was never gonna go belly-up with Kevin.'

In addition to his aversion to early rises, it didn't take long for Kev to get bored with the work itself. He recalls, 'The first couple of years were great because you were learning new stuff all the time but after that it became very monotonous. What made it great was the characters I met.

'There was one time I was working with a French sparky, and we were trying to find a fault. We were working on what they call bins, huge steel silos that feed the powdered nickel ore into the furnace for the smelting process. The furnace then turns the powdered nickel into a molten state, which is then sprayed through a powerful jet of water, turning it into tiny little glass-like pebbles.

'So here we are, me and the Frog, up there working on this bin, and it was a new one at the time, and one of the electrical installations was showing up faults in the control room. Between the control room and where we were was the actual furnace and when we opened the electrical cabinet, a single wire fell out.

'The Frenchman says, "What is zis?" 'cos it wasn't ended off or anything. It was just a thirty-two-volt insulated wire which had been stripped about a quarter of an inch from the end, ready to be installed, but it hadn't been installed anywhere. It was just hanging loose in the cabinet.

'So the Frenchman is thinking out loud, "What is zis thing?", and as he grabbed it, it sparked on the metal cabinet. He asked me if I knew what the wire was for, so naturally I grabbed it and sparked it on the side of the cabinet again. We were trying to figure out what its function was, and why there was power running through it, and during that process we probably zapped it about nine or ten times on the edge of the metal frame of the cabinet.

'What we didn't know was that every time the rogue wire made contact with the cabinet it blew out a complete switch-board panel back at the control room. Not only did this cause tens of thousands of dollars' damage to each successive panel, it also shut down the heating process of the entire fuckin' nickel smelter, and a smelter ain't a smelter without fuckin' heat. What then happens is that after about twenty-four hours' downtime, the hot part of the furnace cools down, the bricks that line it start to cool down and contract, and then the bricks dislodge and simply start to fall. The whole smelter staff, including all the bosses, had to stay on the job for about four days straight, and they reckon if they hadn't got it in time they'd have had to rebrick the entire smelter, at a further cost of fuckin' millions, all because we were up there fuckin' around with a stray wire. We shut the whole fucking plant down with thirty-two volts.

'The Frog got sent straight back to France, where he probably got a job with the French secret service sabotage team, while I became a fuckin' legend for providing my mates with four days of triple overtime.'

Kev's take-no-prisoners approach to comedy was already evident during his days as a sparky in the mid-seventies. He grins as he remembers another incident from that time. 'There was a train station at the nickel smelter where they loaded all the processed nickel onto the trains. The carriages were enclosed, and they'd pour the nickel into them and then cart it almost seven hundred kilometres to Kwinana on the coast. These carriages were huge, and this bloke, a complete wanker who nobody liked, decided to write his name in huge white letters all the way down the side of one of these carriages: DEXTER. I saw him do it and I watched where he hid the spray can, so when he was out of sight I added a few more letters: DEXTER *IS A CUNT*. That was funny shit, but what made it even funnier was that poor ole Dexter's pedigree was being read by everyone from Kalgoorlie all the way to Kwinana.'

Like everyone else at the smelter John Merry hated the early starts on winter mornings, but it was on one of those cold August mornings that John witnessed some of Kev's very early, very best work.

'There was a bit of union argy-bargy at the smelter, and everyone was cold and grumpy. At the time Ansett Airlines had a commercial where all the staff used to get together and dance in a conga line. They used to sing, "We're all going to be a little bit more friendly." So Kevin came in and just started this conga line. Within a couple of minutes you had a workshop full of electricians, mechanics, fitters, boilermakers, even foremen, dancing along in the conga line hanging on to Kev as we all went around the shed. There must have been sixty of us doing the conga around the workshop.

'It was so spontaneous, it was just brilliant, and that was the sort of thing that he could do. There was tension in the air, mates were against mates, foremen against tradesmen and all that sort of stuff, and he just defused it in a matter of minutes. It was just very funny and it was also very clever.'

Having a second baby wasn't something Betty thought she'd be doing until several more years down the track, but once again the timing turned out to be beyond her and Kev's control.

'Because we were still struggling financially and we didn't have our own home, we thought we'd wait a while,' says Betty. 'The Valiant was parked in the garage at that point because we couldn't afford to get it registered. I think I couldn't afford to get my prescription for the pill redone . . . it was extra money that we didn't have, so then Tammy came along. Travis and Tammy were born twenty-two months apart, which I think is great now, but back then I thought, "What the hell are we gonna do?"'

As Tammy's birth approached Kev was working almost around the clock, so Betty's father offered to come to Kalgoorlie to help look after Travis when Betty was due to go into hospital. He stayed with the family for a couple of weeks waiting for Betty to have the baby, but nothing happened. After dinner one night he went for a walk with Betty and politely explained that he could not stay in

Kalgoorlie forever because he had things to do back in Perth, and could she please hurry up and have the baby. Betty dutifully followed her father's instructions and went into labour later that night.

It was 27 March 1972, and Tammy Jo Bryant was ready to make her grand entrance. Kevin dropped Betty off at the hospital and said he'd come back at lunchtime, but everything happened very fast after that, as Betty recalls. 'I had Tammy much quicker than anyone thought I was going to. I was busting to call someone but there were no phones. I was so excited that I'd had a girl, so now I had a boy and a girl, but I couldn't tell anyone.'

Upon returning to the hospital during his lunch break Kev was surprised to see Betty sitting up in bed with her knees up under the blanket. 'I thought she was still pregnant. I said, "What's happening? You haven't had the baby yet?" and she told me we'd had a little girl.'

As with Travis, Kev wanted to give his new daughter a name straight out of the American country music almanac. 'My favourite singer was Tammy Wynette, she was married to George Jones. So, Tammy Jo.' These days Tammy Jo is also known as TJ (by her friends and fans), T (by her husband), and by her most recent stage name, Jenny Talia from Australia.

Travis was not allowed into the hospital to meet his new sister, and had been constantly asking for his mother during the week she was away following the birth. Betty can still remember his reaction when she finally returned. 'Mum's not there, so it's like I've deserted him. So when I came home with this new baby he wouldn't even come to me. He wouldn't give me a kiss or a cuddle. He just went straight to his father and ignored me. I was heartbroken. I couldn't believe it. It took me a week to get him back. And from then on every time I tried to feed Tammy he was all over me going, "Right, you've got her, I wanna be on the other arm," so it sorted itself out pretty quickly.

'Tammy was not a good baby for the first few months. She struggled because I had a bit of a problem. I had dermatitis and it was all over my breasts, so I couldn't feed Tammy because of the ointment I was using. She couldn't take her bottle, and as soon as she did she'd throw it back up. I didn't feel good at all, because I'd fed Travis and he was so good and it felt so right to do the breastfeeding. And then for three months nothing went right with her. She wasn't sleeping at all. She'd sleep for an hour then wake up crying. It really does affect your mind and your body. You don't sleep, and of course you've got another child as well. It's really quite tough.'

Kev was busy too. He had his day job as an apprentice, the gigs he was doing at night with Alley Katz, plus he was working part-time at the local radio station, 6KG. (That's a whole other story that we'll get to in the next chapter.) At the same time Kev was expanding his musical horizons. Alley Katz were not just a country music act; they also played the contemporary hits of the era, everything from Neil Diamond to the Beatles to Jimi Hendrix, and most of it was music that Kev had never previously been exposed to. Kev enjoyed his time gigging with Alley Katz, although he did get sick to death of playing Neil Diamond's 'Sweet Caroline' over and over again at cabarets for the pissed punters, as you would.

The members of Alley Katz had been gigging hard in and around Kalgoorlie, and they decided to reward themselves for all their hard work, as guitarist Tex Curran recalls. 'At the time we were doing cabarets four or five nights a week, so money was coming in, and we were sitting around one night and we decided that we should all go overseas together.'

Kev's suggestion was a weekend on Rottnest Island, a forty-five-minute ferry ride from Perth. Thankfully, nobody took him seriously, says Tex, or it would have been quite possibly the lamest overseas journey ever. 'Everyone went and got brochures and we all got together at Kev and Betty's place and agreed on where to go. We came up with a trip to Singapore, Hong Kong and Japan, and then back the same way. We worked hard for that. Once we set a date, every spare cent went straight in the bank.'

It was 1977, and Kev and Betty were finally off on their long-awaited honeymoon, albeit seven years after the wedding and with the rest of the band tagging along. They were both buzzing as they jetted off on the first of many overseas adventures. 'It was amazing to be walking up the stairs of a British Airways 747 jumbo jet,' Kev recalls. 'I'd been in an aeroplane before but never overseas and this thing was just fuckin' amazing.'

Travis was dragged along to see his parents off and remembers being similarly impressed. 'It was the first time I'd ever seen a 747. It was at Perth airport where you could stand at the wire fence and see all the planes—where the domestic terminal is now, pretty much. Back then I never thought I'd be a pilot, let alone flying one of those big buggers.'

Travis and Tammy stayed with Betty's parents while Kev and Betty went to Japan, and Kev left some instructions for Travis. 'He made me write a diary every single day. I got about five days into it and then I asked Nanna Pascoe to write it.'

In Japan, Kev was struck by the friendliness of the people. 'One of the things that really impressed me was when we were walking past a high school and it was snowing. A whole group of girls were shooting basketball nets, and Betty and I stood at the gate watching them for about thirty seconds. They stopped playing and two of them came over to us, and one of them handed the ball to Betty, then took her arm and escorted her into the schoolyard to shoot nets with them. Imagine if that was Japs walking past an Australian school. The Aussie kids would probably be picking up rocks and chucking them at the cunts.'

For Tex Curran, this was a trip of many firsts. 'It was the first time most of us had seen snow, although Kev had already seen it during his touring days through the Snowy Mountains of New South Wales. But for all of us, Kev included, this was just amazing.

'We went to the foothills just below Mount Fuji and there was a Japanese chap there . . . strange, that. He had a kid with a little plastic toboggan. One of us asked if we could have a ride, so we borrowed this little kid's toboggan, hopped in it and slid down the smaller slopes of the mountain. So for three-quarters of an hour we're all playing with this kid's toboggan while the Japanese bloke just stood there with this little kid.'

The whole band had a go, including Kev. He recalls, 'The trouble was, we'd all bought new denim jeans in Hong Kong on the way up to Japan, so every time you came off the toboggan you'd leave a fucking big blue stripe in the snow.'

As part of such a large group, Kev and Betty needed to occasionally duck off by themselves if they were going to make this trip feel in any way like a honeymoon. 'We had honeymoon times when we got back to the hotel, bloody duty-free alcohol and wild sex. It was great, a proper holiday.'

Shopping was another activity that dominated Kev's Japanese adventure. 'The women were mad on shopping for watches and things like that. Betty and I treated ourselves, and then we bought a big silver trunk and just crammed it full of toys for Travis and TJ. We missed them like buggery. It was great when we came back to Australia to be coming home to the kids and bringing them presents. We also noticed in Travis's diary that he'd progressed to running writing.'

As a kid who loved electronic gadgets, Travis was impressed by the contents of the big silver trunk. 'They brought back all sorts of really cool stuff that you couldn't get in Australia at the time. I got a remote control car, and I'd never seen one in my life before, so that was pretty good. TJ got a doll that could piss itself.'

Upon his return from Japan, Kev went straight back to work. Around this time a new form of musical and comedic expression was creeping into Kev's on-stage persona. Says Kev, 'When I was in Kalgoorlie I had a copy of an album called *Bawdy Barroom Ballads*, and they were all old songs like "Charlotte the Harlot", "The Good Ship Venus", "The Hairs on Her Dicky-Di-Do", stuff like that. It amazed me that there wasn't anything contemporary being written . . . some of these songs were over a hundred years old and, worse than that, they sounded like they had been sung by a drunken pommy rugby team to the accompaniment of an equally drunken piano player and recorded on a fuckin' two-dollar tape recorder.

'Another idea probably got filed away at that point: why weren't they recorded properly? Why hasn't somebody had a crack at doing proper recordings of these sorts of songs? The other thing I found strange about that album was that they were using expressions like "I'll be blowed" instead of "I'll be fucked", which I thought was a bit timid.'

Before too long Kev was coming up with his own bawdy ballads and trying them out on the Kalgoorlie crowds. He wasn't consciously trying to reinvent himself as a comedian, he just needed more songs to fill out the set list every night. So in effect, Kevin Bloody Wilson was born out of necessity.

'We were playing four nights a week, so no matter how big your set list is you're going to run out of songs. I started to throw some of my self-written songs in, and instantly we'd get a better audience response to these new bawdy ballads than to most of the pop tunes we were playing at the time. All I was doing was writing songs for my mates, about my mates.'

With the Alley Katz, Kev was also continuing to write bastardised versions of other people's songs—his 'decompositions'. 'They'd compose 'em, we'd decompose 'em. The audience response was always encouraging, and we gave our home crowd, as well as ourselves, a fuckin' piss-funny night out. It also gave me the impetus to continue writing more of them.'

As Tex recalls, 'It became part of almost every gig: Kev was always introducing his new songs while we all continued to fuck up the old ones.'

Kev had also been bouncing some of his safer songs off Travis, who remembers 'one song by Johnny Chester, called "You're Always Welcome at Our House", and it was about a visitor coming to the house, a salesman or something like that, and one member of the family would knock him over the head with the broom and they'd put him in the broom cupboard. Dad would change that song around to suit us and we'd play it for relatives when they came over. We'd have little singalongs.'

Another of Travis's childhood memories is of his dad's early starts at the nickel smelter. The kids were too young to be left at home on their own, so they had to drag themselves out of bed before sunrise and jump in the car with Betty when she drove Kev the forty-kilometre round-trip to the smelter. Travis remembers finding it much easier to be up before the sun than his father did. 'Dad hated getting out of bed—Mum had to prise him out some mornings, particularly after he'd been gigging the night before. Mum would have his breakfast ready when he woke up and all he would have to do is get dressed and have breakfast on his lap in the car on the way out to the smelter. He absolutely hated it. As a kid I couldn't understand why he did it, but I totally get it now.'

Kev wasn't too sure why he was doing it either. 'My pay packet was about fifty bucks working a forty-hour week at the smelter, but by then I was makin' a coupla hundred bucks for sixteen hours as a fuckin' musician. It was just beyond comparison, so my focus certainly wasn't on being a sparky. The reason I stuck with it was for the family. I was determined to finish what I'd started. I also thought the kids deserved to have a dad with a *proper job*.'

However, Kev's focus on having a proper job wavered more and more as the exhaustion of trying to juggle all of his commitments started to get the better of him. 'Sometimes I'd finish a gig at eleven pm, race home, put my clobber on, then I'd go and work night shift at the smelter.'

There were compensations, though. Towards the end of his apprenticeship Kev was able to take on a more senior role in the smelter's pecking order. 'I used to have fun convincing new apprentices they had to hold hands with me as we walked down the main corridor of the smelter, the five-hundred-metre road that goes from the electrical workshop past all the other trades' workshops, down to the control office. I told these young blokes that they had to hold hands with me so everyone knew they were *my* apprentice. I never did let them in on the joke, so to this day there's probably heaps of 'em out there who still think I'm as gay as two blokes fuckin'.'

In spite of his long hours, Kev and Betty's house in Kalgoorlie was always full of friends. TJ remembers falling asleep on Friday nights to the sound of laughing, singing and guitars in the lounge. 'It was great. It was such a musical home. I thought everyone's dad was in a band, 'cos all my dad's friends were.'

Still, Kev and Betty weren't seeing a lot of each other. As Tex Curran points out, 'Only a certain sort of woman can put up with that sort of thing, where the husband is away five or six nights a week as well as working during the day.'

Kev concurs. 'Sadly, it's not like you're compensating during the day or even on the weekends, you're just never there. I don't think there's a dad in the world who wouldn't have liked to have spent more time with his kids while they were growin' up.'

Like any guy with a young family, Kev had been doing whatever was necessary to put food on the table. 'By now, though, it wasn't like we were completely broke. We were all starting to see some reward for our efforts. The band was doing really well.'

While things were looking up for Kev as a performer, his smelter days were numbered. All he wanted to do was to get his ticket as an electrician before he or Western Mining ran out of patience. John Merry could see the writing on the wall. As entertaining as Kev's antics at the smelter were, the guys who ran the show were finding Kev a bit difficult to manage.

'He was always in trouble at the smelter in one way or another,' says John. 'I think it was about the time when he finished his apprenticeship and there had been some problems, especially for the nickel smelter's chief engineer, Doug Marshall. We were all in the workshop, a big bunch of us this particular morning, and someone came in and shouted, "Marshall's coming!" So of course we all went to the benches to look busy, people started sweeping up, and we all knew that he was going to tell Kev off. Kev just walked into the middle of the shed, tucked his thumbs in his electrician's belt with the pliers and screwdrivers and things hanging there, then walked bow-legged the length of this massive shed.

'He waited by the door. As Doug Marshall walked in, Kev just stood there and then, with his best John Wayne stance and accent, challenged him: "Marshall, this town ain't big enough for both of us!" Everybody cracked up, we couldn't stop ourselves. Poor Doug Marshall had steam coming out of his ears. He turned around and walked out the door. He had no comeback. It was just beautiful. I can remember it as clear as day.'

Betty recalls the night Kev decided he'd had enough of being a sparky. It happened just weeks after he finally got his qualification as an electrician. 'He came back home one night, only about an hour after he'd left for work, and he said, "I'm not doing that shit any more." He said, "I'm up to my nuts in nickel dust and I fuckin' hate it," and he never went back again.'

CHAPTER 7

Radio days

'Don't let people without a life dictate how you should live yours.'
Kevin Bloody Wilson

In the years after he quit his job at the nickel smelter Kev had more time to focus on his various other passions, including his radio gig at 6KG, a part-time job that he started before— and continued throughout—his five-year apprenticeship as a sparky. In typical Kev fashion, despite having no prior radio experience he gleefully threw himself into learning yet another new skill.

Says Kev, 'I was always a huge country music buff, and before I started at 6KG they used to have a country music show on the air from nine until ten Sunday mornings, and it was left up to the jock doing the shift to find the records to play. They didn't have any information. They didn't even seem that interested. They were just playing a big pile of records that were left in the studio for them, hence it was not a good show.'

One night in 1972 after a gig at the Exchange Hotel, Kev spotted 6KG's station manager in the audience and wandered over for a chat. 'I said to him, "I'd be happy to give your disc jockeys the information I have in my books and all my press clippings on country music," and he said, "You've worked with microphones and stuff, why don't you come over and do an audition yourself?" and so I did. They taught me how to work the panel, which took about a minute and a half, and I pretty much started straight away.'

Kev's radio name was the same as his stage name at the time, Bryan Dennis. Kev didn't think he was particularly great on the radio to start with, but at least he was very passionate and informed about country music. 'All your mates are listening to you, so was the whole fuckin' town, so at first it was a bit intimidating. I eased my way into it. "Time on 6KG is ten past seven!" "Good morning, this is Bryan Dennis! Welcome to 6KG!" I didn't launch into talking straight away about what I knew about the artists, but eventually I loosened up and started to ad-lib and have some fun with it.'

Within three months Kev turned the whole format around and personally found sponsors for a three-hour show called *Country Countdown*. He was also the panel operator for other people's shows, including the Sunday morning sports show.

One of his regular listeners was guitarist Tex Curran. 'He was very good on radio. It was a very popular show. Once again he used the same recipe [as performing with Alley Katz], playing songs that were hits. You can't go wrong if you play that stuff. On the radio he was a little subdued, but still funny. He'd go to a place that was just on the borderline—he knew just how to do that.'

Travis was a fan too. 'Dad was really good on the radio. He was popular, he was professional, and in that industry at the time—especially in Kalgoorlie—I don't know if it was even that important to be professional. He didn't have to be.'

This professionalism was not necessarily reflected within the radio station itself. Kev and the rest of the weekend staff at 6KG would get their breakfast delivered from the BP service station down the road; Kev recalls, 'One morning I had a sausage left over from breakfast at the end of my shift. The Sunday morning sports reporter, Milton Cairnduff, was sitting opposite me reading live to air, and I was pushing the buttons for him. While he was reading I casually unzipped my fly, stuck the sausage out of my pants and left the panel and walked around to where Milton was sitting, then started to wave this big fat pork sausage in his face. The poor bastard was trying not to break up, but I could see I was gettin' to him.'

Kev then decided to up the stakes by producing a pair of scissors out of nowhere and chopping the sausage in half. 'The dispatched knob-end of the sausage rolled across Milton's script, leaving a trail of tomato sauce all over the page. But just before he slipped into uncontrollable belly laughter, Milton blurted, "We'll be right back after this commercial." It was all I could do to stop from screaming, "Fuck you, Milton!" 'cos I had to run back around to my side of the panel to push the button to start the fucking ad break. The result: sports reporter, one; Kev, nil.'

Alley Katz had enjoyed a long run as Kalgoorlie's premier party band, but Tex Curran felt the time was right for him to move on. 'I wanted to have a bit of a break for a while. My wife and I went on to run a hostel for geographically isolated children—there was no high school in Laverton or Leonora so the kids would come and stay at the hostel and go to school in Kalgoorlie. So I pulled out of the band and they got another guitarist to replace me, [New Zealander] Jim Williamson, plus his talented singing wife, Anne. With Kev and our keyboard player Terry Carlsson they formed a new band called Delta.'

Delta lasted around three years but disbanded when Jim and Anne returned to New Zealand, at which point Tex Curran rejoined the band. By now Kev's reputation and profile as a musician, presenter and entertainer was well established in the goldfields area and Kev put that profile to good use, naming his new band Bryan Dennis and the Country Club.

'That's where we really cornered a market, as Bryan Dennis and the Country Club,' says Kev. 'We did support shows for all the cabaret acts that came through town, from the A-listers like Normie Rowe, Duane Eddy, the Platters, the Drifters and Judy Stone through to all sorts of really weird acts.

'Cabaret was huge in Kalgoorlie at the time, all sorts of strange things, whip-crackers and fire-eating hippie jugglers and shit. I remember one time this family turned up—Mum and Dad, the spunky big-titted young daughter and the drunken, drug-fucked son—with an act that was something straight out of the twilight zone. A whole family of fuckin' cowbell ringers. How could parents be so cruel? Why would you bother passing that shit on to your kids? How do you get good at that shit? *Ding-a-fucking-ling-a-ling-a-ling*; daughter wobbles tits; *ding-a-fucking-ling-a-ling-a-ling*; Dad juggles cowbells; *ding-a-fucking-ling-a-ling-a-ling*; son plays out-of-tune guitar; more *ding-a-fucking-ling-a-ling-a-ling*. While

Mum, on her own little planet, provides an even more out of tune yodelling soundtrack. It was a monstrous musical train smash. *Ding-a-fucking-ling-a-ling-a-fucking-ling-and-a-yodel-diddle-leddy-dee.* Fuck, I miss Kalgoorlie.'

Kev has always been a true country music enthusiast, and he felt his radio show was being held back by the lack of availability of new music by the artists he was enjoying reading about. To solve this problem Kev joined the Country Music Association in Nashville under the disc jockey charter. He wrote to their newsletter and explained that he wanted to get hold of some albums by new country artists so he could play them on his radio show.

A month or so after his letter was printed Kev began to be bombarded by packages from American record companies containing all sorts of country music nobody in Australia had previously heard. Kev was the first disc jockey in the Southern Hemisphere to play many of these legendary artists on the radio, making him the most progressive and informative country music presenter on Australian radio at that time.

One of the artists Kev was interested in playing on his radio show was Buck Owens. He'd first heard of Buck back in Proserpine when his song 'Act Naturally' came on the radio. Kev thought it was completely different to the Slim Dusty and Reg Lindsay songs he'd been listening to up to that point; now he decided to write Buck Owens a letter explaining that he had a radio show and would like to play Buck's music if he would be so kind as to send him an album.

A few weeks later Kev checked his post office box and was thrilled to discover that Buck Owens had sent him not one, not even a dozen, but *thirty-six* albums, along with a handwritten note which read, 'From your friend Buck

Owens'. For Kev this was not only an enormous thrill; he also committed it to memory as a lesson in the importance of the relationship between an artist and the media.

Kev had long ago lost touch with his old mate from his Sydney days, Wayne Pride. Wayne had moved to Perth and in 1977 they reconnected and have stayed in touch ever since. Says Wayne, 'I went to Kalgoorlie for my honeymoon and we renewed our friendship. He interviewed me on 6KG and we did a show at the country music festival at the Kalgoorlie racecourse, and we also did one in Esperance.'

While in Kalgoorlie, Wayne went along to see Kev play at the Victoria Tavern. That's when Wayne first noticed that Kev was veering off in a unique musical direction. 'He's up there with his band and they started singing "Sadie the Hay Street Lady", you know, like John Farnham's "Sadie the Cleaning Lady", but they had the Hay Street brothels up there in Kal, so they'd be singing about "Sadie the Hay Street Lady, her trusted little towel and pail of water". He's always, as he says, decomposed songs.'

It was not unusual for Kev to drive all over Western Australia as part of his work with 6KG. Occasionally he would even travel six hundred kilometres down the road to Perth to do an interview. That's how Kev got to meet one of his heroes, as he recalls.

'I did an interview with Charley Pride in Perth for 6KG when he was on his first tour to Western Australia. We became friends. I went to the concert and got invited backstage. One of the things I noticed was that there were about two thousand people in the concert hall and after the show

Charley sat there and just signed autographs. I'm thinking, "How good is that?" So I guess on a subconscious level I took a note of that. I looked at it from the fans' point of view. What a treat to meet the artist after the show, fuckin' amazing.'

Charley Pride's story had always fascinated Kev, in particular the fact that Charley was one of the few African-American musicians to have success in the almost all-white world of American country music. 'In the redneck areas of America, people at the back of his concerts would hold up signs that said *Fuck off nigger*, but Charley's biggest asset was his ability to ignore all that shit. That is what DILLIGAF is all about. Don't let people without a life dictate how you should live yours.'

Part of the bedrock of this friendship is that Charley has always been amused by Kev's use of Australian colloquialisms. 'Last time I saw Charley Pride he asked me, "Hey Kevin, have you rooted any more chooks lately?"'

On the airwaves of Kalgoorlie Kev continued to hone the subversive humour that would one day become Kevin Bloody Wilson's trademark. His radio broadcasts were, by all accounts, as funny as hell. 6KG hired a new station manager, a bloke by the name of Graham Harvey.

'I knew him as Bryan Dennis,' says Graham. 'I started there [at 6KG] as sales manager and shortly thereafter became station manager. Kev was an incumbent. I inherited Kev.'

Despite the legendary differences of opinion he and Kev had at 6KG he still remembers Kev fondly. 'Personally I found him to be a really likeable, easygoing guy. I think he had a good heart and worked well in the community, and on air he was a smooth operator. He was just a natural communicator, and pretty proficient on the panel. He did all of the things that you would expect an on-air professional to do, but he did always want to stretch the rules a bit.'

Kev's employment at 6KG was not without incident for Graham. Actually, there were plenty of tense moments. 'One incident I remember was the morning I heard Kev play a song that was not on our playlist—not that he played much that *was* on our playlist. I mean, he was running a country music program, so it was pretty much his own bag, but he played a song that had some swear words.'

The song in question, according to Kev, was called 'Heaving on a Jet Plane' by a band called the Barron Knights. Graham explains that the problem was the repeated use of the word 'bloody': 'The first time I heard it I thought, "OK, maybe that song doesn't really fall within the rules of the radio station, but no great damage done." And then about an hour later he played it again. So I rang him in the studio and said, "OK, Bryan, you've played it twice, do me a favour, don't play it again," and he said, "When did you get religious?" That was his response.' Graham put the phone down and continued to listen to his radio station, and that's when he and the rest of Kalgoorlie got to hear Kev's response to Graham's programming input. Graham almost spat his morning cup of coffee all over the room.

'Guess what, listeners?' said Kev when the needle reached the end of the Barron Knights track. 'The boss just rang through and he says I can't play that song again 'cos apparently it's inappropriate. But if you want to hear it again, give me a call in the studio. If I get five phone calls, I'll do it.'

Needless to say the switchboard went into meltdown. Kev played the song again and was summoned to Graham's office the next day. Says Graham, 'We had a little talk but that was nowhere near the end of the deal. That was just a little incident I remember where Kev was doing his own thing. He was not absolutely brilliant at taking direction.'

One of Graham's charters at 6KG was to expand the station's on-air hours. On Sundays, for example, 6KG would start broadcasting at eight am and finish at ten pm. 'I called Kev into my office and had a discussion with him. I said, "Hey, we're starting earlier on Sundays. I now need you to start at six o'clock." His response was to laugh and tell me to fuck off.'

Kev was usually out gigging until all hours on a Saturday night, so a six am start the next day would have been a bit of a stretch, but that wasn't the main reason for his objection. 'I didn't really mind the early start too much, but Graham wanted to move the whole country music show forward to an earlier start. It was being moved from a prime spot, which I'd worked hard to establish, from nine in the morning, to fuckin' six o'clock. No cunt is awake in Kalgoorlie at six o'clock on a Sunday morning.'

Kev proposed a compromise, which was for Graham to get someone else in between six am and eight am so that Kev could cruise in at eight and do his country music show. Graham wasn't having a bar of it. 'Kev and I weren't getting much agreement on that, but I have to say that this was a friendly and cordial discussion. We never came to harsh words or blows at any stage, but one of his issues was that he didn't want to be playing some other sort of music and maintaining the overall station format until eight am when his country music show started.

'We agreed we needed to find an answer, and that we would both ponder on it and talk again in the next week or ten days. Then, a few days later, I woke up to the headline in the *Kalgoorlie Miner* that said *Bryan Dennis sacked by 6KG*.

Obviously he'd decided that he wasn't getting up to start at six o'clock and his idea was a pre-emptive strike in the form of a headline. You can get stressed about it or you can laugh, and I'm not sure what I did. But anyway, after that we had a chat but he had clearly made his decision. So after nine years, that was the severing of ties. He'd turned the whole thing into a terrific headline. It's just that it had absolutely no basis in fact.'

News of the 'sacking' of the most popular DJ on 6KG spread around town like wildfire, and before long fans of the show were standing outside Woolworths asking passersby to sign a petition to get Kev back on the air. All of this self-generated publicity soon attracted the interest of the ABC, which hired Kev to present its afternoon drive-time show.

Now that he was working for the national broadcaster, Kev had to read the news every day at four, five and six pm. The ABC, or Aunty as it is sometimes affectionately known, is a pretty serious outfit. For a natural comedian such as Kev with a questionable attention span, this presented a considerable challenge, as he recalls.

'They had their own newsroom and two journalists, one guy who went on to become quite a prominent politician in Western Australia, John Bowler, and there was Dean Cox, who at that stage was still a cadet. Stanley Brown was the station manager at the time and was just a wonderful man who happened to like whatever the fuck I was doing on the ABC. I had to read news occasionally when I was with 6KG but it was just local news. The ABC news was the real deal.'

Radio newsrooms tend to work at a hectic pace, and often a breaking story is typed up and handed to the newsreader as the news theme goes to air, leaving no time to pre-read the new story. Kev's colleagues in the ABC Kalgoorlie newsroom, Bowler and Cox, took the opportunity to put all sorts of rude words into the script just to see if Kev would crack up laughing or, worse, read out all of the words in front of him. Kev somehow managed to navigate this period without dropping any f-bombs or c-bombs on air. However, a few times he did break up laughing in the middle of a bulletin, and before too long trying to get Kev to lose it live on air became the newsroom's number one sport.

'Fuckin' Fridays were the worst,' Kev remembers. 'There would always be a court story from that morning, usually something like some bloke in Nanny-goat Hill had beaten his missus round the noggin with a cricket stump, and I'd be reading the story and I'd look up and the rest of the blokes in the newsroom would be behind the soundproof glass in the studio next door acting out the event as I read the story live to air. Once, they started pulling each other's pants down and pretending to pork each other up the freckle while wrestling with a fuckin' cricket stump. I managed to get through that news bulletin without losing it somehow, but I haven't been able to look at the Ashes in quite the same way ever since.'

CHAPTER 8

Mr Dennis the music teacher

'They call it playing *music for a reason. "It's gotta be fun."'*
Kevin Bloody Wilson

As if he wasn't busy enough, there was yet another pursuit Kev had become involved in during his time in Kalgoorlie: teaching guitar. It had started when he worked at Musgroves music store, and customers would come into the shop, buy a guitar and ask Kev if he knew where they could get guitar lessons for their kids. Kev being Kev, he offered to teach both the kids *and* their parents how to play guitar.

In this way guitar teaching started out as a sideline for Kev, but after he quit his job at the nickel smelter he made some enquiries and discovered that the local education department had no program for teaching guitar in schools. Kev then sat down and documented his own method, and presented it to the superintendent of education in the gold-fields, Rod Curruthers. It was accepted on a trial basis, and

Kev was invited to teach guitar to the world's most isolated students.

When it comes to great Aussie inventions, the School of the Air is up there with the Hills hoist and the ute. It was founded so that school-aged kids in remote areas of Australia could stay at home on their farms or mine sites and do their lessons each day via a two-way radio link. Music had always been one of the hardest subjects to teach on School of the Air, partly because there wasn't yet a system in place to teach it and partly because the extreme heat in many of Australia's remote areas would play havoc with both the tuning of musical instruments and the two-way airwaves themselves.

Kev recalls, 'They gave me ten kids to start with but then they opened it up to other schools and I ended up with three hundred and sixty kids a week, in groups of ten, all because of the success of those initial ten kids on School of the Air. Slim Dusty came in and did it with me a few times. Now whenever I can I go and chat to the kids on School of the Air. I've done it out of Alice Springs, Broome, Port Hedland, Mount Isa, all over the place. Most of these kids don't know me, but their parents seem to know who I am.'

To take his teaching method to the next level, Kev roped in his old mate Tex Curran. 'Kev put a proposal to the education department and they set it up under a program called DCAP, the Disadvantaged Country Areas Program, and then Kev sort of called me in on it. In those days we ran school camps, so we were the bosses of the school music camps over teachers. There were no police checks or anything like that. The town knew and trusted you.'

Kev tested his method of teaching guitar out on his own kids, both of whom were given their first guitars the

Christmas when Travis was six and TJ was four. Travis tries to recall the first song his dad taught him to play. 'It was probably "Hang Down Your Head Tom Dooley", I'd say. Just a simple two-chorder. The good thing about his teaching was he was teaching easy songs which were out at the time rather than just teaching you scales and boring shit like that.'

Kev and Tex had bugger-all interest in teaching their students to read sheet music—that was a distraction Kev himself was still studiously avoiding—but they could teach them how to play by ear and by feel. Kev's system of teaching guitar turned out to be so effective, and so enjoyable for the students, that it is still used today by the education department in Kalgoorlie. As Travis explains, 'It was fairly revolutionary the way he was doing it, teaching you to play by ear rather than by sight-reading music. If you had an idea of the song in your head you could try to learn how to play it, and a lot of the kids would do that after a while. They would learn to play songs all by themselves because they had developed an ear for music straight away.'

First, Kev would show his students how to play a D chord. Then he'd show them an A chord. Once they got the hang of that they learned an easy rhythm using both the A and D chords. Next, Kev got his students to start singing as they played, and after a few lessons a few more two-chord songs, and once they knew their way around the fret-board a bit better he would introduce a third chord.

Kev didn't even care if the guitar was in tune as long as it was in time. His students were learning and enjoying the rhythmic or percussive aspects of playing guitar in the exact same way Kev himself had started on his homemade ham-tin guitar. Tex Curran noticed the results straight away.

'The kids could have their lesson, go home, and be singing "Tom Dooley" to Mum and Dad after their first lesson. The parents thought that was just great, and of course at school assemblies the kids would be out there in a ten-piece guitar band with the rest of their classmates singing along.

'Kev insisted on keeping it fun. The kids had a good time, and on quite a few occasions the teachers used it as a disciplinary measure—if any kids were playing up they'd say, "Right! You're not going to guitar lessons this week!" and the kids would just become perfect. Quite a few kids that were real problem students thrived with those guitar lessons.'

One student in particular remains in Kev's memory. His name was Chad, and he suffered from the then often-misunderstood learning disability of dyslexia. Says Kev, 'The education department had all these special programs for dyslexic kids and young Chad struggled with all his other subjects, but he loved music. So I taught him how to play guitar, and pretty soon he was up there with the best of them playing in school assemblies. Because of his dyslexia, young Chad didn't succeed academically, but he was up there playing guitar in front of the whole school, and it was really good for him. Now he's a qualified diesel fitter. I'd like to think that those guitar lessons helped him to get his confidence rolling. He's a big boy now—if he called me a cunt I'd ask him who told him.'

It was not only the kids who took Kev's guitar lessons who got to enjoy the benefits. Kev's lessons effectively filled the whole school with music, as he explains. 'Our students were let out of their normal classes to go to guitar lessons, but the payoff was that they had to take the guitar back into the classroom after the lesson. So every song we taught the

Hazel and Cecil Bryant 'family pramming', long before the advent of family planning.

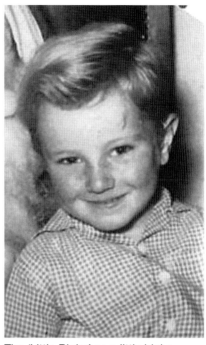

The 'Little Bloke' as a little bloke.

Kev on his second birthday with a model of a Sydney tram made by his dad.

The Bruvvers.
Brother Terry (bass),
Ian Stafford (lead),
Ron 'Fred' Palmer (drums),
15-year-old Kev (guitar).

Kev on his first
Australian tour with the
Buddy Williams Show
1965.

1966–67.
Two more laps of
Australia with The
Rick and Thel Show.

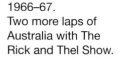

ALL STAR
WESTERN
VARIETY
SHOW

An early publicity shot of handsome young country singer Bryan Dennis ... the world wasn't quite ready for Kevin Bloody Wilson in the mid sixties (but he was working on it)!

then...

..and now

The Alley Katz. From left Tex Curran, Kev, Terry Carlsson and Graham Bignell.

Delta. Graham Bignell, Kev, Ann Williamson, Terry Carlsson, Jim Williamson.

Betty Pascoe and Kev on their first date.

Kev and Betty's second date.

Betty and Travis a week
before the birth of Tammy.

And then they were four.

Kev and 13-year-old son Travis playing bass on Dad's latest album.

Belated first honeymoon, Japan 1977.   Second honeymoon, Bali 1991.

From teaching kids in Kalgoorlie to rehearsing his American musicians for live concerts in Nashville.

Passionate Territorian Wayne Cubis helping Kev discover the wonders of the Top End.

Singing 'Livin' Next Door to Alan' for the people of Oenpelli, Northern Territory.

So that's how they got there!

Kev with tour manager Sue 'Cactus' Maloney.

Travellin' baggage with Buddy Holly Airlines.

Kev with co-author of *DILLIGAF*, Gavin Miller.

Kev's nickel smelter workmate John Merry.

Tex Curran from the Alley Katz today.

Long-time friend and IT guru Bruce Tuffin.

Kev with comedy legend Peter Dee and Wayne 'It'll never work' Pride.

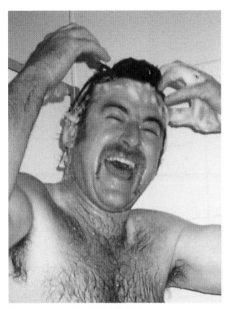

First manager Brian Booy.

Betty and Kev with Greg 'The Rev' Evans.

Ben Dover and Phil McCaverty, the awesome twosome—Kev and tour mangler Peter 'Hollywood' Heeney takin' the high road to Scotland.

Brother Terry and wife Lyn pretending to look happy.

The Both Barrels 'A' Team. Tour front-man Kevin Bloody Wilson, tour coordinator Skye 'Blue' Humphreys, tour mangler Peter 'Hollywood' Heeney.

Kev, the official tennis court jester, makin' a racquet with Australia's Davis Cup Team, including Todd Woodbridge, Lleyton Hewitt and Pat Rafter.

Front page headlines *Kalgoorlie Miner*, April Fool's Day 1999.

Kev, TJ, Betty and
Travis with Nana
and Pop Bryant,
Lismore 2001.

'Search & Destroy'
helping Pop with
a sound check,
Broome 2003.

The 'Dung Beetles'. Search, Destroy, Macaroni, Leadbelly and baby Magoo.

Growing old is mandatory, growing up is optional.

Kev with Scoota the foul-mouthed labrador. Scoota called the dog catcher a 'stupid old cunt', yet Kev got the blame!

Search & Destroy upholding the family motto: 'standing shoulder to shoulder, takin' the piss.'

kids they then had to teach to the rest of their class. We gave the class song sheets so they could sing along, and the little guitar players who had been missing for forty minutes once a week gave the music back to their class.'

Kev loved this particular aspect of being a music teacher because he has always believed that music is something that should be shared, as he tastefully notes. 'It's very much like a vagina. You can go out and give it away all night and still have enough left over to share around the next morning.'

At this time Kev was a heavy smoker (Marlborough Reds), until the day one of his young guitar students said something that made Kev—who the kids called Mr Dennis— quit smoking forever. 'I remember walking into guitar class at Kambalda Primary School and this little bloke looked up at me and said, "Gee, Mr D! You smell of yucky cigarettes!" I said, "Well, I'll tell you what, Jason, I won't have one at lunchtime then." So he came back later and asked, "Did you have one at lunch?" I said, "No, I didn't, Jason," and thanks to that little bloke's suggestion, I haven't smoked since.'

To this day, Kev still smiles whenever he thinks about his time with School of the Air. 'Besides what I'm doing now, teaching was the most rewarding job I've ever done, but it must worry the fuck out of a lot of the goldfields mums and dads knowing that Kevin Bloody Wilson was alone with their kids for forty minutes every week. If their kids turned out to be arseholes, they probably blame me. But, DILLIGAF, I'm OK with that, as long as they turned out to be funny arseholes.'

It isn't always easy being the child of a performer, as Travis recalls. 'I don't know if Dad's even aware of this, but among my friends I felt like a bit of an outsider. His job was so different. He was an entertainer, and all my mates' dads had office jobs or worked at service stations and stuff like that. Every year at school you had to fill out a form and say what your mum and dad do for a job, and I could never work out what to put for Dad. I think eventually I put down "entertainer" or "music teacher", and people would say, "What does he do?" and I'd tell them he played in a band and they'd go, "What sort of music?" and I'd say country music, which to me wasn't that cool. Had he played in a rock band it might have been different.'

Kev was barely able to juggle all of his commitments at this point in his life, and this did not escape the attention of his young son. 'He'd be teaching all day, then in the afternoon he'd do the ABC radio show and then he'd go out that night and do a gig. That's a pretty big day, so he'd sleep in until he had to get up for teaching the next day. And on the weekends he'd do more gigs and host the Sunday morning sick parades. That's a pretty full-on schedule.'

Lingerie shows were huge in the pubs of Kalgoorlie in the seventies and Kev was a natural choice to host what used to be known as the Sunday morning sick parade. It was Kev's job to entertain the crowd between catwalk shows; this was the perfect audience for Kev to try out some of his bawdy ballads.

Already in Kev's arsenal in those early days was a song that would end up being included on the first Kevin Bloody Wilson album: it was one Kev felt compelled to write after he got a visit from some evangelists—or, as he puts it, 'God-bothering door-knockers who made the mistake of tryin' to sell me Jesus on my own doorstep'. He called it 'The Festival of Life'.

The Festival of Life

Aaah the festival of life keeps trying to save my fuckin'
    soul
They don't want me drinking piss or screwing round no
    more
They got fuckin' Buckley's chance, I'm giving you the
    score
Ohh, the festival of life keeps trying to save my fuckin'
    soul.

It's Saturday afternoon at last, it's what you've waited
    for all week
Relax and put my feet up, turn the footy on TV
You're expecting Vern and Bluey round
They'll probably stay all night
A couple of mates and a couple of beers, aw Christ this
    is the life
Well, here they are already, I just heard the car door
    slam
Ya wedge yourself out of the chair; ya get up to let 'em
    in
But it's some wanker that you've never met
With a briefcase in his hand
Some prick just out of bible school who thinks he's
    God's right hand.
Hallelujah hallelujah hallelujah.

Aaah the festival of life keeps trying to save my fuckin'
    soul
They don't want me drinking piss or screwing round no
    more

They got fuckin' Buckley's chance, I'm giving you the
    score
Still the festival of life keeps trying to save my fuckin'
    soul.

'I'm Elder Robbins, he's Elder Pyke, we'd like to talk to
    y'all
About eternal salvation, won't take but a minute or
    more
Got a book we think y'all should read about how y'all
    should live
My what a charming home y'all have, y'all mind if we
    come in?'

'Well, I'd love to invite you in you know
But the joint's a fuckin' mess
And there's an orgy raging in the lounge
And every cunt's undressed
And I'd love ya to meet the missus Shirl
But she's a bit crook in bed
She says she's got a real sore throat through giving too
    much head.
Gobble gobble, gobble gobble, gobble gobble.'

Or you're all snuggled up on Sunday mornin' and you
    wake up with a horn
Ya grab the missus on the ass
Aw Christ she feels so warm
The scene is set, the mood is right
You're about to slip it in
Then knock knock
There's that fuckin' door again, fuckin' bastards!

'Good morning sir, did I get you up?
Sorry, I'm David and this is Pam
We're missionaries who've come to talk of God's eternal
    plan
And to discuss the holy future, and to reflect the holy
    past.'
So you flash ya dick and scream, 'I'll holy shove this up
    your arse.'
Up your arsehole, up your arsehole, up your arsehole.

Well, it's not like it's just once or twice it's every damn
    weekend
Now how'd you think they'd like it if we done the same
    to them
You know, turn up at their doorstep at a time they'd
    least expect
Try and ram our way of life down their fuckin' necks
Just imagine for a minute the reception that you'd get
With a couple of stick books in your hand and a carton
    on the steps
And your missus chewing chewing gum in a really low
    cut dress
And you in thongs and overalls, you know your fuckin'
    Sunday best.
What a yobbo, what a yobbo, what a yobbo.

'G'day, we're pissed-up Testicosticles
I'm Kevin and this is Shirl
We've come to introduce you cunts to a whole new
    fuckin' world
We've come to preach the good news
It's what we think you need to hear

*We'll show you more fun in five minutes than you've
      had all fuckin' year
Now you sweetheart can come with me and I'll teach
      you how to sin
And sister Shirl ol' son will suck ya sack until your head
      caves in.
Aw shit your missus just fainted so we won't bother
      comin' in
We'll just piss off back to our place just drop ten dollars
      in the tin.'
Another carton, another carton, another carton.*

*Aaah the festival of life keeps trying to save my fuckin'
      soul
They don't want me drinking piss or screwing round no
      more
They got fuckin' Buckley's chance, I'm giving you the
      score
Still the festival of life keeps trying to save my fuckin'
      soul.*

On stage, on the radio and in the classroom Kevin Bloody
Wilson had well and truly made his mark in Kalgoorlie.
As he kept on writing 'decompositions' and watching the
crowd double over laughing when he played them live, a
new thought began to bubble to the surface. It was a thought
that would cement Kevin Bloody Wilson's destiny. 'I started
to think to myself, "I wonder how this shit would go down
outside Kalgoorlie?"'

CHAPTER 9

Your average Australian yobbo

'One of the biggest things that made it work for me is that it didn't happen when I was seventeen. I was thirty-seven when I first recorded as Kev, and by the age of thirty-seven your world is pretty safe. Your objectives, priorities and ambitions are all in place.'

Kevin Bloody Wilson

A year before Travis was ready for high school, Kev and Betty decided it was time to leave Kalgoorlie. Kev wouldn't have minded at all if his kids chose to work in the mining industry, but first he wanted them to finish their schooling in a city where every other career option was also available to them. Kalgoorlie had been kind to Kev and his family, but Kev knew in his heart that it was time to go. As it turned out, it was a very good move.

At one point they were planning to relocate to Cairns in far north Queensland, as Kev thought it sounded like a great place to bring up kids, but fate soon stepped in and sent the family further west. Kev's mate Wayne Pride, who had worked with him on the Le Garbage Bins show all those years ago, suggested to Kev that he should come to Perth for twelve months and give it a go.

By that time Wayne had carved out a successful career for himself in and around Perth working as a solo artist in various restaurants and bars, and he suggested to Kev that he could easily do the same thing. 'Kev said he was gonna go to Cairns to live and I put him in touch with a few Perth agents to get him some work. There was a lot of work in Perth.'

While the move to a bigger city with better opportunities for the whole family seemed like a great idea to Kev and Betty, young Travis needed convincing. 'I remember not wanting to go. Kalgoorlie at that stage was the whole world for TJ and me. We used to go to the skating rink in Kalgoorlie all the time, and it was opposite the train station where we eventually caught the train to Perth. As the train was pulling out of the station, us sitting inside it, one of the blokes who worked at the skating rink ran out front and waved us off. TJ and I bawled our eyes out, thinking, "That's it, we're never coming back."'

The Bryant family arrived in Perth on New Year's Day 1981, and for the first two weeks they stayed with Betty's parents in Morley before renting their own digs in Duncraig. In those days, before the height of the mining boom and the population explosion that went with it, Duncraig was still considered to be a far-flung suburb despite being just sixteen kilometres from Perth's CBD.

Kev says, 'I remember Betty's dad saying, "Duncraig? That's out in the bush! Jesus Christ!" But it was a lovely home.'

The kids had to adjust quickly to life in a new city, as Travis recalls. 'Once I got my first day of school over and done with, I felt great. Pretty much from that point on the hard part was over.'

The transition was not quite as effortless for TJ, thanks in no small part to her footwear. 'I showed up for my first day of school and I realised how different I was. I had sandals on, like all the kids did in Kalgoorlie, but these city kids had brand-new shoes. I thought I was going to have to learn how to fight.' Much like her old man, though, TJ quickly figured out that her greatest fighting weapons were not her fists. 'It was my mouth that got me into a lot of trouble but it definitely got me out of trouble as well.'

A little-known fact about Kevin Bloody Wilson is that during his early days in Perth he recorded an album called *Bryan Dennis Sings Sad Songs and Waltzes* in a little recording studio not far from his house. According to Kev it was, to put it politely, a limited release. 'Mum had a copy and I'm still trying to find out who had the other bastard.'

Instead of going to the expense of employing a backing band for this recording, Kev used backing tracks sent from America. 'Wayne Pride told me you could get these backing tracks, and they were on cassette, so you can imagine the quality. These cassettes were the forerunner of karaoke backing tracks, and they were as rough as guts. It was in the early eighties when everything seemed to have three blocks of echo on it. That album never made it into shops, it was just to sell at Bryan Dennis gigs.'

Travis remembers that album, but for all the wrong reasons. 'I remember I played it on the tape deck at home, and one of my high school mates was with me, and he heard part of a song and he instantly started laughing. And he went, "Who the fuck's *that*?" and I said, "That's my dad," and he goes, "Oh, sorry mate, I didn't realise." It was just one of those moments and I felt so bad for Dad. I viewed my mate's reaction as a sign that this entertainment thing might not work out for Dad.'

Ironically, the chorus from the title track on *Bryan Dennis Sings Sad Songs and Waltzes* went, 'Sad songs and waltzes ain't selling this year.'

Indeed, being a professional entertainer in the big smoke wasn't always as easy as Kev had expected. 'It was only after I came to Perth that I realised how hard it was going to be on my own after fourteen years performing with a band in Kalgoorlie. In the first three months I would have happily put my tail between my legs and gone back to Kalgoorlie. My motivation was my family: I'd uprooted them from a comfortable, stable life in Kalgoorlie and felt compelled to offer them a better life in Perth. Solo giggin' was initially fuckin' hard work. In Kalgoorlie we were the top turd on the live music dungheap, and we were each getting paid anywhere between a hundred and two hundred dollars a night as Bryan Dennis and the Country Club, but when I came to Perth as a soloist I was on sixty-five bucks less ten per cent commission. That fuckin' hurt, and so did having to do a three-hour show by myself.'

Kev's musical and comedic horizons had continued to broaden, thanks in part to Wayne Pride, who returned from a trip to America with an LP by an American group called MacLean and MacLean. 'They had a song on there called "Dolly Parton's Tits".' Kev was excited to know that someone else was writing bawdy songs too.

The Bryant family had been hit hard by the taxman before moving to Perth—'A so-called *mate* dobbed us in'—and their

Kalgoorlie property took longer than expected to sell, so things were pretty lean for a while. To supplement the family income, Betty got a clerical job at Imperial Typewriters in Stirling Street. 'I used to ride the bus to work because we only had one car then,' she remembers. 'I used to love sharing that bus ride with all those strangers, what with their smelly armpits and all.'

The lack of available funds didn't stop Kev from slowly saving up for the things he and his family really wanted, and in the process he taught Travis a lesson that remains with him to this day.

'We wanted a video recorder so badly, and Dad wanted the first stereo video recorder that came out. It was this huge thing, a Sharp VCR. He opened a special passbook account to put the VCR saving into, because there were no EFTPOS cards or anything, and he'd show us what he saved from each gig he played and what the balance was up to. We needed about a thousand bucks for this video, and he was only earning about sixty-five bucks a gig.'

It took about a year to save up the money they needed, and Travis remembers his excitement as the balance on the passbook account slowly crept up towards the magic one-thousand-dollar mark. 'I thought, "Bloody hell, we're gonna get this video. We're gonna have a stereo video in the house! I can't believe it! It's gonna be like a cinema!" Eventually we had this stereo VCR sitting on top of the telly, and it was the best day. Of course the first thing he did was give it to me to set up, 'cos he didn't have a bloody clue.

'I think the underlying lesson was that the things you really want can take time, so work hard for them and you can have whatever you want, which I totally got. That was the only time I was ever aware of what Dad was earning. We would never talk about money. I wouldn't have a clue what he earns now. In fact, he probably doesn't know either. But as he says, he's never been dollar-driven.'

One of Kev's main sources of income between moving to Perth and the success of the first Kevin Bloody Wilson album was MCing and performing his bawdy songs at lingerie shows. These shows were a poor attempt to circumvent the laws that prevented strippers from performing in a licensed venue. In Kalgoorlie, tits were the norm. In Perth, bare breasts were illegal. Kev was a natural at hosting these sorts of shows, and he worked out a clever way to give the audience exactly what they really wanted: tits, tits and more tits. 'I'd like to think that I'm the founding father of the wardrobe malfunction. I'd prearrange it with the girls backstage, then on stage I'd go up and say, "Oh, this thing's not done up properly . . ." and rip their fuckin' bra off and go, "See? I fuckin' told ya!"

'I also got lots of Sunday morning gigs with the local footy clubs—local Perth clubs like Wanneroo, Armadale and Swan Districts in the metro area, then bush gigs like Bunbury and Geraldton, and on occasion I even went back to Kalgoorlie. Perth audiences, just like the Kalgoorlie mob, started to call them the Sunday morning sick parades. These gigs usually involved me as MC, a couple of strippers, a chook raffle and a couple of hundred seriously hungover blokes who looked like they'd been fucked all night and hung up wet.'

About this time Kev also started to notice that all these gigs were coming to him via referral and not through booking agents, yet the agents still held their hands out for a ten per cent commission. In Kev's mind this was another embedded system that needed changing. Wayne Pride recalls Kev's decision to sever his ties with the agents he felt were fleecing him and his peers. 'We were doing a lot of comedy shows together, but he got to a point where he said to me one day, "Mate, listen, these cunts are ripping us off." But I played on the safe side of things; I was doing pretty well. He said, "No, I'm not putting up with this shit any more, I'm going out on my own. I don't need them." I thought that would either be the end of him, or it would be the beginning of something. He virtually told them all to go fuck 'emselves and he never looked back. He was confident enough to do that because he already had this ever-expanding following.

'The key to it all is that in the early days we earned our stripes as musicians. We did the hard yards with those shows, the Buddy Williams show and the Rick and Thel show. That was hard work, and you didn't get paid a lot of money, but boy you learned your trade, and you learned how to connect with all sorts of audiences.'

The time had come for a new persona to be created especially for the funny stuff, and Kev looked to his own family for inspiration. 'I have a brother called Kevin, and he's the biggest fuckin' yobbo on the planet. He's more Kevin Wilson than I am, and I pretty much just borrowed his first name and forgot to give it back. I also wanted a name that was pretty ordinary. I didn't want to be Lorenzo Studebaker or Billy Bob Butt-Fucker or anything like that. So I thought I'd keep it simple, Kevin Wilson.'

Kevin Wilson wasn't a bad stage name, but Kev thought it needed an extra word to make the name stick. 'The Bloody came to me when my brother-in-law told me this story. He was on holidays, walking on the beach with his wife—my sister Maureen—at about six in the morning and draggin' himself along the beach is this poor bloke who had obviously had a big night out. He had spew all over the front of his T-shirt, and underneath the vomit you could barely make out the words *Poor Bloody Fred*. I imagined this bloke crawlin' along the beach trying to get home, and I thought, "How funny is that?" That's when I decided to stick Bloody in the middle of the name. I thought it would give it some empathy, as well as letting you know that it was Australian and, more importantly, that it was of an adult nature.'

Kev started sharing his idea for a new on-stage persona with some of his close friends, including Wayne Pride. Says Wayne, 'I was around at his place having a cup of tea one day and he looked at me and said, "What do you think of Kevin Bloody Wilson?" I said, "Who?" and he said, "Kevin Bloody Wilson." I said, "Never heard of him," and he said, "Well, that's me," and I said, "Mate, that will never work." He started telling me what he was going to do and I said, "Mate, you're crazy, you're gonna get yourself in the shit, don't do that." I just didn't think the world was ready for him, 'cos the way he was doing it was pretty full on.

'But he was pretty stubborn about it and he will probably always be like that with the way he conducts his business. He backed his own judgement totally. I remember a couple of years later we were sitting out on the balcony of his new three-storey home and he said, "Yeah right, Jock, it'll never work . . ." I'll never forget that comment. He wasn't being a smart arse, but he'd certainly got it going by then. Now it's history, what he did after that.'

The name Kevin Bloody Wilson was created primarily to separate Kev's work as a bawdy balladeer from the straighter gigs he was still doing, but people who had seen Kev in both performance modes wouldn't tend to let him get away with it quite that easily.

'I'd be doing a performance at a wedding—yep, I was even a fuckin' wedding singer—and punters would approach me and say, "Hey mate, aren't you the same cunt who was playing all of those fuckin' funny songs at the buck's night? How come your name's changed? Who the fuck is Bryan Dennis?"

'But the other thing that happened was, when I was performing the Kevin Bloody Wilson songs, blokes kept on coming up to me, time and time again, and saying, "Why don't you record some of this shit? We'll buy it!" So eventually I did, and they kept their promise.'

Slowly but surely, Kev gigged his way out of the financial pressure he and his family had been under when they moved to Perth. His kids got to see more of him too, as TJ recalls. 'During school holidays he was around in the afternoons for us, because Mum had a day job. Back in Kalgoorlie he wasn't around at all. There were always at least two jobs, usually three. When he came to Perth there was only one job, and it was at night, so in the afternoons he'd take us to the beach or to the music shop. It was a really happy time for Travis and me, and especially for Dad.'

Wayne Pride remembers, 'Occasionally we would work together. We were doing a thing called the Aussie Arna Pub Show at the Chelsea Tavern in Claremont. We ran this sort of gong-show talent quest, and there was this bloke and his wife and their three young kids from Kalgoorlie. Kev knew these people and he told me how they operated. They used to exploit their kids in talent quests trying to make money. Ours was just a fun show, but they sent one of their kids up and he sang "House of the Rising Sun". He wasn't very good. This other guy got up, pissed as a fart, and he did an impression of Benny Hill. He was a big guy, and he ended up stripping down to his jocks. Just near the end of his act he fell forward and the stage collapsed. So naturally Kev, myself and the audience voted him the winner.

'Then the parents of the kid who sang "House of the Rising Sun" came up and started abusing Kev and me. I said, "You're all idiots, this is not a serious thing, it's a bit of fun, and there's not much in prize money anyway." Kev jumped in and proceeded to tell the parents, in fairly blunt language, to take the kids home and stop trying to exploit the poor little buggers. With that the father arced up and took a swing. I managed to grab him and shoved him out the door and told them both to piss off. So that was the end of that, we thought.

'The next week Kev went up to Kalgoorlie to do some solo shows, and I did the Chelsea Tavern Aussie Arna Pub Show by myself, and the cops came because these people had made a complaint about us. I told them it was all a bit of sham, and all we got was a reprimand. That would have been Kev's first run-in with the cops as Kevin Bloody Wilson and the prick wasn't even there for it.'

CHAPTER 10

Cock on the block

'That will never work.'

Wayne Pride

After some months performing under his new name, Kev felt the time was right to have a crack at making a Kevin Bloody Wilson album. He quickly found the studio where he wanted to record it, but there were four thousand things still standing in his way. 'It was going to cost four grand to record an album, and this is back when houses were about fifty grand. Betty and I knew there were other things we could've been spending four grand on, but I believed in it and Betty was behind me all the way. And by now I was convinced there was a market out there for this kind of stuff.'

Despite being hailed as an x-rated Henry Lawson, Kev has never written poetry for its own sake, but as any Kev fan will tell you, when you forget about the music and focus solely on the words, Kev's lyrics are up there with some of the funniest poetry ever written. This has recently been formally recognised with the inclusion of the entire Kevin Bloody Wilson catalogue, both lyrics and recordings, in Australia's National Film and Sound Archive. Says Kev, 'I bet they'll have fuckin' fun with that in a hundred years from now . . . '

Kevin Bloody Wilson songs don't just rely on the punchline. There's always a story that runs through the verses, and if you listen carefully to the last verse there's almost always a payoff in there somewhere.

Travis, himself an accomplished musician, explains his father's songwriting method. 'When he writes he looks at the song from a lot of different angles. Initially he looks at it from a humour perspective, and then he thinks about who's going to enjoy the song and what parts they are going to be singing along to when they're at his shows. And musically he likes his recordings to be pretty good too, even though on stage there's only him and a guitar.

'It might be reggae or it might be country or jazz or whatever but it's the same simple chords and simple progressions. Most people wouldn't even notice though, because the stories and the words are all so different. One of the secrets of Dad's songwriting is that he's never really nudged off the simple open chords he started with.'

Another year or so of relentless gigging yielded the money Kev needed to record his songs at his chosen location, a funky but run-down operation called Shelter Studios in Perth's northern suburbs. Now that he had an album's worth of songs to record, and access to a recording studio, all Kev needed to do was assemble his band.

For his first recordings Kev gathered some of the best musicians in Western Australia. Brian Booy, who was also managing Kev at the time, played drums on some of the songs, while the rest of the drumming was credited to a character called O.B. Heimer (really the Oberheim drum machine). 'We had Jimmy Fisher on guitar, fiddle and a bit of piano, and a recent arrival from America, Lucky Oceans, on pedal steel. I did most of the rhythm and bass, and Travis was on it too.'

Or was he? It is widely accepted as fact that Travis played guitar on Kevin Bloody Wilson's debut album, in no small part because Kev has mentioned it in many interviews over the years. Oddly enough, the only person who disputes this is Travis himself. 'Back then I was only a bedroom musician. I had an old Fender amp of Dad's in the bedroom and I had a bass guitar in there which I used to play, and I used to try and copy all the new romantic pop shit that was on the radio at the time. Then one day he just gave me a go. He said, "Come into the studio. I wanna use you to do this track." He says I recorded the track and it went onto the album but I know it didn't because I wasn't stupid enough not to recognise that it wasn't my playing. I listened to the album and thought, "That's Dad playing." He still says it to this day, he tells people I did my first session when I was fourteen— well, yes, I did do my first session when I was fourteen but it didn't make the final cut. Maybe my bass playing was so bad back then that he didn't want to hurt my feelings.

'Just about everything I've played on his albums has made the cut since then, though. Since I was about eighteen I've been involved in one way or another. For *Kalgoorlie Love Songs* I played most of the instruments on the whole album; the *DILLIGAF* album was pretty much all me as well. I also did the recording engineering on that one, so I'm absolutely sure that it was me on the records.'

Most of the arrangements for the songs that ended up on *Your Average Australian Yobbo* had been figured out before Kev got into the studio. He was, after all, paying for it by the hour. But a couple of songs were written on the spot in the studio. One was 'Wow Did I Get Whacked' and the other one was 'Arr Fuck (The Instrumental)', which, like many of Kev's greatest creations, came about completely by accident.

It all started when Kev and his band were mucking around in the studio one day, and one of Kev's band members (none of whom is prepared to take personal responsibility) was playing a solo and completely botched the last note. Without thinking he let out an 'Arr fuck' and started the solo all over again. At the end of the second attempt he played the wrong note again, at which point the whole band went, 'Arr fuck . . . two, three, four!' and kept playing.

As the idea developed, everyone in the band had a go at playing a solo with a dodgy last note, and each time the band would go 'Arr fuck . . . two, three, four!' and do it all over again. From conception to completion, that song took less than an hour.

'I Gave Up Wanking' was a song Kev wrote out of necessity, or so he tells people. 'I used to play at a place called Godiva's in Applecross on Tuesday nights and these pommy blokes used to request this English song called "I'm a Wanker". The lyrics went, "I'm a wanker, it feels so good when I'm pulling my pud, I'm a wanker." They were all from a darts club and that was their song and they kept pestering me to sing it, but I couldn't get hold of it. Finally I wrote one of my own; that's how I appeased them: "I don't know that particular one but I do have a wanking song of my own." So it was just me trying to write a funny song about wanking to keep these blokes happy.

'I got the idea for my version from an old Kalgoorlie mate named Dick Yates, who well into his seventies would always delight in telling me, "I gave up wanking this morning." Thanks, Dick.'

I Gave Up Wanking

I give up wankin' this mornin'
I never thought that I could
And I'm feeling better already
And this time I'm off it for good.

When I first wanked I thought I was so clever
And all of me mates they were mugs
Thought I was the first bloke here on earth
Who'd ever played with his slug.

It was me own little secret
I never told anyone
And the feelin' I got this first time I shot
Was like chooks flyin' out of me bum.

So I'm givin' up wankin' tomorrer
I never thought that I could
Then I won't get these bad headaches
Then I'll be off it for good.

I've wanked in some unlikely places
The shower, the beach and the pool
The dunny, a tram and the pictures
And biology class at school

And once me grandmother caught me
Wankin' meself in me room
But to her surprise, I just shut my eyes
And imagined her standin' there nude.

So I'm givin' up wankin' on Tuesday
I never thought that I could
Then I won't squint like I do now
Then I'll be off it for good.

Me dad says it's gonna take willpower
There really is no easy trick
I honestly thought I'd need surgery
To help get me hand off me dick.

Me dad's been a great inspiration
He really has been a great help
He knows what I go through, and just what to do
'Cos he give it up yest'day himself!

So I'm givin' up wankin' next Friday
I never thought that I could
I won't have to wear these thick glasses
And then I'll be off it for good.

So if you say you don't wank you're a liar
And a fool if you say you do
So next time you see Prince Charles on TV
Remember he's wanked himself too.

So I'm givin' up wankin' next Easter
I never thought that I could

And I'll sell me dog and me white cane
Then I'll be off it for good.

'Stack the Fridge' was Kev's first recorded homage to smoking pot. Kev had figured out that a lot of people in his audience liked a choof, and he knew he would find a new way to connect with them if he could come up with a funny song about smoking weed. 'I'd never really heard any songs about dope. The only funny one I'd heard was a thing called "Wildwood Weed" by Jim Stafford, but even that was pretty tame. So I wrote one of my own.'

Stack the Fridge

There's an uptown party on tonight that we're invited
  to
All the jet-set people there and the finest wine and food
Sip some champagne, snort some coke and maybe swim
  some in the nude
But they can stick that trendy shit 'cos that's not me
  and you.

A night down at the local pub is nearer what we like
Play the pinball, shoot some pool, if the atmosphere is
  right
But sometimes it's too crowded there, or some dickhead
  wants to fight
So stack the fridge and stoke the bong we're staying
  home tonight.

Stack the fridge and stoke the bong we're staying home
  tonight
I'm a lover, not a fighter and I'd rather fuck than fight

*And we'll get smashed on booze and hash and then
    we'll screw all night
So stack the fridge and stoke the bong we're staying
    home tonight.*

*We don't need no people round for us to have some fun
To me a good night out with you means staying home
    alone
And I'd rather share my highs with you than share with
    anyone
We'll drink some booze and smoke a joint and turn
    each other on.*

*Then we'll just lay down on that big ole rug then we'll
    dim the lights
Stick a dirty movie on and just wait for a high
And then we'll hump, screw and fuck till our brains are
    fried
So stack the fridge and stoke the bong we're staying
    home tonight.*

*Stack the fridge and stoke the bong we're staying home
    tonight
I'm a lover, not a fighter and I'd rather fuck than fight
And we'll get smashed on booze and hash and then
    we'll screw all night
So stack the fridge and stoke the bong we're staying
    home tonight.*

Now that wanking and weed were represented in his song catalogue, Kev moved on to the subject of cats, specifically his intense dislike for them.

'I fuckin' hate cats. Kittens should come with a recipe. "That Fucking Cat's Back" was just a series of stories I'd heard about cats which I strung together. Tex Morton had a song called "The Cat Came Back" and that was the only guideline I had for that song.'

Needless to say, Kev's lyrics would have made poor old Tex blush.

That Fucking Cat's Back

I was pissed and disorderly again last Friday night
I got thrown out of the pub just after nine
It's not the first time that that's happened, but if I
*   remember right*
I think they caught me pissin' in the fire!

Waltzin', trippin' to the carpark, took a shortcut down
*   the lane*
When a fuckin' cat jumped out a rubbish bin
So I picked the cunt up by the tail and looked him up
*   and down*
'N thought, 'Fancy throwin' away a perfectly good cat
*   like him!'*

I took all the back streets, goin' home that night
'Cos I didn't wanna end up in the can
And I'd just turned into my street after stoppin' at the
*   lights*
When some big prick went and trod all on me hand.

But I finally got to my place and tripped arse-up on the
*   lawn*

Then I spewed me guts up on the cat
I remember eatin' peanuts and a crusty pie with sauce
But I'm fucked if I remember eatin' that!

But that fuckin' cat's back
Now how did he do that?
I slammed me foot right up his bum
And kicked the cunt to Kingdom Come
Now where the fuck did he come from?
That fuckin' cat's back

I slipped in beside me missus, the wrong way up in bed
With me feet where me head was s'posed to be
I thought her bedsocks was her nightcaps and her
    kneecaps were her tits
But her rotten breath still smelled the same to me

And I just crashed like that till mornin', the wrong way
    up in bed
And Christ I had the horrors when I woke
I thought me missus' snatch was that fuckin' cat again
And worse than that, some cunt had cut its throat!

But that fuckin' cat's back
Now how did he do that?
I slammed me foot right up his bum
And kicked the cunt to Kingdom Come
Now where the fuck did he come from?
That fuckin' cat's back.

After around two intensive weeks of recording his songs
onto two-inch sixteen-track tape, the recordings were mixed

and transferred onto cassette and for the first time Kev was able to listen to the finished product all the way through. Admittedly, it wasn't exactly *Abbey Road*, but for four grand the production was still damn good. 'I listened to it in the car, on an unlabelled cassette, and it was a pretty good feeling. The only thing weighing on my mind was not the money side of it. I was more concerned if my mates were going to like it.'

Kev needn't have worried about getting the approval of the punters who had already seen him perform his bawdy ballads and decompositions, but there were many others who were quick to warn Kev about the dangers of releasing this kind of material on an unsuspecting and often conservative public. 'I was giving it to other musicians to have a listen to and they're going, "Mate, if you release this you'll never work in taverns again," and I haven't.'

Wayne Pride was one of those who voiced his concerns to Kev about how he thought this material was likely to be received. 'Back in those days you weren't allowed to be rude and swear on stage. But Kev was having too much fun with it. More importantly, he was getting away with it. He just kept getting better at it.'

Betty didn't care too much about whether or not Kev could recoup the costs of recording *Your Average Australian Yobbo*. The thing that kept on running through Betty's mind was the possibility that Kev could find himself in more hot water than their family could handle. 'My dad said to him a couple of times, "You're not allowed to say that, are you?" Dad's very reserved and I suppose I was back then as well. I thought, "What happens if he does get into trouble? We have a family here. What if he gets arrested?" Everyone was saying, "You can't say this!" and "You can't say that!" and he just used to say "Fuck 'em, I can say what I like.

Everybody swears!" But you really weren't sure if he'd be arrested, because nobody had done this sort of stuff before, at least not upfront the way he was doing it.'

The idea of his dad being thrown in jail for public indecency didn't sit too comfortably with Travis either. 'I can understand why Mum probably thought that, because it was serious shit. Rodney Rude was doing it around the same time, so Dad had an ally there I guess, but it was a different world back then. Dad was getting arrested at shows. I never saw it happen, but I know police were involved on several occasions.'

Even before *Your Average Australian Yobbo* was released, Kev was getting grief from publicans all over Western Australia about the content of his live shows. 'I got asked not to come back again by a couple of pubs. I'd been a regular at this particular pub for a while. The blokes were loving it, but the snobby sheila who was rootin' the boss and fucked her way into managing the joint came up to me one night to impress her chardonnay-sipping cronies. The bitch blew cigarette smoke in my face and said, "Darling, we don't pay you to do that sort of filthy stuff. Just host the show and sing nice songs." I thought, "Fuck you, lady! I'm not doing this for you or your fucktard friends, I'm doing it 'cos the audience love it."

'I didn't bother arguing 'cos she just didn't get it. She basically told me to fuck off and not come back, but when the Kevin Bloody Wilson thing hit six months later she was on the phone like my newest best friend ever, asking me to come back because, "Darling, I've always loved your sense of humour." So that's when you delight in saying, "I'm sorry, precious, I can't make it, I'm fully booked. So feel free to go 'n fuck yourself with a pineapple."'

The front cover of *Your Average Australian Yobbo* features a photo of Kev sitting on a beer carton, holding a guitar painted with the Australian flag, and sporting a DILLIGAF grin. A sticker on the front cover reads: *This recording contains offensive language and is not to be purchased by, or played to, minors or wowsers.*

By wowsers, Kev meant politically correct types who would be easily offended by his lyrics. 'That was a word that didn't translate all that well in England. The first time I toured England the promoter asked, "Wowser? What does it mean over there in Australia?" I told him it meant a do-gooder, a party pooper, that kind of thing. He told me it means something completely different over there. In England a wowser is a poofter, so their interpretation would have read: *Not suitable for minors or poofters.*'

Kev needed to be careful not to lose his international audience in translation, but he wasn't about to change any of the words he used in his songs or his live shows. Kev's solution was to include a full glossary of the Australian terms and slang in his lyrics in the liner notes of his overseas album releases. 'If they still didn't get it after that, well, DILLIGAF. I let it all hang out. Who gives a fuck if you're offended?'

Getting his new songs committed to the sixteen-track tape recorder at Shelter Studios was one thing, but preparing his cassette tapes for purchase was another matter entirely. Fortunately Kev knew exactly where to find some people who would help him execute his plan without expecting to be paid the full market rate for their services.

One typically sunny Perth Saturday morning in June 1984, Kev arrived at the family home in Granadilla Street,

Duncraig, brandishing a large cardboard box. It contained two hundred unlabelled cassettes, four hundred stickers (one for each side of each cassette), two hundred unfolded cardboard album covers and two hundred plastic cassette cases. Kev, Betty, Travis and TJ sat around the kitchen table and spent the evening preparing the first two hundred cassette copies of *Your Average Australian Yobbo* by hand.

Kev quickly struck up a deal with the kids. They would get ten cents per cassette, to be saved up and used as their spending money when the family went on their next big holiday. Travis spent every spare moment he had making cassettes. 'I remember being in the upstairs lounge doing it, watching the telly. We used to have to fold the sleeve. Originally when he got them they didn't have any fold marks so we had to make our own fold marks using a ruler and then we had to put the stickers on the actual cassette. Once you put these stickers on they stayed on, so if you stuffed it up after one attempt it was a wasted product.'

TJ also felt the pressure of putting the labels on correctly. 'You'd have days where you just didn't get one right. Some would be crooked, with the little bubble in the label, and I'd just put it in the case and think "Please don't let that be the one Dad picks up."'

Kev's plan was to sell each cassette for twelve dollars, and he figured that if he could sell all two hundred in the six months before Christmas he would make $4800. If he could achieve this he would have recouped his recording costs with enough money left over for an overseas trip to reward the kids for putting the cassettes together.

The plan was put to the test the very next day when Kev hosted a Sunday morning sick parade at the North Beach Rugby Club. He took ten cassettes with him, wondering to himself as he left the house if he was being overly ambitious taking that many.

Those ten cassettes sold out within minutes of him finishing the first set, so Kev rang Betty at home and asked her to drop into the venue with twenty more. Betty did just that, and after Kev's next set they were all sold out too. Kev called Betty yet again. 'You might as well just bring the entire fuckin' box with you this time.'

Kev made a point of counting the number of people in the room that morning. There were exactly one hundred and five including himself, two topless barmaids and a stripper, and he somehow managed to sell eighty-seven cassettes before heading home. When he put all the money he'd made that day on the kitchen table, the kids' eyes bulged.

There was another part of Kev's homemade marketing campaign that turned out to be a clever move: each cassette had six little coupons squeezed into it which read, *Don't Let Your Mates Borrow This, They'll Steal It. Fuck 'Em, Make Them Buy Their Own!* Printed underneath that message was a postal address for ordering more copies of the cassette. Three days after the initial burst of sales, Kev checked his mailbox and found that he had received around a hundred orders. By now it was starting to become apparent that Kev might just be on to something here.

'It was very back to front as far as the music business was concerned. There was no radio airplay, it was purely word of mouth. I started selling the cassette, which was the only format we were available on, at live gigs. Then it grew because people were going into record stores and asking for Kevin Bloody Wilson cassettes. I learned a lot about the business in those days and one of the things I learned was that usually people like to buy music on Thursdays,

Fridays and Saturdays—that was the general trend—but my stuff was selling on Mondays, Tuesdays and Wednesdays, and that came about because people were hearing it on the weekends at parties and then they'd go out looking for their own copy early in the week.

'Trouble was, other than one store in Geraldton, I wasn't in record stores at that stage, so the shopkeepers were asking, "Who the hell is this Kevin Bloody Wilson?" A couple of the more entrepreneurial record stores around Perth, and even Adelaide, simply read the label which included my postal address and phone number, and rang up and ordered in bulk these seemingly hard-to-get cassettes.'

So instead of selling individual copies of *Your Average Australian Yobbo* at his live shows, all of a sudden Kev was now selling boxes of two hundred to roadhouses and record stores around Australia. The only problem with selling box after box of cassettes was that they all still had to be prepared by hand. The job was starting to test Travis's patience. 'When you got a spare moment in the day you'd just go up and do some. Some nights you'd ask yourself if this was ever going to end. Every week you'd get a phone call from Dad's outlets and they'd be irate 'cos they needed two hundred more cassettes, so off you'd go upstairs and try to make two hundred so they'd be ready for a pickup. And that kept getting more and more and more until eventually he had to shop out that work. We just couldn't keep up with it in the end.'

TJ figured she didn't need the job any more because she thought she had already set herself up for life. 'Dad told us that if we got these cassettes done that we could have money to spend on this trip we were planning, and back then even a hundred dollars would have been unbelievable. So, once we got up to around the eight-hundred-dollar mark between us we were going, "Dude, this is gonna be enough for the rest of our lives! Get someone else to do it! I'm gonna go buy a house!"'

Your Average Australian Yobbo went on to sell twenty-two thousand copies in its first year on the market, all on cassette. At twelve dollars per cassette, that's a gross of over a quarter of a million dollars. Not bad for a guy with no record industry experience who was selling his albums without the help of radio airplay.

Says Kev, 'I see that as an advantage. It's what's got me to where I am. Instead of getting my songs played on the radio, it all came from mates telling mates, which is the best kind of recommendation you can get.'

CHAPTER 11

The boardroom barndance

'All I was armed with was common sense and bush nous.'
Kevin Bloody Wilson

One of the early signs for Kev and his family that his new career was really taking off was that they were able to get rid of what the kids had dubbed the Six Million Dollar Van. Kev recalls it less than fondly. 'I had a Ford Escort van. Mustard coloured. Every time I turned the key on it it'd cost me a grand.'

This van had a long and chequered history with the Bryant family, as Travis explains (while shamelessly dobbing his old man in). 'He was getting fairly busy and he needed a vehicle to take him around, so he bought this Escort panel van, and his auto-orchestra and the guitars and everything would go in the back, but it was a piece of shit. It would break down all the time, that's why we called it the Six Million Dollar Van.

'He got done for drink driving coming home in it from a gig in Fremantle one night. He lost his licence for three months, and for a few weeks there we were going to all these gigs with him, and then he found himself a driver, a teenage bloke who'd just got his licence. That van brought him a lot of bad luck. He always threatened that he was going to take it out onto a salt lake, put a stick of dynamite under it, and blow the fucker up.'

Kev gleefully recalls the weekend when the family finally parted company with the Six Million Dollar Van. 'I had a gig in Geraldton and on the way back the van conked out for the umpteenth time, so I fuckin' left it there on the side of the road. I hitched a ride to the nearest roadhouse, where my mate worked, then he drove me back to my car. We threw my stuff in the back of his ute and my mate and I struck a deal. I said, "You drive me back to Perth with all my gear in the back of your ute and you can have whatever's left of that fuckin' van when you get back to it." Done deal. I gave it away.'

Betty was amazed that Kev was now in a position to give away the Six Million Dollar Van. 'All of a sudden he's talking about buying me a new car; twelve years earlier we couldn't even afford to register the Valiant.' Kev bought a Holden Calais for himself, and he also took great delight in buying Betty her dream car, a convertible red Toyota Celica.

Kev's first manager, Brian Booy, decided to step down when Kev's career took off beyond a point anyone had dared predict, as Kev recalls.

'Back then, when I was doing straight stuff, the going rate had increased to about one fifty a gig. And yet as Kevin Bloody Wilson I was making two thousand a gig plus the cassette sales. So it was getting bigger and bigger and Brian said, "I don't think I'm gonna be able to handle it." I thought that was a huge call 'cos most other blokes would have only seen the money to be made, but Brian was a totally honest bloke, and he proved to me by making that decision that he only had my best interests at heart.

'A few months later I ran into Ross Mitchell at one of my footy club gigs and we got to know each other. Ross had managed Johnny O'Keefe for the last four years of Johnny's life, and he'd just started an agency in Perth.'

Ross took over as Kev's manager, and the money kept rolling in. In the mid eighties, the Kevin Bloody Wilson business was a lucrative one; for Kev, being able to take his family to Bali for a holiday was the realisation of another long-held goal. It was also the kids' long-anticipated reward for putting all those cassettes together. Says Kev, 'That was one of the first things we did as a family once the money started rolling in. It was exciting to be able to buy shit. We bought a video camera for that trip. The camera was the size of a fuckin' ghetto-blaster, coupled with a suitcase-sized battery pack. Travis did the filming on that trip. He became the self-appointed family cameraman, and he loved it. He stood there on the beach all day watching surfers and naked ladies. He was about fourteen at the time.'

TJ was excited to finally get her hands on all the loot she had earned by packaging up Kevin Bloody Wilson cassettes. 'We were just not able to spend it all. It was so much money when you would get ten T-shirts for a dollar. And we bought lots of cassettes—I remember the bottom of my suitcase being lined with them.' TJ fell in love with Bali instantly. 'It was like a movie—beaches and palm trees. Travis and I just ate ham and cheese jaffles with vanilla milkshakes. That's all we ate the whole time, because as kids the local food just didn't taste right.'

Travis shot about six hours of footage of that holiday, then edited it all together once he got home. 'I made a three-minute surf movie. It's probably still hanging around somewhere. It was to the tune of "Melting in the Sun" by INXS. It sort of worked, and it had titles and everything.'

Now in Year 7, TJ kept her brother busy with other home-video projects once he had finished editing the movie of the Bali trip. 'We made a music video. Travis directed. It was me in my Wanneroo hockey club jumper with taped-on black plastic fingernails from my Perth Royal showbag, miming "Beast of Burden".'

Kev could also now afford to stop renting and buy a house. He found one in Telopia Drive, Duncraig, just around the corner from the family's rental property in Granadilla Street. 'Because of the volume of money that came in initially I was keen to invest wisely. I figured the whole Kev thing wouldn't last that long. I was very aware that, in general, entertainers very rarely went the distance through to retirement, and so I invested money in my own home.'

Ever the showman, Kev took his kids for what they thought was a casual walk around the block and showed them their new house for the first time. TJ thought she must have been dreaming. 'He took us down there and said, "What do you think of this house?" It was enormous and it had a pool. We were amazed. He said, "Kevin Bloody Wilson bought this house," and I remember thinking, "I don't care who bought it, this is great!" I wrote to my friends in Kalgoorlie and told them that my house had an upstairs 'cos, you know, we had outdoor plumbing in Kalgoorlie.'

For Betty, it was starting to feel like she'd hit the big-time. 'We had two bathrooms, I couldn't believe it. I'd come from having a toilet out the back to this house with an ensuite bathroom right next to my bedroom. It was just beautiful.'

Kev was on a roll. *Your Average Australian Yobbo* was outselling Dire Straits and Jimmy Barnes in Western Australian record stores, which was an incredible feat in 1985 when absolutely every Australian seemed to own a copy of *Brothers in Arms* and *For the Working Class Man*. The fact that you couldn't hear Kev's songs on the radio was the very thing that seemed to be driving his sales. If you wanted to hear what all the fuss and laughter was about, you couldn't just tune in and hear one of Kev's songs on your local radio station—you had no choice but to go out and buy the album. Not surprisingly, the big record companies soon came knocking on Kev's door.

TJ remembers when the record company people started sniffing around, literally. 'That's an expression that Dad uses, that they came sniffing around, but they really did. I remember guys, business types, standing at the screen door asking, "Is Kevin Bloody Wilson home?"'

RCA was the first company to fly Kev to Sydney to make him an offer. It was the first time Kev had ever sat at a boardroom table, and he was surrounded by guys in suits who were all trying to convince him to sign a deal that was clearly much better for the record company than it was for Kev.

After patiently listening to their pitch, Kev said, 'Fellas, I'm not sure how your system works, but my system works like this: I'm making one hundred per cent and you're offering to give me eleven per cent of that . . . so how exactly does that work?'

The suits replied, 'That's how it is, we take care of everything,' to which Kev spat back, 'I'm already taking care of everything!'

Clearly, the suits weren't getting it. 'But Kev, you won't have to do all of that work any more!'

Kev replied, 'But I enjoy doing all of that stuff. And by the way, gentlemen, that plane ticket you bought me—is that a return ticket?' The suits said it was, and Kev ended the meeting by smiling and saying, 'Well, thank you very much gentlemen, I'm flying home now, and you can all go fuck yourselves. Have a nice day.'

The next record company that attempted to sign Kev was CBS, which later became Sony. Kev explains, 'I had written the second Kevin Bloody Wilson album by then and that was the one they were interested in. I've since found out from one of the execs at Sony that they were looking for another Rodney Rude. Rodney was popular at the time but he was on EMI, so all CBS wanted was another Rodney Rude.' As it turned out, they did better than that.

Kev's first meeting with CBS was in Perth with their CEO, legendary Australian music industry stalwart Denis Handlin, who recalls, 'As mad as Kev was, CBS Records didn't have anything like him on the label. Kevin was truly unique and we could see that he was connecting with the Australian public.' Denis had a special approach to getting Kev signed to his label. He pretended to be the cleaner. 'There actually was a real cleaner in the office making a big noise and Kev said, "What's going on?" I acted out being a cleaner too, saying something like, "I started cleaning the floors in the company in 1970," and I told him I was still doing it as I believed in multi-tasking. Later on we had a million laughs about that.'

Denis made his pitch about how good CBS could be for Kev—'But how would he know, he was only the cleaner'— but Kev wasn't really getting into Denis's comedy routine. Says Kev, 'I wasn't paying attention anyway. I was too busy checking out the cardboard cutout of Bruce Springsteen in the corner of the boardroom.'

It was a life-sized version of the iconic photo from the cover of *Born in the USA*, which happened to be Betty's favourite album at the time. Kev told the CBS suits that his wife would love to have that cardboard cutout, and was promptly told that there was only one of them in Western Australia and that if they got any more they would be giving them to their major clients. 'In other words, "Get fucked!"' says Kev.

Kev returned home from that meeting feeling distinctly underwhelmed, and the next morning he rang his manager and asked him to send CBS a telegram. It read: 'BECAUSE OF THE DRUNKEN NATURE OF YOUR CLEANER DENIS HANDLIN, I NO LONGER WISH TO NEGO-TIATE WITH CBS MUSIC.' Ross asked Kev if he was absolutely sure he wanted to send the telegram, to which Kev replied, 'Abso-fuckin'-lutely.'

Exactly one hour after the telegram was sent there was a knock at Kev's front door. A courier was standing there holding a big box of CBS albums along with a note asking Kev to please consider flying to Sydney at CBS's expense for a face-to-face meeting. Kev noticed another guy standing behind the courier, gently rocking back and forth in the breeze. It was the cardboard cutout of Bruce Springsteen.

With her very own cardboard Bruce Springsteen and the large box of Bruce Springsteen LPs that came with it, Betty was now officially sold, and she had some advice for her husband, who was enjoying the chase but was still far from convinced. 'Just sign with these people, will ya?'

Wayne Pride was another person in Kev's inner circle who encouraged him to take the offer that was on the table. 'I was in Kev's house one day and they rang. He hung up the phone and said, "That was CBS." He virtually told them to piss off and I thought, "Jesus, mate, just take what they're offering you! From memory he was offered something like ten grand to sign on with them plus an extra twenty-five hundred to do a film clip, and he said no. I heard him say to them when they rang him back, "No, that's the deal. If you don't want it, forget about it." I said, "You're crazy! Just take what they're giving you. It's a big label, you know? Just go for it." He said, "Nup, they can pay me what I want or I won't do it," and he told them again to go away—not in those words, in Kev's speak.'

It was now becoming apparent to Kev that Wayne Pride, given his track record, was to be consulted before making any business decisions. If Wayne said 'Kev, it'll never work', then Kev felt quite sure that it would work, and Kev was almost always right.

It seemed as though CBS were willing to do just about anything to sign Kevin Bloody Wilson at that point, and Kev was keen to maximise the experience for himself and his family. TJ remembers fondly CBS's courtship of her father. 'Dad told us to make a list. He asked us to write down every album we'd ever wanted. Travis and I were both music fans by then so we wrote this list and four days later these boxes full of records started turning up at the house.'

By now CBS was clearly starting to see the value in getting Kev's family on side, and it was an angle they worked shamelessly when it came to TJ. 'My favourite singer back then was Cindi Lauper. CBS paid for me to go to Sydney and I went to both of her concerts and I met her and hung out backstage.'

Despite all the attention CBS was paying Kev and his family, the second meeting went much the same way as the previous meeting: the suits tried to convince Kev to sign a deal with them, assuring him that they would do all the hard yards for him, What they hadn't taken into account was that Kev loved doing those hard yards himself, and he was already getting amazing results without the help of a record company. He enjoyed booking his own gigs, packaging his own albums and doing his own marketing, and he wasn't willing to surrender control of his own career to anyone.

However, as any successful artist will tell you, this approach only works up to a point. Eventually, when the performer's stature as a recording and touring artist has reached a certain level, it becomes impossible for them to do all the work themselves, and the time they should be spending creating their next big hit becomes time spent on the phone, in meetings with suit-wearing non-creative types, or buried under a mountain of paperwork. For this reason, Kev had secretly started to warm to the idea of signing with a record company, but no way was he going to do it for an eleven per cent share of his own profits, and no way was he going to let the suits from CBS know that he was even remotely interested in what they were offering.

During a smoko break at the second meeting with CBS in Sydney, one of its accountants made the mistake of saying to Kev, 'You may not realise this, but if you sign with CBS today we'll make you a millionaire by Christmas time.'

Kev instantly replied, 'Mate, you're supposed to be a fuckin' accountant, so if you'd done your homework you'd have worked out that I already *am* a fuckin' millionaire!' With that Kev slipped quietly out of the building.

In the cab on the way back to the hotel, which CBS was of course paying for, Kev's ashen-faced manager was convinced that Kev had really blown it this time. 'They won't want to have anything to do with you now,' he told Kev.

They continued their conversation back in the hotel room. Kev's approach was pretty clearly defined. 'Fuck 'em! I'll continue to do it myself. I've already got the systems in place. Let's go home.'

There was a knock at the hotel room door. This time it was a limo driver, all dressed up with the suit and the funny hat. 'Mr Wilson?'

'Yes?'

'CBS has postponed your flight back to Perth until later this afternoon, if that's all right with you. They would very much like to see you again—if you would be so kind as to come with me now, please, sir.'

Kev and Ross got into the limo and returned to CBS, where they were presented with a contract that had every-thing Kev was asking for and more.

Many record company executives probably would have stopped trying after the second or third rejection, but not Denis Handlin. 'Well, in many ways it was good old-fashioned persistence,' says Denis. 'We stayed on his case—in a good way—because we believed in his unique talent.'

The terms of this record deal were unheard of at the time, and have rarely been matched since. TJ explains, 'He says it's the Kev clause, and he was proud of that. It was the best record deal ever, because he didn't need them. He didn't need to sell a million albums. He could make that much selling a hundred thousand. He didn't need them, and he loved all of it.'

The hell that Kev put CBS through was all worth it from Denis Handlin's point of view. For him, this was more than just a sound business decision: Denis Handlin was a fan. Says Denis, 'Kevin had the great gift of true Australian humour and he is a very clever man and great fun to be around. It was a fascinating part of my career working with Kev, and it is something I will never forget.'

CHAPTER 12

Kev's back

'I'd like to be a better songwriter, a better musician. You are always "pleasantly unsatisfied". Your next song is always gonna be your best.'
Kevin Bloody Wilson

Over the years, many an artist has fallen victim to a condition known in the music industry as difficult second album syndrome, crumbling under the pressure to follow up a hit debut album with something as good or better. But not Kev.

'I think my second Kevin Bloody Wilson album, *Kev's Back*, was my defining moment. That's when I knew I was in it for keeps. The second album was a better recording, with better songs that had been better thought out. I spent a bit more time on that one. I'd also had about a twelve-month run-up to road-test all the songs in front of people, which I didn't with the first one.'

Kev now had the logistical and promotional support of a large record company; he'd also added to his repertoire a new song that was destined to become part of Australian pop-culture history.

To this day, at the mere mention of Kevin Bloody Wilson's name the first words that will fall out of people's mouths are: 'Hey Santa Claus, you cunt . . .!' For better or worse, in terms of Australian cultural history, a line like 'Hey Santa Claus, you cunt . . .' is right up there with 'I love a sunburnt country . . .' (And when you really think about it, Dorothea MacKellar must have had a pretty wicked sense of humour herself: all she needed to do was drop the last syllable of that famous line of hers and she'd have been just as outrageous as Kev.)

So what's Kev's big issue with Santa Claus? Did he really miss out on getting a bike off Santa when he was a kid, and is that where the song comes from? 'No, not at all. We did actually get a bike from Santa as kids—not a bike for each of us, one for the whole family—but I was too small to ride it.'

The idea of calling Santa a cunt was a little bit out there, even by Kev standards, but Travis was surprisingly under-whelmed when his dad played a rudimentary version of the song for him after school one day. 'When he played it to me on acoustic guitar I didn't really think it was that funny, to be honest.'

Kev didn't take Travis's lack of interest to heart. He spent the next few weeks working away on the song then tried it out on Travis again, this time with far more encour-aging results. Travis recalls, 'When he did it in the studio, and he delivered it properly, the way he wanted to, all of a sudden it was just this monster. My mate who was with me when we heard the recorded version for the first time was holding his cock, rolling around on the ground trying not to wet himself. Dad was leaning back in his chair laughing. It was just a funny day. I'll always remember that moment when I first heard that song properly, it was just incredible.'

As Travis says, to really get the full effect of the song you have to hear the studio version, although the lyrics do make for some pretty interesting reading.

Hey Santa Clause

Hey Santa Claus, you cunt!
Where's me fucking bike?
I've unwrapped all this other junk
And there's nothing that I like.
I wrote you a fucking letter
And I come to see you twice
Ya worn-out geriatric fart
You forgot me fuckin' bike.

If I wanted a pair of bloody thongs
I would have bloody asked.
And this cowboy suit and ping pong set
You can shove right up your arse!
You've stuffed me bloody order up
It's enough to make you spew
But it's not just me who's snakey, mate
Me sister's dirty too!

Hey Santa Claus, you cunt!
Where's me fuckin' pram?
You promised me you'd send me one

And you'd remember who I am.
'Cos I'm the little girl
Who you made sit right on your hand
I'll give you fuckin' ho ho ho
You forgot me fuckin' pram.

Next time I come to see ya
I'm gonna punch ya in the guts
And I'll let your fuckin' reindeer loose
And kick Rudolph in the nuts!
You just wait till next year
When you get back to that store
And me and me little sister
Come stompin' through the door
And we'll say, yeah you wait for it.

Hey mums and dads just smell his breath
And check his bloodshot eyes
And don't listen to him boys and girls
'Cos he tells fuckin' lies.
He's just a piss tank and a pervert
And he's not even very bright
'Cos the old fuckin' wanker
Forgot me fuckin' bike.

Twelve-year-old TJ was roped in by Kev to do some backing vocals on *Kev's Back (The Return of the Yobbo)*. The song in question was 'It Was Over (Kev's Lament)', and TJ's is one of the voices you hear doo-wopping all the way through it. She had no idea what she was singing about, which is probably just as well. 'They took away Dad's master vocal so I couldn't even hear what he was singing. I would go in with the other ladies, the professional session singers, and I'm sure because I was the boss's daughter they were very patient with me. This really lovely lady called Lucy would tell me what all of my parts were. *Ooh aah, do it do it, come come.* That's what I sang. As a backing vocalist they're just words and harmonies. You lose sight of the meaning of the words.'

It Was Over (Kev's Lament)

I remember back on our very first date
In the back seat of me car
I wanted you to go all the way
But you wouldn't go that far.
I wanted you to hold me dick
You wanted to hold me hand
And when I accidentally brushed your tit
I just blew it and cum in me pants
And it was over . . . before it began.

Blouses and buttons and bras and buckles
And 'Stop it I'm gettin' cold'
First time I'd had a tit in me mouth
Since I was nine months old.
I had lover's balls and you had no idea
Of the pitch of me passion and pain
Tryin' to stay cool with me knacker on fire
I cum in me pants again,
And it was over . . . before it began.

But you wouldn't give and I wouldn't go
And we couldn't seem to agree

You got the giggles and I got the shits
Then you wouldn't talk to me
And when we made up and we started again
Your dad banged his fist down and he yelled,
'What are you two kids doin' in there?'
And I shit meself as well
And it was over . . . before it began.

You hear people say that they'd love to go back
And do things that they did in the past
But if you reckon they were the good old days
You can go stick 'em right up your arse
'Cos when I look back how I came and I went
With a tear in me eye I recall
How me, I had a cunt of a night but me undies had a
*   ball*
And it was over . . . before it began.

Kev talked wife Betty into making her recording debut on 'Dick'taphone'. 'The singer who was supposed to sing the operator parts turned out to be a born-again Christian,' he grins. 'When she read the lyric sheet, she stormed out of the session saying she wouldn't lend her God-given talent to a song like that, so I got Betty in the recording booth to lay down a demo track but it turned out so well that we left Betty's version on the album. She did it brilliantly, but I haven't been able to coax Betty back into the recording studio since then.'

'Dick'taphone' is one of those Kevin Bloody Wilson songs that can sometimes get stuck in your head for days at a time. Kev wrote it out of frustration. 'We've all been frustrated by phones. Back when I wrote it we used to have operators,

now it's just automated systems; now you've gotta press five
to tell someone to get fucked . . .'

Dick'taphone

Hello, Operator? I'd like to make a call
Can I have 477 3104?
'I'm sorry, sir, could you repeat that number once
again?'
477 3104, did ya get it then?

'Could you speak a little slower?
477's all I got.'
3104, are you bloody deaf or what?
'Look, I got the first bit
But I just can't get the last.'
Well, stick that fuckin' phone
Up your fuckin' arse.

'Good morning, I'm from Telecom
Come to disconnect your phone
For a breach of regulations
Just a couple of days ago:
You upset our operator
With a pretty nasty call.'
What are you fuckin' on about?
It was all her fuckin' fault!

'Well, she claims that it was all your fault
She really was distressed.'
What about your customers?
She upset me first!

'We've got her written statement
Which shortly will be read
But it might help if you'd recall
Exactly what you said.'

I said . . .
Stick that fuckin' phone
Up your fuckin' arse
You're supposed to fuckin' help
Not make it fuckin' hard
I'm just tryin' to make a call
But you're just being smart
So you can stick that fuckin' phone
Up your fuckin' arse.

'Well, that's not exactly on, sir
It's just not on at all
You must use common etiquette
If you wish to make a call
And "please" and "thank you" also help
You can't talk to her like that.'
'Please' and fuckin' 'thank you'?
Well, you fuckin' tell her that

And she knows without a telephone
I'm really in the shit.
'Well, perhaps if you'd apologise
That just might help a bit.'
Apologise? Apologise?
Apologise to who?
'Just go in and ask for Operator 42.'

KEV'S BACK

'Good morning, are you waiting?
Is there something I can do?'
Yes, I'd like to speak to Operator 42.
'I'm sorry sir, I missed that
Could you repeat what you just said?'
Ah shit! I don't believe it
Here we fuckin' go again.

Operator 42, look I'll just write it down.
'Oh Operator 42, I'll see if she's around.'
Jeez, they're bloody useless
I'm sure that they're all deaf
No wonder I did me quince
No wonder what I said.

Why don't you . . .
Stick that fuckin' phone
Up your fuckin' arse
You're supposed to fuckin' help
Not make it fuckin' hard
I'm just tryin' to make a call
But you're just being smart
So you can stick that fuckin' phone
Up your fuckin' arse.

Now they'll make me sit around
And wait all bloody day
Just so they can make me sweat
And have the final say
That's like the public service
How they make you scrape and bow
Ahh shit, she's fuckin' ugly
If that's her coming now.

'I'm Operator 42
I'm busy, make it fast.'
Did a bloke tell you to stick
That fuckin' phone right up your arse?
'Yes he did, the filthy animal
I remember now.'
Well, you'd better brace yourself
'Cos they're bringing it around.

Well you can stick that fuckin' phone
Up your fuckin' arse
You're supposed to fuckin' help
Not make it fuckin' hard
I'm just tryin' to make a call
But you're just being smart
So you can stick that fuckin' phone
Up your fuckin' arse.

Another memorable track from Kev's second album is 'Mick the Master Farter'. I asked Kev if Mick is a real person.

'Mick the Master Farter is a combination of two great mates, both of whom are named Mick: Mick Cook, now a resident on the 'Mates' Star' who I went through school with in Sydney, and Mick Kaart, a fair-dinkum work-hard, play-hard truckie from Kalgoorlie. Both of these mates shared a common talent, the unique ability to fart on cue and, incredibly, for the most part in tune.

'Fart jokes still make me laugh. They make everybody laugh. Even the Queen farts. Even the corgis fart.'

Mick the Master Farter

I first met him in the classroom
Back in 1963
We seemed to hit it off pretty good
We were mates, Mick and me.
He wasn't such a big kid
Even back then at the start
And he wasn't all that clever either
But Jesus he could fart.

I first found that out in class one day
When things were going pretty slow
And just to keep us all amused
Mick let this fucking ripper go.
Well, you should have been there
Look, I'd describe it if I could
But I just turned around and I said,
'Hey Mick, you're fucking good!'

And at the end of school Grand Final
On the rugby field that time
We were getting beaten
They were twelve and we were nine
And play was three yards from our goal-line
When the referee called a scrum
And Mick said, 'Don't worry fellas
We've as good as got it won.'

So we just locked ourselves down in the scrum,
And we held each other's nose
And Mick, our little hooker

He let this fucking ripper go.
Well, it stung their nose
And it burnt their eyes
And it even scorched the grass
And I twigged right then and there,
He had a double-jointed arse.

Mick, me mate the master farter
Put the art back into farting
With his custom-tailored farts.
Mick, me mate the master farter
Broke new ground in breaking wind
With his double-jointed arse.

And it was just a couple of years later
We both went to see Kamahl
It was a really poshy sort of show
In this great big bloody hall
All the blokes were dressed like penguins
Well, you should have seen the sorts
And Kamahl himself wore a sheila's dress
Like a bloody black Boy George.

We were all locked in there like sardines
For the show to get underway
But the tuba player didn't lob
He'd booked off crook that day
And Kamahl said, 'Without a tuba player
I cannot commence the show.'
So old Mick jumps up and says,
'Sambo, mate, I'll have a fucking go!'

KEV'S BACK

Well, from then on in I honestly thought
That the whole show would be ruined
But he just winked at me and picked that tuba up
Just like he knew what he was doing.
Then the maestro tapped his little stick
To tell the band to start
And Mick just shut his eyes and cocked his leg
And then began to fart.

Well, you could have heard a pin drop
That night there in the hall
And it's hard to say who sounded best
Mick farting or Kamahl.
Then the audience just went apeshit
They cheered and clapped and stood
And Kamahl smiled as if to say,
'Hey Mick, you're fucking good!'

Mick, me mate the master farter
Put the art back into farting
With his custom-tailored farts
Mick, me mate the master farter
With his true-pitch perfect, calibrated
Double-jointed arse.

Well, good news travels fast it seems
And it wasn't very long
Before Mick got this midnight phone call
From Ben Lexcen and Alan Bond.
They said, 'Mick, we've got this specialist job
And we're prepared to pay ya,
Mick old son would you consider
Farting for Australia?

'We'll just prop you on our brand-new yacht,
When there's no sea breeze blowing
And get Mick the master farter to start her
And keep the bastard going.'
So Mick went into training
On sausage rolls and pies
And Vegemite and Foster's beer
And a scholarship from Heinz.

The world had never seen before
A yacht so finely groomed
Or a crew so fit and young and strong
Or an arse so finely tuned.
The Yanks weren't even in the race
Not even in the same class
What with Ben Lexcen and his secret keel
And Mick's fuel-injected arse.

Well, he come back a bloody hero, didn't he,
The all-Australian boy
And government commissioned this bloke
To build a big statue of his coit
And I can still see Mick standing there
When they confirmed his knighthood
And Bob Hawke pinning it on 'n saying,
'Hey Mick, you're fucking good!'

Mick me mate the master farter
Put the class back into farting
With his designer-label farts
Mick me mate the master farter

With his true-pitch perfect-calibrated,
Turbo-thrusted, fuel-injected,
Wynns-protected double-jointed arse.

One song on Kev's second album attracted a bit more attention than the others. Some people who heard it immediately branded Kev a racist and others thought he was right on the money, but nobody who heard the song has ever forgotten it.

Alan Bond is arguably Australia's most infamous businessman. Like Kevin Bloody Wilson he came from humble beginnings, working as a signwriter before getting into the property development game, founding in 1959 what would become Bond Corporation. He expanded his business interests to include gold mining, TV and that most Australian of entrepreneurial pursuits, brewing. He was named Australian of the Year in 1978 after financing Australia's challenge for the America's Cup, and in 1983 he paid the bills which helped wrench the yachting trophy from American hands for the first time since 1851. Ben Lexcen was the designer of *Australia II*'s winged keel. Bondy was a real Aussie hero for a while there, especially in and around Perth, but that was before he found himself at the helm of one of Australia's biggest-ever corporate collapses.

It was impossible to live in Perth in the eighties and not be aware of Alan Bond. One afternoon when Kev was driving to a gig several hours out of Perth, Smokie's 'Living Next Door to Alice' came on the radio.

I don't know why she's leaving or where she's gonna go
I guess she's got her reasons but I just don't want to
know

*'Cause for twenty-four years I've been living next door
    to Alice.*

Kev passed the time on the long drive by decomposing
Smokie's song, changing Alice to Alan. He was singing the
chorus to himself under his breath as he unloaded his gear and
set up for the gig. It probably didn't feel like a career-defining
moment at the time, but history tells us that's exactly what it
was.

Livin' Next Door to Alan

*They come down from Meekatharra
In a burnt-out blue FJ
That farted and just shit itself
In Jutland Parade
Right next door to Bondy's.
When the smoke had cleared a voice said,
'Eh, this place look all right
We'll tell the government it's a sacred site
Dead fuckin' easy.*

*'G'day Mr Alan Bond, how you goin', bloke?
Eh, I'm your brand-new neighbour
Eh mate, you got a smoke?
And I think I'm gonna like it 'ere
Livin' next door to Alan.
Twenty-four kids, nine adults and fifteen dogs
A dead roo on the roof rack and bootload fulla grog
And I'm flash as Michael Jackson
Now I'm livin' next door to Alan.*

'The first thing that we gotta do is get another car
'Cos the one sittin' out the front
Won't even fuckin' start
We'll call that bloke again from the government
He's all right, eh?'

So they called the bloke in charge
Of all the government grants
And the next day in the driveway
Was a new Mercedes-Benz.
'Eh, come and have a look at this one, Edwin
This one's got a wireless! Look at this, eh!

'G'day Mr Alan Bond, how you goin', mate?
You got a real flash car
But my one's flash one, eh?
And I believe that my one's faster than yours, Mr Bond
'Cos mine's a red one! Look at this!'

Twenty-four kids, nine adults and fifteen dogs
All squeezed in the front seat
With the wireless turned full on
Listenin' to Slim Dusty
Now they're livin' next door to Alan.

So Bondy called Ben Lexcen and said,
'I want another yacht
Twice as big and twice as fast
As what I already got.
That'll fuck 'em!'
So his neighbours called some welfare mob
Not to be outdone

And got *the* HMAS Melbourne
On some sorta government loan.
It's got me knackered
They just said they wanted to go fishin' for yabbies in
     the river.

'G'day Mr Alan Bond, how you goin', mate?
You got a real flash boat, but my one's flash one, eh?
And I think I'm gonna put him in the river next door to
     Alan's.'
Fifteen dogs, nine adults, two dozen screamin' kids
With lines strung from the flight deck tryin' to catch
     some fish
Swimmin', fishin', pissin' in the river next door to Alan.

So Bondy threw a party, the likes you've never seen
And invited everybody, from the Premier to the Queen
And the Leyland Brothers
So his neighbours baked bungarra on a barbie on the
     lawn
And invited all their relatives from Meekatharra to come
     down.
'Hey, Edwin,
Don't you forget to bring a big flagon of woobla
There's a party on at my 'ouse!'

I don't know why he's leavin' or where he's gonna go
He says he's got his reasons and I reckon that I know
He just never got used to livin' next door to Abos.

He's jumpin' up and down
And he's makin' such a fuss

At least we don't got fuckin' coons
Livin' next door to us!
Now we gotta get used to not living next door to Alan
Now we gotta get used to not living next door to Alan.

Says Kev, 'There was only ever one Aborigine who took us to task over that song, and it turned out he and his white manager were out to line their own pockets, and in the end they both got charged with extortion with menaces. They both lived in Darwin, and this was the same Aboriginal bloke that had already tried to sue the Collingwood Football Club for being racist and put a curse on them—as if Collingwood needed a fuckin' curse. This same bloke claimed that he was offended by my song and that all his people were offended by it, but he said that he was prepared to forget all of that if I gave him and his manager forty grand or a brand-new four-wheel drive. They were both committed for trial but got off on a legal technicality. It's interesting to note that more recently the white manager was charged and jailed for trading drugs for sex with underage girls, and the black fella was charged and jailed for having sex with underage boys. So, black or white, once a cunt, always a cunt.'

When Kev first started touring the Top End in the mid eighties he was amazed and somewhat relieved to discover just how much Indigenous appeal his music had. 'I was in the Northern Territory doing a beer commercial with my mate Wayne Cubis from the NT Brewery. We called in for a drink at the Gunbalanya Sports and Social Club in Oenpelli near Kakadu when this Aboriginal fella, a tribal elder, came up to me and said, "Eh Kevin, if we were to get you a right-hand guitar, would you play some music for us?" What he meant by that was that they only had left-handed guitars in the community because when the missionaries had gone in there in the 1930s, one of them taught them the guitar but he was a fuckin' kacky-hander, so everybody learned, then passed the guitar down as left-handers.

'Luckily they were doing some construction there at the time and one of the construction workers had a right-handed guitar, so I borrowed it and played some songs. As it was nearing Christmas I sang "Hey Santa Claus", and then he said, "Hey Kevin, would you sing for my people 'Living Next Door to Alan'?" I said, "I'd fuckin' love to, but make sure your mates don't start chuckin' fuckin' spears at me." That's when he said to me, "Kevin, my people love your music because you make us laugh."

'So I did the song, and they fuckin' got right into it, particularly when I did a broad hand gesture and sang the line "Least we don't got fuckin' coons livin' next door to us". They fuckin' lost it. I've never heard that line work better. For the next hour the whole mob were repeating the hand gesture and line from the song while directing it at each other. They were literally cryin' laughin'. When we were leaving, my newest mate and a couple of his friends took me to a shed that was just full of absolutely magnificent Aboriginal artwork, and he said, "Kevin, you take what you like." I said, "Thanks, but you don't have to do that." "Come on, Kevin, we want you to have this for makin' my people laugh." "OK then, you pick one." He chose for me a striking and detailed Aboriginal bark painting. I've still got it hanging prominently on the wall in our home. I have no idea what it's worth, but to me it's fuckin' priceless.'

Kev still gets asked in interviews whether Alan Bond ever heard 'Livin' Next Door to Alan', and if so what he thought of it. The answer is yes, and he thought it was the second funniest song he'd ever heard Kev do.

Alan Bond had been telling friends that he was a big fan of Kevin Bloody Wilson ever since the release of Kev's debut album. According to the guy who used to park Alan's Rolls-Royce at Perth airport, there was never anything other than a Kevin Bloody Wilson cassette in Bondy's car stereo.

Alan's wife Eileen, who Kev refers to as Rough Red, famously went into 78 Records in Perth's Hay Street and bought forty copies of *Kev's Back (The Return of the Yobbo)* to give as presents to her and Alan's friends and family. Not long after that Kev found himself being pursued by the family of another Western Australian mover and shaker, Alister Norwood.

Alister had started Jeans West in 1972 with one Perth outlet, and by 1984 he had twenty-eight stores across Western Australia and was well on his way to making Jeans West a national brand. Alister's family were planning a surprise fortieth birthday party for him, and—party because Alan Bond would be at the party—they wanted Kevin Bloody Wilson to perform.

Kev reflects, 'I didn't like the idea at first, because I didn't want to be there as some kind of plaything for the rich, performing in front of them as they looked down their noses at me. When I was initially approached by the Norwood family I remember writing down my telephone number on a piece of paper and giving it to them. They thought I had written down my fee and the stupid pricks agreed to pay it, so I turned up and did the gig.

'I did about a twenty-minute set and I finished with "Livin' Next Door to Alan", which was a weird experience, playing the song and watching Bondy himself laughing along to it. Eileen Bond came up to me at the end of it and said, "Kevin, why don't you play 'That Fuckin' Cat's Back'? That's Alan's favourite!" So I came back and did it as an encore.'

When Alan Bond was thrown in the slammer in 1997, legend has it that as he was walked to his cell for the first time all the other inmates were singing 'Livin' Next Door to Alan' at the top of their voices. As Kev points out, 'He probably doesn't like the song as much as he used to.'

CHAPTER 13

How lucky can you get?

'Luck comes in two forms, good and bad. Sometimes they travel together . . .'

Kevin Bloody Wilson

The controversy Kevin Bloody Wilson's second album created was not always easy to manage. In an attempt to protect his family's privacy, Kev invented false names for them. These false names became part of the Kev mythology, a series of falsehoods that were designed to give Kevin Bloody Wilson a believable backstory while protecting the innocent.

As far as Kev's fans were aware, Kev was born in Kalgoorlie, he was a raging pisshead, and he had a wife called Shirl and two kids called Greg and Sharon. None of these things were true, but many of his fans believed every word of it—Kev still meets people who *swear* they went to school with him in Kalgoorlie. 'If I'd sat next to everybody that told me they sat next to me in school, that fuckin' school bench would have been three hundred metres long. I never challenge them on it, because they've probably dined out on that for years, so why ruin their fun?'

Kev's brother Terry has also heard the 'I went to school with Kev' stories. 'One day in Kalgoorlie sitting next to a bloke and his mate and this bloke's telling his mate that he went to school with Kev, sat next to him at school in Kalgoorlie . . . I never said a thing. I let him have his five minutes.'

Travis, aka Greg, was beginning to feel unsettled by some of the trappings of Kev's initial success. 'My most vivid memory is from just after he'd got his record deal with CBS, and we had a party for the record company people. There were a lot of randoms there and I remember Mum was bringing some food out to the backyard and some bloke yelled out, "Go and get us another beer, Shirl!" and I thought, "You wanker, you don't even know us and I don't even know you, and you're talking to my mum in that way."'

TJ understood why her dad was referring to her as Sharon on stage. 'I kinda got it because it was all part of the character that Dad had created. We were well and truly in our twenties before he would say our real names on stage.'

Betty—or Shirl—was impressed by the progress her husband was making with his career, even though she was now starting to feel a bit excluded. 'I thought, "Wow, a record deal!" I didn't know any other person who was signed to a record company. That was pretty big, but I'd never met anybody involved in it at all. I was at home with the kids while he was out there organising all that.'

While Travis enjoyed some of the trappings of being the son of a famous father—including swapping copies of his father's albums for packets of cigarettes at school—it was not always an easy ride for him. 'I felt like all of a sudden we'd been shot into Hollywood or something, and there were all these clingons—and they *were* clingons—hanging around the house. Not only hanging around the house but ringing you up and saying, "Is Kev there? It's his old mate from Kalgoorlie" or whatever. It was unbelievable.'

The Clingons converged, and when record companies come in there is a certain type of person they bring in with them. TJ explains: 'You could just look at them and know they wouldn't be my dad's friend if he wasn't Kevin Bloody Wilson.'

Travis is exceptionally proud of his dad's achievements both on and off stage, but he has his reasons for not telling people who his father is until he feels he knows them well enough. 'I guard it pretty fiercely. If people find out too early, especially when you're trying to develop friendships with people, it taints it from the very beginning and you really don't know whether they're your mate 'cos they like who you are or if they're your mate 'cos they're interested in who your dad is. You make sure you get to know people before they find out.'

Kev was good at attracting a crowd, but he was even better at attracting trouble. Wayne Pride recalls the first time Kev got him fired from a gig. 'I was working at a tavern restaurant in Subiaco called Henry Africa's. I'd been there every Tuesday night for five years at that point. This night I took a break and I looked over and there's Kev. I said, "What are you doing here?" and he said, "I've got a presentation tonight." He was being given this award by the people from Ampex for gold sales of his album using Ampex recording tape. When that was all over he came up to the bar and he was having a drink. Everywhere I used to go and play he'd turn up and we'd sing a song by Waylon

Jennings and his wife Jessi Colter called "Storms Never Last". So he got up and we did that song as a duo. Then we sang Everly Brothers songs and just did a bit of straight music.

'So we're having a nice little time, and there's this girl sitting at the bar. She was half attractive, and she's sorta looking at us and then she looked at her watch and grabbed her handbag and started walking out the door. Kev just turned around and looked at her and said, "Where the fuck are *you* going?" on the microphone. My heart sank. I thought, "He's gonna get me in the shit now." Well, the girl kept walking out the door but everyone in the tavern came alive, and after that he launched into some Kevin Bloody Wilson songs. We were there till half past one in the morning and the publican's filling us with piss and he reckoned we were the greatest blokes in the world. But the next day I was told that I was sacked, after five years of playing there regularly.

'Another night Kev turned up at a gig I was doing at the Craigie Tavern. He was there with Martin Jenner, who played guitar with Cliff Richard. Inside this tavern there was an old-fashioned red phone box, and one of them—or possibly both of them—went in there and took a piss. They were pretty maggoted, but I didn't get the sack that night, 'cos I told the boss I didn't know them. These days, every time he asks me where I'm playing I tell him I can't remember.'

Kevin Bloody Wilson was now a household name all over Australia; he was having a wild time around Perth and he was on the verge of becoming a successful international recording and touring artist. This sudden ascendency had brought with it many advantages for Kev and his family, but what Kev failed to notice was that at the exact same time as his career was taking off, things were beginning to crash and burn on the home front. Betty was doing her best to go along for the ride, but being a fundamentally shy person she was not always comfortable with the trappings of her husband's success.

Shortly after signing him to the label, CBS held a dinner in Kev's honour to celebrate the launch of his second album. As Kev recalls, he was 'sitting there at the head of this big table in front of everybody with all the CBS execs holding up gold albums and stuff like that, and Betty's stuck in the corner with one of her girlfriends from Kalgoorlie'.

Betty was beginning to feel that she had become non-existent. 'They were all kissing his arse or whatever it is they do, and I guess I didn't want to be in the limelight as such, but I really didn't feel like I belonged. I thought I was in the way. Nobody knew me. I was his wife but nobody knew that. Nobody bothered to say hello or introduce me to anyone. It wasn't really Kev's fault because they just kind of took him and whisked him away.

'Then it all hit home and I just took off. I said to my girl-friend, "I need to go, I can't be here," and I left. And the next day this lady rang us at home, a reporter, and she asked for Kev. I said, "I'm sorry, he's not home," and she said, "Who is this?" so I told her I was his wife and she said, "Oh! Why weren't you there yesterday?" and I thought to myself, "I *was* there, bitch!"

'I think the more success he had, the bigger he got, the worse it was at home, because he was going on tour and then when he'd come home he still wasn't ours. We never got to do stuff. There was never time for the kids or me or anything like that. I felt like I was there to wash his clothes and cook for him and then he'd be off again. I'm not blaming him as such. It was just a situation that took off that perhaps I wasn't ready for. I tend to blame myself a bit more now because I think I didn't cope with the success when it first hit. There was not much communication between us, because there just wasn't time.'

Travis was also feeling overwhelmed by the effects of his father's initial success as Kevin Bloody Wilson. 'We all felt a bit left behind. It was happening to all of us. As soon as the Clingons started ringing up and coming around to the house we all just sort of disengaged, because this *thing* was a force of its own.'

If Betty and the kids were waiting for 'the Kev thing' to die down a little so they could see more of the man they still knew as Dennis Bryant, it soon became apparent that they would be waiting for quite a while. Propelled in no small part by the success of 'Livin' Next Door to Alan' and 'Hey Santa Claus', *Kev's Back (The Return of the Yobbo)* won an Australian Recording Industry Association award, otherwise known as an ARIA, for best comedy release of 1987. Kev's ARIA was presented to him by a jittery Elton John. Kev says, 'I reckon he was on one of his cocaine binges at that stage, so you didn't get to know him, you didn't get to see him backstage or anything, but I've still got the photo of him and me together from that night so I'm happy about that.'

Kevin Bloody Wilson had come from relative obscurity to become the most in-demand performer in Australian comedy in two short years. He couldn't quite believe his luck. But luck comes in two forms, good and bad, and sometimes they even travel together.

'So, suddenly all this stuff I'd never even dreamed of turns up in my lap. The record deal, sold out concerts, an ARIA award, and a fuckin' marriage break-up.'

CHAPTER 14

Ground zero

'Mate, they can take everything else away from you but they can't take your talent. Focus on that.'

Kev's mate Bruce Tuffin

To understand why some men treat the women in their lives the way they sometimes do, it helps to go back a generation and look at that man's own upbringing.

According to Kev's brother Terry, 'Our old man would go to the pub on his way home from work. A few times the old girl had to go down the road and drag him out.

'Being Catholics, Friday was fish and chip night, and Dad would bring home the fish and chips. Sometimes he wouldn't turn up, Mum would have to go and get him from the pub, and all of us kids would be starving hungry. But all the fathers did that in those days. None of us boys have ever done it, though. None of us are regular drinkers. We'll have a beer on the weekend or whatever but we don't drink every day like he used to.'

When Terry started seeing some things in his brother he didn't like, he took Kev aside. 'I pointed out to him that I didn't like the way he was treating Betty. Coming from our background you could understand why he needed to adjust his attitude to women, 'cos you got bashed at home by your mother and then you went to convent school and got bashed again by another woman. I s'pose for whatever reason a lot of men were chauvinists in those days, but some of the things I saw him do to Betty . . . fuck me dead.

'There was an intercom system in their house. One day I was in the bedroom talking to Kev and Betty was downstairs, so he called her up on the intercom. "Betty, can you cook me some breakfast and bring it up?" She asked him what he wanted, and he said bacon and eggs. So Betty cooked it all and brought it upstairs and he didn't even fuckin' touch it. He just left it there to get cold, got out of bed and went downstairs and had a coffee. I wondered why on earth he would do that. Maybe he was trying to show her that he was the boss, I don't know.

'I had my own business then and he was working weekends, as a muso does, so every Monday night we'd go to the local pub and inevitably we'd end up in town some-where. At two o'clock in the morning I'd suggest that we get a cab home, and he'd go, "Aah fuck it, I'll phone Betty up." Betty had a job in the city, so she'd have to be up early, and I'd tell him not to phone her. But he would, and she'd turn up and she'd be fuckin' wild. He did that a few times.'

Prior to the break-up of their marriage Betty showed very few outward signs of strain, to Kev or to anyone else. She explains, 'I held it in for a long time, and looking back that was probably a mistake. I knew when we got married that he was never the sort of person who would help out around the house, and I just accepted it all. I think we came from the school where Mum always did the housework and everything 'cos Dad was the one who was out working, and mums generally weren't working back then. I'd started work so I was leaving home early, making beds and doing all that stuff before I went to work, and getting back late. And when I got back, in the dark, even though he'd be there, I'd still have to make dinner. There was no time to sit down and have a chitty-chat 'cos there were kids who needed to be fed.

'There were times where I'd try to speak to him and he'd say things like, "For God's sake, it's only the garbage, can't you just take the fuckin' bins out? You're always on about the fuckin' garbage . . ." and I'd say to him, "Well, it's not *just* that, that's just one thing that comes to mind while I'm running around doing all of it and you've got your big fat arse on the couch." Bottom line, I just felt like I was the fucking housemaid.'

As Kevin Bloody Wilson's career took off, the trappings of fame were all his for the taking. There were some, such as hard drugs, which he flat-out rejected, but others, such as the tantalising offers he got from female fans after his shows, he occasionally found much harder to resist. For a long time Kev assumed he was getting away with it, but Betty knew at least some of what was going on. What Kev didn't know was that Betty had a secret of her own: at work, Betty was the object of a much younger man's affections.

Says Betty, 'It was really nothing to start with because he was so much younger than me, but he just paid me all this attention and did all these very gentlemanly things for me. It started just as a friendship thing, and then it moved into me thinking, "I quite like this . . . This person doesn't think I'm a household appliance. This person thinks I'm a nice person."

We were friends for a long time and then we started seeing each other secretly. It was grinding inside me all the time, trying to keep this secret and then going home and seeing that the situation there wasn't getting any better. And Kev didn't even notice that there was something wrong, which was part of the problem.'

Kev recalls, 'The day in 1986 that Betty told me she was leaving me was the worst day of my life. She told me on a Saturday morning, and I had a show to do on Saturday night. She said, "We need to have a talk," and I'm going, "Jesus, what?" I was gutted, absolutely gutted. I didn't see it coming. She just held it in and held it in, and then the time came.'

Kev and Betty were completely unaware that while they were talking, Travis was overhearing parts of their conversation. 'I was asleep on the couch, which was pretty close to where the kitchen and dining table was, and they were sitting over there talking. I heard Mum saying stuff like "Well, what about TJ? Where is she going to go?" I heard that, and immediately I knew that something was pretty serious, but I didn't think they were going to break up. I went over to my girlfriend's house that morning and I told her there was something serious going on with Mum and Dad, but I didn't think it was *that* serious.'

When Travis returned home after talking it over with his girlfriend Robyn—now his wife—his parents asked to speak to him. 'They called me into the upstairs lounge room. Dad was sitting at one side of the room, I was sitting up the end where Mum was, and they told me they were splitting up. That was probably the worst day of my life I reckon. When you're sixteen years old that was as bad as it gets, because everything that you do revolves around that family unit. No matter what you do, you believe that family is always going to be there, and that's your safe haven in life. When that goes your brain turns to mush, you don't know what you're there for. It's a really strange feeling.'

Now a husband and father himself, these days Travis has little doubt as to the reasons behind Kev and Betty's split. 'She'd had enough. He wasn't a good husband. He was a great father, but he wouldn't have been a good husband. He would have been a bastard to be married to because he was old-fashioned. The wife did everything and that was the way the house was run.'

Kev didn't handle very well the news that Betty had a much younger boyfriend, but as TJ points out her father hadn't exactly stuck to his marriage vows either. 'I know that back in Kalgoorlie Dad was screwing around. He later told me that he was married for a few years before he realised he was married. It took him a while. He has a saying that family comes first, second and third—he's said it for as long as I can remember. Before he and Mum split up I know he believed it, but he couldn't live it. He wasn't able to, and a lot of the dads of his generation couldn't.'

TJ arrived home an hour or so after Kev and Betty told Travis the news, and she knew as soon as she walked through the door that something was up. 'The house was just weird. It wasn't unusual for Dad to be doing his thing and Mum to be doing hers, but there was just a mood in the house. Not an angry mood, just really weird.

'I was playing the piano upstairs, and Mum came and sat down next to me. I don't think she even gave me any heads-up on it, she just said, "Your dad and I are separating." I was fourteen and I was a total drama queen, so I immediately threw myself over the piano like a bad movie, going, "Oh my God! What am I gonna do?" I just remember looking at her and going, "Why? No one's unhappy." I had friends whose parents were divorced and with that there was a lot of screaming and yelling. I'm sure my parents fought too, but it was not an unhappy house.'

Once she picked herself up off the piano, TJ went downstairs to see her dad. 'He was sitting on the lounge, and he was just a mess. I didn't know what to do. I was the kid. I'd never seen one of my parents in that sort of distress. I remember thinking, "Do I hug him or what?" I remember he was on his way to a big festival, and he was going, "There's fifteen thousand people out there waiting for me to be funny, and I've never felt so fuckin' unfunny in my life," and he was just sobbing.' TJ decided she needed to get out of the house for a while. 'So I got on my bike and I rode to Uncle Terry's house, because he was in Warwick at the time. When I told him he was more upset than I was. I wasn't at home a lot after that. I didn't want to know about it.'

Kev was destroyed by the day's news, but he still had to get through that night's show. 'That night I put in what my manager says was the best fuckin' performance he'd ever seen me do. You have to go into a zone. You can't afford to let your mind play on it for even a millisecond 'cos it will fuck you up. After the show I walked off stage and straight into his arms and I fuckin' cried like a baby. I couldn't do any signing or anything. I was just fucked, and I had felt like that all day except when I was on stage.

'To me that was the most critical moment in my life, when everything in my life was just gone yet at the same time I was suddenly making more money than I'd ever dreamed of. I learned a monumental lesson out of that, which is I would have gladly got all the fuckin' cheques that CBS and everybody shoved in my fuckin' pocket and just said, "Here, have them back. I just want my fuckin' life back." You think you'll never get through stuff like that, but you do.'

Travis recalls the awkward period after his parents announced their separation. 'Mum was sleeping in the downstairs room. Dad was upstairs. It went like that for a week or so and then Dad moved out. He had enough money to go and get a townhouse. So he moved out and I was still at home.' Travis would occasionally go and stay with his dad in his new place at North Beach.

'I really started going downhill. I started giving up on a lot of things. School became less important. Everything just became less important to me, and I couldn't be bothered with anything.'

A few weeks later the family made a shared decision that Betty would move into the North Beach property and Kev would move back into the family home. Travis stayed there with Kev. He remembers, 'TJ decided, without talking to me, that she was going to live with Mum. I think if I got the first choice I probably would have lived with Mum, because Mum knew how to do everything. She knew how to cook dinners, and Dad didn't know how to do any of that shit.'

TJ adjusted pretty quickly to her new living arrangement. 'I think Travis had a much harder time than I did because, for a lot of that time, Mum was happy. Dad wasn't. I was around the happy one, and Dad had a series of girlfriends, mostly idiot bimbo twenty-something-year-olds, which you should have if you can get 'em in your forties. Why not? If you can get a root from a blonde chick with big tits who is twenty years old then why are you gonna go for the forty year old?'

One thing about TJ: like her dad, she knows how to tell

it like it is, or at least like she remembers it. 'Dad turned into an arsehole. Even at the time I remember thinking he was acting like an animal that has been hurt and is in attack mode. I remember coming home from school and seeing my mum walking up the street just laden with shopping bags. I'm like, "What are you doing?" "Just doing the food shopping." "Why are you walking?" "Your dad took the car." And that's the sort of stuff that he did back then, for no other reason than to go "Fuck you".'

Now that Kev and Travis were living on their own, one of the first things Kev had to figure out was how to cook for the two of them. So that Travis would have plenty of food to eat even when he was left to fend for himself, Kev enrolled in a microwave-cooking course at the local TAFE. Says Travis, 'He'd go on tour for a few weeks at a time, and before he went he'd have a cooking day where he'd cook me three weeks worth of meals, like steaks and rissoles and all sorts of things like that, and then store them all in the freezer and go, "Right, there you go. You're fed for three weeks." He would also give me five hundred bucks to buy incidentals while he was gone.'

Incidentally, Travis spent his incidentals money on cigarettes, alcohol and lighting for his start-up band and for the parties. Whatever was left over, he spent on two-minute noodles. He didn't go near most of the frozen meals Kev had cooked for him, and his sister certainly wasn't going to eat them either. TJ remembers her dad's cooking as 'basic to say the least. The meals were nutritious enough but they were incredibly boring. He'd come home after the tour to a freezerful of those meals. By then Trav had discovered two-minute noodles, so Dad stocked him right up. You'd open the pantry and there'd be fifty packs of two-minute noodles.'

As much as TJ still loved spending time with her father, she felt that she had made the right decision in choosing to live with her mother. 'I was smarter than that. I went with Mum, someone who knew how to iron. Travis would come over when Dad was on tour, and he wouldn't have brushed his teeth for a week. His hair would be everywhere and Mum would go, "Let me guess, your father's away."'

Travis had the house to himself for much of the first year of Kev and Betty's separation. He would occasionally get a surprise visit from his Uncle Terry, who recalls now, 'I go round to the house one day and here's the fuckin' band set up in the kitchen. The whole band. I said, "You don't wanna be playing too loud around here 'cos all the neighbours will be telling your old man, and he'll go off his head. You'll have to clean this place up before the old man gets home."'

Whatever Travis may have lacked in terms of domesticity, he well and truly made up for it with his social skills, which was in turn a bonus for TJ. 'Travis threw the best parties. I don't know how many Dad found out about, but it was always a case of "Kevin Bloody Wilson's on tour: party at the Wilsons"!' They were organised, there were fliers passed out at school, and on the day of the party everyone would wag school to go over and move the furniture. Trav even had Mum come to one of the parties so if anything happened he could say she was there. Like she wasn't in enough shit already.'

After one particularly messy party Travis went to great lengths to clean up the house before his dad got home. As TJ explains he would have got away with it, if not for one small oversight. 'He got caught because the carpet cleaning bill came, and it was in Dad's name. He'd used Dad's name because he knew he'd get a discount. He'd think it through but then that last ten per cent would always bring him undone. He'd never get the details exactly right.'

Terry remembers the time Travis was caught red-handed. 'I was with Kev. He'd done a show, and we were supposed to be going directly up to Lancelin after the show but he had forgotten something so we had to go home. When we got there Kev saw this sixteen-year-old kid hanging outside his house. Kev asked this kid what he was doing there and he said, "I'm here for the party." Kev told him, "There's no fuckin' party here, kid, so you and your mates can fuck off!" I think Travis threw a fair few parties, but what kid wouldn't take advantage of the situation?'

Kev worked through the pain of his marriage break-up by throwing himself even further into his work. 'I have a mate, Bruce Tuffin, who said to me at the time, "They can take everything else away from you but they can't take your talent." That became my mantra over that period; I rested on that idea really hard for the next couple of years.'

Terry could tell that Kev still hadn't come close to letting Betty go. 'It was always on his mind that he was going to get her back, always. He's always tried hard to be positive. At the time he had the choice of any woman that he wanted, really, and he had a few, but Betty was the only one that counted. He'd go on stage and perform and everything would be fine and then the minute he was off he was a wreck. That's why I started touring with him, to keep my eye on him.'

Terry became what is lovingly referred to in show business as the 'merch bitch', selling Kev's recordings and T-shirts at the shows. According to Terry, though, his talent and involvement extended far beyond this. 'I had my own stage name given to me by the band when I was on the road. They called me Terry Cougar Melancholy. I'd do knock-knock jokes and sing "Song Sung Blue". So whenever I walked into rehearsal the band would see me and automatically start into "Song Sung Blue" just for a joke. I never actually performed—for whatever reason I was never asked. Obviously he didn't want to exploit me, but I was willing to give it a go. It would have been a tough support act for Kev to follow: knock-knock jokes and "Song Sung Blue".'

Kev's live shows were going off like never before, thanks in no small part to his new tour manager, the woman Kev calls Cactus. Sue Maloney is a bona fide legend in the touring business, having piloted successful treks for artists as diverse as Elton John, Billy Connolly, Barry Humphries, the Wiggles . . . and Kev.

'Kevin and I hit it off really well from day one,' says Sue. 'Betty wasn't around when I started working with Kevin. They had just broken up. He was an absolute mess without Betty, absolutely he was, but Kevin was always incredibly driven. Kevin was amazing to work with. He never said no to interviews or anything like that, he loved connecting with people in the media. He always worked really hard. There was never an opportunity that went untouched.

'I worked out with Kevin what we wanted to do and then we just booked the tour. We booked the venues, went out and did some artwork, did some advertising and ticketing, and we did all the logistics. Air travel, ground transport, accommodation, everything. We were doing theatres and he had a band, so it was a high-end, big theatre-type production.'

Kev liked working with Sue, and to ensure that she felt like part of his crew he assigned her a nickname. Sue recalls,

'I kept saying, "No, I'm fine, I don't need a nickname." He said, "No, no, everyone's gotta have a nickname." So after weeks and weeks of me refusing to have a nickname he said, "OK, you've got two choices: Snot Sleeve or Cactus Pubes," and I said, "I don't like either of those." I knew that which-ever name I was given, it would eventually be shortened to either Snot or Cactus. I chose Cactus.'

On the road Cactus witnessed Kev's behaviour as a newly single man—not that she noticed much that she considered out of the ordinary. 'He had two girlfriends that I knew of, and I don't even remember their names now. They'd come on and off the road, but I don't remember him taking girls home at night or doing much of that. Mind you, we were pretty busy. We'd finish a show at ten thirty and wouldn't get out of there until eleven thirty, and then back on the road at nine the next morning, so there wasn't a lot of time for him to be screwing around.'

In 1987 Kev released his third album, *Born Again Piss Tank*. By now he knew precisely what his audience expected of him, and with songs like 'The Kid (He Swears a Little Bit)', 'Rootin' in the Back of the Ute' and 'Supa Mega Fugly' he delivered.

In 'Kev's Love Song (Dinkum 'Bout Ya Darlin')', Kev used one of his favourite lyrical devices. It's the old set-up and knock-down, where a romantic and innocent line is followed up by something completely unexpected. Hence, 'I'm dinkum 'bout ya darlin' . . . 'cos I've had a fat all day'. (Another fine example of the set-up and knock-down is a line Kev wrote many years later that goes, 'I'm missing you . . . suckin' my cock'.)

At the end of the *Born Again Piss Tank* album, there's an indecipherable message. To hear what Kev says, the tape needs to be reversed, pitched down and slowed down. That's an impossible task on a domestic CD player so to save you the trouble, and as a reward for buying this book, here's the decoded version: 'My life's been made different, I'm a born again piss tank, and the wowsers can go fuck 'emselves.'

CHAPTER 15

Long service leave

'If that's what it took to wake me up, it was worth it.'
Kevin Bloody Wilson

Kev's private life may have been in tatters, but creatively he was on fire. Disturbed as she was by what she describes as the 'constant parade of blonde bimbos' in her father's life, TJ was still impressed by her dad's work ethic. 'It was all he really had at that point and after that it really took off for him, I believe because he put everything into it. All of those big things in his career came after that and I remember them all well because for so many of those events I was his date. I did all the awards shows and stuff like that.'

There was, however, another skeleton in the family closet that was about to be revealed: it turned out Travis and TJ had a half-sister called Donna. Although Donna was born well before Kev met Betty, her existence came as a complete shock to TJ. 'Donna had known who her dad was for years but she only came on the scene after Mum and Dad split up.

That's one I didn't cope with at all, and that caused a big rift between Dad and me. It didn't seem to bother Travis as much, but I'm going, "*I'm* your daughter!" Looking back on it now it obviously threatened who I was; my place in the world was as his daughter, with one brother, one mum and one dad, and now who is *this*? I probably wouldn't have been as bothered if it was a son, but during that tumultuous time in our lives, everybody's emotions were running red-raw. Now that things are different and our lives are back on track, Donna and I have spent time together and she's a really great girl.'

The tour to promote *Born Again Piss Tank* took Kev all the way to a venue that most performers only ever dream of playing in; in order to book that gig, however, Cactus had to be a little bit sneaky. 'We decided that we would play the Sydney Opera House, which Kev still refers to as the Bennelong Workers Club, so we booked it and we didn't tell the Opera House who the act was until they got the contract back. They weren't very impressed.

'We quickly went on sale. Back then you could do these big four-sheeter street posters and we literally covered Sydney in these posters. So on the Sunday night the posters went up everywhere, and they were really simple: they were red and blue and they just had *Kevin Bloody Wilson at the Sydney Bloody Opera House*, and the date of the show and the date the tickets went on sale. Of course, on the Monday morning the Sydney Opera House people and the government people are driving to work and they are on the phone to us in a heartbeat. "How *dare* you defame the Sydney Opera House like this? Take those posters down!" From what I remember that was kinda the plan anyway, that we would shock everybody. By the time we ordered the street posters down we'd sold out our shows, so we were very happy. It had worked.'

As Sue recalls, there was another reason the Sydney Opera House staff would remember Kev's show. 'We actually broke the bar record there. Ten minutes before the show they'd sold out of beer and they had to go and get more beer for interval. When this ran out the crowd consumed everything else in the bar like a plague of locusts. I believe Kevin's audience still holds the record for the most alcohol consumed during an Opera House performance.'

Kev remembers that show at the Sydney Opera House as the pinnacle of his performing career up to that point. 'I'll always remember driving to the Sydney Opera House in a limo with my parents and my agent at the time, Harley Metcalf. We were driving past the front of the Opera House and there were queues of people, and Dad said, "There must be an opera on tonight." Harley explained, "No, Cecil. They're not here for the opera, they're here for your son." That was a pretty amazing moment in my life, watching the look of recognition on my father's face.'

TJ was also in that limo, but with a completely different look on her face. 'The limo came to pick us up and he had a date. It bothered me that this was such a momentous thing in Dad's life and this woman—who as far as I knew had been on the scene for twenty-four hours, maybe a week, I don't know—was there. I remember getting out of the limo, and all the TV cameras were there. Nan and Pop got out, Dad got out, and then I got out. Then she went to get out and I shut the door on her head. That was the exact kind of behaviour I would have got belted for in the past, but during that time I got a pass on all of them, so I just kept doing it.'

Once inside the Opera House Kev went backstage to prepare for his show. He was unusually nervous, and asked

TJ to come and see him ten minutes before he was due on stage. 'He wanted to talk to me backstage before he went on, probably just to have someone there who wasn't a Clingon.' Unfortunately, TJ had loaned her backstage pass to Kev's date, possibly in an attempt to offset the guilt she felt for slamming the limo door into her head. 'I wanted to get backstage and see Dad, but I didn't have a pass and this chick wasn't anywhere around. I had promised Dad I would go backstage and I thought he was going to get mad, so I started bawling. I eventually found someone from CBS who told security I was his daughter and to let me through.'

With five minutes to go until show time, TJ raced into her father's dressing room to find him slumped in a chair. Kev looked up at TJ, his eyes filled with tears, and said, 'Your mother should be here for this.'

For the most part, Kev tried not to show how much his separation from Betty was hurting him, but his distress was always very evident to TJ. 'I have since run into a couple of the nicer ladies he dated in that time and they'd say, "It was never going to work: I wasn't Betty." The ones with half a brain worked that out pretty quickly. Mum was in a relationship pretty much the whole time they were separated and Dad couldn't speak to her while that was going on. He'd come to pick me up at the place Mum and I shared, but he'd never come inside to get me. There was just too much anger around. At the time I thought he was being such a dick, but now that I'm older I get that it was just hurt.'

There was no shortage of people who were prepared to kiss Kev's arse. As he became more and more famous the Clingons were steadily increasing in numbers, but the only people Kev felt he could really open up to were those who had known him before the Kev thing took off. His old mate Wayne Pride was one of those people. Says Wayne, 'He wasn't happy in that time he was apart from Betty, I know that. One night we were driving back from a gig, I forget where we were, and we sat in the car outside his place and had a very long talk. He won't remember, 'cos he was maggoted, but we were in the car for probably an hour and a half, and he totally poured his emotions out that night.

'When you get to the level and the height that he's reached, you can go a bit Hollywood. You can get a bit big for your boots, and it's hard not to because when you're doing as much as he was doing and getting all the attention he was getting, it's easy to let go. He wasn't himself for that little time, I know that for a fact, but he always soldiered on with his work.'

Another person who Kev felt he could confide in was Sue 'Cactus' Maloney. Says Sue, 'I think we all knew that he wanted to be with Betty, and he would talk about it to me when we were on the road together sometimes, but not a lot. He talked more about how he hated Betty's boyfriend at the time. He never put Betty down, he'd only ever put the boyfriend down.'

During Kev and Betty's separation, a time they now refer to as long service leave, Kev worked as hard as he could to maintain his relationships with his kids. With Kev being on the road for long periods of time this wasn't always easy, so Kev and Cactus came up with a solution. Cactus explains, 'We used to have TJ and Travis come out on the road with us during school holidays, and that's when TJ and I became really close, like sisters, so I watched the kids kind of grow up on tour.

'Travis came on tour once. He actually came out to work, because he'd decided that when he grew up he wanted to become a roadie. Kevin said to me, "Don't do him any favours, he's gonna have to work like everyone else." So within twenty-four hours Travis was drinking and smoking and doing all that stuff, however within three of four days he was completely exhausted. They'd driven the truck, loaded in, done the show, loaded out, partied hard, grabbed a couple of hours' sleep then driven to the next town. Travis was just comatose, but he was so determined to make this work, so he stopped drinking and stopped smoking and he knuckled down. He was just a fantastic asset on the road, but he quickly realised that being a roadie was not a glamorous job.'

TJ falls apart laughing as she recalls her brother's short-lived career as a roadie. 'He was the skinniest, scrawniest, kid and you'd see him halfway through the tour and he'd have big black rings under his eyes and he'd be limping 'cos he'd dropped something on his foot. You'd go, "How are you, Trav?" and he'd go, "Good . . . good." I'm sure he could have easily made it as a roadie, but now he's an airline pilot, so I think the roadie experience helped change his mind.'

During long service leave Kev went the extra mile when it came to gift giving. There was one birthday present from his dad that will be forever etched in Travis's memory. 'I came home on the morning of my seventeenth birthday from a driving lesson, and walked in the back door of the house and there were these four topless chicks waiting there with *Happy Birthday Travis* written in lipstick across their tits. The rest of the morning was spent with them in my bedroom jumping all over me in particular poses. They all had their knickers on but they had their tops off. Dad wanted to make it look like this all-encompassing orgy, and he's still got the photos. Mum couldn't believe it.'

Given Travis's history of throwing legendary parties when his dad wasn't home, Kev figured he should be at his son's eighteenth birthday party the following year, to witness the carnage firsthand. Betty was there too, and it was awkward for everyone involved, but it meant the world to Travis to have both his parents with him that night. So began the process that would soon see Kev and Betty get back together again.

Kev's anger and hurt had started to cool; in fact, he was settling into his mid-life bachelorhood rather comfortably. Meanwhile Betty, realising the relationship was never going to go anywhere, had called it quits after two years with her younger partner. Although this occurred five months before Kev and Betty started speaking again, Kev was unaware that Betty was now single.

TJ knew what was happening in her mother's personal life, but it wasn't a subject she ever considered broaching with her father. 'On Christmas Eve 1998 Travis and I and our partners were going out and I remember saying to Mum, "You're sitting at home by yourself, Dad's sitting at home by himself, you know you could be friends. There's enough of a history here that you could be mates." We were trying to encourage Mum and Dad, not to get back together at all, just to be civil and to make our lives a bit easier.'

Terry was also relieved when Kev and Betty started talking to each other again. 'The thing is, my wife Lyn and I have always loved Betty. We tried to stay in touch with her through the whole thing, 'cos I could understand where she was coming from, but she just cut off all relations with us. I guess it was because I was his brother, but she was really good mates with Lyn. But after a while she started coming around to see us again, and not long after that Kev and Betty got back into the dating thing.'

When Betty revealed that she was single again, it came as no surprise to Terry. 'We all knew that from Betty's side it was never gonna last, it never does. She was with a younger bloke, so they're light years away in interests. Sooner or later you've gotta talk to them, haven't you?'

Kev and Betty's first 'date' was at a restaurant in Northbridge. Betty was all dressed up—not because she was treating this as a special occasion, just because she likes to get dressed up, she says. 'After dinner on that first date we went for a walk and linked arms. That's when I felt something again. We didn't say anything to each other at the time, but we talked about it a few months later and we both agreed, that was the magic moment when it happened for both of us.'

There were three more dates, and on the fourth date Kev and Betty slept in the same bed together for the first time in three years. Betty giggles like a teenager when she gets to this part of the story. 'That was nice. Well, what can I say? That part of our life was always special; now it seemed even more special.'

When Kev and Betty started discussing the possibility of moving back in together, despite the fact that he had spent the last three years desperately missing Betty, Kev had some doubts. He explains, 'I was the one who resisted the idea initially. I told her I was enjoying my lifestyle at that point and that I needed some time to think about it. The reality was, I didn't ever want to be hurt like that again.'

By now, Travis had all but given up on the idea of his parents reuniting. 'Separations don't have a very good track record, do they? I thought they were finished. I thought they were only seeing each other under the guise of having stuff they needed to talk over, not for a romantic evening. Those meetings turned into dates, I guess. I'd moved out of home at that stage, I'd moved in with Robyn, and I got a call from Dad to say that they were getting back together. And I'm sure he expected me to go, "I can't believe this, this is the best news I have ever heard." I was just infuriated. You've just got used to them being apart and that's the way the rest of your life is going to be, and they're busy avoiding each other for three years and then all of a sudden they say, "No, we love each other again and we're getting back together. What do you think of that?" Well, fuck you. Thanks for putting us through all that for the last three years. And TJ was exactly the same.'

Well, not *exactly*. TJ recalls, 'I was about seventeen by then so I had my own life and a car and I wasn't home that much, but I remember waking up one morning in the unit in North Beach that I lived in with Mum. It was six thirty in the morning and there was a sneeze downstairs, and I thought, "That's my dad, *in this house!*" He'd never been inside that house since I'd lived there. So I went downstairs and there he was sitting in the kitchen looking all sheepish.' TJ put two and two together and immediately went into a tailspin. She ran back upstairs, threw some clothes into her backpack, slammed the door behind her as loudly as she could, and raced around to Travis's place. 'I banged on his door and I said, '"Dad slept at our house last night!" He goes, "Eew, fuckin' gross! Get in here!"'

Once the initial shock subsided, Travis soon warmed to the idea of his parents reuniting. 'After a while TJ and I both realised that we were pretty lucky to have them back together. Dad has had to wise up. Before he makes a decision he has to consider Mum, which he always does now. He's still not perfect, nobody is, but he's two million per cent on what he was, and he knows how to cook without a microwave oven now too.'

Before Betty moved out of her North Beach pad and back into the family home, she set some new boundaries for her and Kev's relationship. There was one new rule that was particularly vital from Betty's point of view. 'We agreed to put it all behind us. No matter what, even if we're having a dummy spit, neither of us can ever bring up anything that happened when we were on long service leave and use it as ammunition. I thought that was the only way we were ever going to be able to make a proper fresh start, and we've both stuck to that.'

Since the end of long service leave it's been more or less plain sailing for Kev and Betty. There have been some changes on the domestic front, too. Although the Wilson family could well afford a housekeeper, Betty still chooses to do it herself. 'When we are home, I still do all the cooking and cleaning, and I've always been happy doing that, that was never the issue. But the thing is he helps out now and he appreciates what I do for him, and he shows me, which I don't really think he ever used to. He's a different person since long service leave, and our marriage is better and stronger now than ever.'

Back when Kev was still conflicted over their reconciliation, he spent three days alone in Lancelin. This is what he wrote:

> *You waltzed right back into my life*
> *Seems our love was too strong to die*
> *We just needed some time on our own for a while*
> *Now you've waltzed right back into my life.*

Sometimes life can get rough
And the best you can do ain't enough
And the one that you hurt most is the one that you love
How did we let that happen to us?
Let the cold winds blow out the fire
Let something so strong almost die
But the storm clouds have gone now, our love has
*   survived*
You waltzed right back into my life.

They're playing our song like before
And as we both listen we know
The harmony's stronger and the words mean much
*   more*
And this time we won't let it go
'Cos we know that we'll make it right
If it takes us the rest of our lives
Livin' and lovin' in three-quarter time
You waltzed right back into my life.

You waltzed right back into my life
Seems our love was too strong to die
We just needed some time on our own for a while
Now you've waltzed right back into my life.

Kev only ever recorded one copy of this song, a demo.
Betty still has that copy. On their twenty-fifth wedding anni-
versary in 1995, they renewed their vows in a small family
ceremony in Las Vegas.

CHAPTER 16

What happens on the road

'I consider myself the luckiest bloke in the world because I get to travel the world with my very best friend in the world. My wife Betty.'
Kevin Bloody Wilson

In addition to his overseas touring—more on that later—Kev still tries to make his way around to just about every town in Australia at least once every two years. That's easier said than done, though, because Australia is a big empty place, especially the middle bits.

'I particularly love the Northern Territory, and I've also found that I write a disproportionate number of songs in the Territory—I don't know if it's the relaxing atmosphere or the creative spirit that's up there. I came up with "Do Ya Fuck on First Dates?" at a place called Groote Eylandt when I was touring up in the Territory. You can't help but feel Australian in the Top End, and you just meet the most remarkable fuckin' characters up there.

'I did my first Top End tour when my brother Terry was

working in Gove/Nhulunbuy and I'd sent him a copy of my very first cassette. He played it to all his mates and they said, "Get him up here!" At that stage I was still doing the Bryan Dennis stuff as well, so I went up and played a Bryan Dennis cabaret on the Saturday night at a place called the Arnhem Club—that was a family show—and then on the Sunday morning we did a buck's show, as Kevin Bloody Wilson, for all the blokes. There happened to be a fella there from the brewery in Darwin, and his name was Wayne Cubis. He said, "Mate, if you wanna do that comedy stuff I can get you some work in Darwin before you go home," and I thought, "Shit yeah, why not?" Wayne took me to some amazing places, some of which don't exist any more, like Lims Cage and the Nightcliff Hotel.

'I remember doing a show where the audience were all Maoris, and they were just woofin' into the piss on a Sunday morning. Between me and the audience there was a mechanical bull. The more piss they drank, the less they could have given a fuck about me, so I spent the entire morning dodging flying Maoris as they got thrown off this mechanical bull—there were flyin' fuckin' Kiwis everywhere, crunching head-first onto the floors, walls and even the fuckin' jukebox while I was singing.

'Another amazing place we went to was the Humpty Doo pub where I played on a stage made out of pallets stacked on top of beer crates. Every time I moved my fuckin' foot went through the open slats of the pallet, so they placed a layer of thirty or forty full cartons of VB cans on top of it then covered it with a tarpaulin. Problem solved, but still fuckin' rough and ready. As the night progressed I noticed that the "stage" began wobbling all over the place until I could barely keep my balance. As I exited the stage for a break I stepped on the edge of the tarp and fell arse over head into a table full of pissed Humpty Doo punters—some bastard had pinched a few cartons from underneath the tarpaulin. By the end of the night the cunts had stolen my entire fuckin' stage from underneath me; with the constant swaying 'cos of the disappearin' VB cartons, Humpty Doo became the first gig I've ever played so far inland and come off feeling seasick.'

The star attraction at the Humpty Doo pub was a water buffalo by the name of Norman. Whenever Norman saw a tourist bus pull up he would casually amble up to the bar—little more than a lean-to—skol beers and pose for photos.

Kev describes the scene: 'The publican would open a can of beer and show the tourist how to put it in Norman's mouth, then ol' Norm would throw back his head and gulp it down. Norman had the capacity for at least two cartons of piss per sitting. He would stagger out of the pub when the tourist bus pulled out, then sleep it off until the next bus arrived. He'd go through up to ten cartons a day, and although he never paid for a drink himself he was the Humpty Doo pub's best customer and favourite patron.

For whatever reason, 'A couple of the locals got together and decided to teach Norman how to waterski. They built this fuckin' great barge and towed it behind a boat; Norm would just stand on this rickety raft following the boat around as they did a couple of slow laps of the lake, but unfortunately one day ole Norm was so full of piss he lost his balance. He flipped it and the barge over-turned and crashed down on his head and knocked him out. The Humpty Doo mob had somehow managed to drown a fuckin' water buffalo.

'Full of guilt and remorse at having killed the pub's top tourist attraction, they decided they should hold a memorial barbecue for Norman, and the whole town turned up to have one last drink in Norm's honour. What a lot of them weren't aware of was that Norm was also on the barbie. Poor old Norman. They'd killed him, cooked him, then cut him up and fuckin' ate him. Not only was Norm there in spirit, he was also right there, on their fuckin' plates, next to the lettuce and tomato.'

These days the only way for Kev to tour Australia properly is to carve it up into several trips. The first trip might be a tour of Queensland, the Northern Territory and northern Western Australia, then after a few weeks back at home it's off to tour New South Wales and Victoria, followed by a trip to South Australia and southern Western Australia, winding up back home in Perth around Christmas time. Every second year he marks this with a Christmas concert at the Burswood Theatre; these shows have been known to run for well over three hours.

Between his Australian and overseas tours, Kevin Bloody Wilson is on tour for up to seven months of any given year, averaging about two hundred shows annually; this is at least twice as many shows as most other touring performers would get through in a year. Barbra Streisand would spontaneously combust if she had to do that many shows.

Kev's touring schedule may be gruelling, but it's also very rewarding as he explains. 'We are, as entertainers, the ultimate egotists, and hearing the crowd get into it is what makes the shows so much fun to do. We all love reinforcement and in our industry you get it a little more often than most people. Nobody would ever come up to you and say, "Wow, this is a great hamburger, man. What's the name of it? McDonald's? Wow! When's your next burger coming out, man?"'

No two Kevin Bloody Wilson shows have ever been exactly the same. The banter in between songs is always ad-libbed, and Kev hasn't worked with a set list since his days playing with Delta in Kalgoorlie. Says Kev, 'Back then it was out of necessity, 'cos you were that fuckin' tired. We'd go out to do a cabaret and you knew you had to do a bracket of barndances and a bracket of quicksteps and the "Pride of Erin" and polkas—all that. We'd write out a set list just to make sure we didn't forget any of the dances.'

These days Kev prefers to decide what songs to play on the vibe from the crowd, though the songs at the end of the set remain the same, mainly so that Kev's crew know when he's coming off stage. But be warned: if you yell a request at Kev while he's on stage you could well end up as his next bit of fodder. 'I love it when someone shouts out, "Play such and such." I tell 'em, "I've already done that one. It's on an album. Go buy the fucker in the foyer."'

Here's another tip for anyone who intends to go to a Kevin Bloody Wilson concert: it would not be advisable to sit in the front row chatting to your friends at the top of your voice throughout the performance. One woman found this out the hard way during one of Kev's first Australian tours. 'I tried to shut her up nicely a couple of times but I'd had enough of this sheila and it was time to get uptight and personal. I stopped the show and said, "Lady, if your cunt was as big as your mouth your fuckin' guts'd drop out." The audience loved that. Yep! Shut her up all right.'

Although he might occasionally let someone in his audience have it if he feels they really deserve it, Kev goes out of his way to connect with his fans after the show.

Kev's former tour manager, Sue 'Cactus' Maloney, notes that Kev's habit of signing autographs at the merchandise stand after every performance is a long way from the norm in the entertainment industry. 'Not a lot of people do that any more. The Slim Dustys and people like that used to do it, but I don't think there was ever a time when Kevin didn't go out and meet the fans after the show.

'We actually restructured the way we did it. He used to be behind the merchandise counter and everybody could get to him and it became quite dangerous because there were so many people, and of course we had money and merchandise, and it just got crazy, it was bedlam. So we had to move Kevin away to a different area, and he had a security guard with him in the end.'

Many a rock star or travelling comedian will tell you at length how hard it is to be on the road, what with the isolation, the constant confusion about what city they are in that day, the strange experience of going straight from a room full of people cheering for you to an empty hotel room, and the drudgery of living out of a suitcase.

When Kev first started touring as Kevin Bloody Wilson he would never be away from home for more than two or three weeks at a time, while Betty stayed in Perth looking after Travis and TJ, who were still in school. Now that the kids have 'grown up and fucked off', Kev can tour for months at a time; these days Betty is right there beside him. Says Kev, 'I didn't want to tour without Betty, I just don't want to be away from her. But Betty wouldn't tour unless she had something to do. She says, "I couldn't just sit in a hotel room for months at a time just watching television, it'd drive me mad." She saw the opportunity and started organis-ing the merchandise, which is now a really big and successful business thanks to Betty's hard work.'

Betty also helps to design and source all of Kev's product lines. The range of Kevin Bloody Wilson merchandise extends way past CDs, DVDs, T-shirts and tour programs. Over his years on the road Kev has flogged everything from Kevin Bloody Wilson penis enlargers (don't ask) to Kevin Bloody Wilson panties. Betty had an interesting time selling those. 'He insisted on designing them so that inside the crutch there was a drawing of his face with his tongue hanging out. That was a bit much for me personally, but they still sold out.'

Kev will be the first to tell you that Betty is unusually tolerant of his shenanigans—so much so that she often stands right there beside him as he partakes in the greatest of all Kevin Bloody Wilson touring traditions, tit signing.

This tradition started many tours ago after a show in country Western Australia when a very buxom fan came up to Kev and said, 'Will you sign my arm?' and without missing a beat Kev said, 'Sorry love, I only sign tits.' She immediately presented her bare breasts to Kev for signing, and to Kev's surprise and delight so did all seventeen of her friends. 'I remember that there were eighteen of them in total, 'cos I counted thirty-six tits and divided by two.' As he was signing the breasts Kev was overheard muttering to himself, 'How the fuck did that happen? I think I'm on to something here . . .' He's been doing it ever since.

Nowdays, tit signing is simply seen as an extension of Kev's larrikin personality and nobody blinks an eye, including Betty. 'Lots of people ask me if it bothers me but why would it? It's not exactly a romantic thing or anything. He's signing that bit of skin for them but I know he's coming back to the hotel with me, so it doesn't really matter.'

Perhaps Betty would be a bit more bothered if she actually read what Kev was writing on his fan's breasts. A particular favourite is *Thanks for the root. Love, Kev*, which must be all kinds of fun for those fans to explain to their husbands later on. So what is it about Kev, according to Kev, that makes these women lose their inhibitions at his shows? 'I think it's because I look so much like Tom Cruise. It's an easy mistake to make 'cos we are the exact same height.'

The number one question Betty gets asked by fans is, 'So what's he really like?' Betty tells them that he's much more of a gentleman in real life than he is on stage. Kev hates that, she grins. 'He doesn't really want me to tell the fans that he's a softy or a romantic or anything like that. He's definitely not the male chauvinist pig or pisshead that he makes out to be. Perhaps he was bordering on that before, but not any more.'

Here's another fact about Kev which will surprise a few fans: in the early years of Kevin Bloody Wilson he used to stumble on stage swilling from a can of VB, or so it seemed to the audience, but the truth is that he has always policed himself on the road, as his former tour manager Sue 'Cactus' Maloney recalls. 'I'd never known Kevin to be much of a drinker at all. Whenever he had a beer can on stage, it was full of either coke or water—that was our job, to always make sure there were cans around and if somebody gave him a beer we quickly just swapped them over. I don't remember seeing him drunk even after a show in those days, but he plays the character so well, so that's what his fans assumed he really was.'

A trick of the trade that keeps Kev in peak condition for each live show is the afternoon nap. This is a throwback to

Kev's days in Kalgoorlie. 'I'd do a day's work, come home and sleep for a couple of hours, then go out and play at night. After I have a nap I'll always wake up thinking, "You bewdy! Show time! Let's go!"'

Kev's not alone in the afternoon nap department, as Cactus explains. 'Every artist has an afternoon nap—they have to, because unlike most people they have to be at their peak at eight pm, so the start of their day is really six pm. Most creative people like a routine, especially on tour, or it can get out of hand. It's crazy.'

Straight after every show Kev gives himself a mark out of ten for the gig he's just done. He is notoriously hard on himself, and surprisingly modest about his act. 'Given that what I do is not stand-up, it's music with talkabout, I can't believe there aren't more people doing it. I reckon the hardest job in show business would be stand-up comedy, to stand up there on stage without a guitar and be funny, whereas it's very easy for me to go out there and sing songs and tell stories. I don't consider myself so much a concert act as a choir master 'cos on any given night the crowd just take over and I pretty much just play rhythm guitar for them. I could go out there with full-blown Alzheimer's and forget all the words to my songs and the audience would still have a top night anyway.

'My starting point in comedy was to entertain my mates at barbecues and parties, then the boys in the cricket clubs and footy clubs around the Kalgoorlie area. It never occurred to me at that time that it would ever graduate out of there and onto bigger stages. I never thought it would translate outside of Kalgoorlie let alone sell out the London Palladium. I remember playing the Palladium two and a half years after I started as Kevin Bloody Wilson and thinking, yet again, "How the fuck did that happen?" It felt like it was only a couple of weeks earlier I was doing the same thing in Kalgoorlie. A lot of comedians see their comedy as just a springboard to something else, like acting, and a lot have done that very successfully, like Robin Williams, Jim Carrey and Billy Connolly. But I'm happy doing what I do. I just love getting up on stage and performing. If something else turns up I'll always look at it, but live performance is the core and the pinnacle of what I do.'

Kev delights in shocking people, but only in situations in which he is one hundred per cent sure that the crowd are with him. 'I don't do guest spots on other people's shows 'cos that's when someone always gets offended. People are always asking me to play at their twenty-first or their fortieth or their engagement party—no, that's *your* show. If they want to see me they can come to a Kevin Bloody Wilson show. They always say, "Nah, you won't upset anybody! My mum loves you," but you will invariably upset somebody at somebody else's show. If they've bought a ticket to a Kevin Bloody Wilson show they're expecting it and if they were easily offended then they wouldn't buy a fuckin' ticket to one of my shows in the first place.'

Offending people has never been a concern for Kev. The people who get the joke absolutely love him. 'And if they don't get the joke, then DILLIGAF. It's not worth worrying about, they don't come to my shows, they don't buy my CDs and DVDs so their opinion on what I do is not worth a cunt full of cold water.'

CHAPTER 17

Buddy Holly Airlines

'My freckle was going five cents, fifty cents, five cents, fifty cents.'
Kevin Bloody Wilson

If words are like fashion, then cunt is the new fuck. In the 1980s, fuck was still considered to be an extremely offensive word to use in public, especially around women. These days the word fuck is used regularly on late-night television, often spoken *by* a woman.

But when Kevin Bloody Wilson started touring around Australia in the mid eighties, attitudes towards swearing on stage were far less liberal. Kev's eyes sparkle as he recalls, 'I got arrested twice in Perth, once in Victoria, and once in Queensland because it was alleged that I said "fuck" on stage. I was playing a show at Festival Hall in Brisbane and apparently I said fuck two hundred fuckin' times or something—they actually counted.'

It was in the late 1980s—at that time the Fitzgerald Inquiry into police corruption in Queensland was in full swing—and it seemed to Kev that the police were keen to get someone else on the front page of the *Courier Mail* for a change.

Cactus was Kev's tour manager at the time, and she recalls that the trouble started well before Kev even took to the stage. 'Somebody had warned me that we should ring and tell the police that we were coming and get approval. So I did ring the police, and told them that we were coming and they said, "Yeah, that'll be fine." When we set up that after-noon I got a phone call saying that the police were coming to record the show. So the police came and they sat across the road for a while and did a noise pollution reading. After that they came inside and sat and watched the show from the back row, and then they took us to court.'

Midway through the show, one of the policemen fool-ishly decided to venture up towards the stage to confront Kev directly as he was performing. Kev describes what followed. 'I was on stage doing the show and this bloke walked up towards the stage, in plain clothes—I didn't know he was a fuckin' walloper. He just stood at the front of the stage lookin' up at me and yelled out to me, "Hey you, get off the stage!" I waited until I finished the song, then I went down the front of the stage and told this dickhead, "Fuck off, mate, I'm working!", which only seemed to piss him off more: "I told you to get off the stage!" I said, "Mate, if you don't fuck off I'll get that big Kiwi bouncer over here to rip your fuckin' head off, then I'll piss down your neck. Now fuck off!" It was around about then that he pulled out his badge. He said, "If you don't get off I'm gonna pull you off," and I said, "Great, I've never been pulled off by a copper before!"'

When Kev had his day in court, at first TJ sat next to him, but in the end she had to leave the room. 'I was sitting in the courtroom and they were playing his song with the lyrics "Having a quiet drink on a Saturday arvo is like trying to have a quiet fuck with a chook." It gave me a real insight into lawyers because I was sitting there and they're asking, "So Mr Wilson, exactly what is your reason behind referencing fornicating a fowl?" I remember pissing myself laughing and Dad gave me this look, so I spent the rest of the day sitting outside. I was sitting outside thinking to myself, "Oh my God, even I know that when he sings about fucking a chook that he's joking, and you're actually trying to go him for bestiality?" Having said that, at that time the Queensland Premier, Joh Bjelke-Petersen, was ordering the police to rip condom-vending machines off the walls in pubs and clubs.'

When it came time for the tape of Kev's Festival Hall performance to be played in court there was a slight technical hitch, much to Kev's amusement and relief. 'Half of it was inaudible. That's what it says on the actual depositions, "Inaudible". You know why? The recording was completely fuckin' ruined by the sound of the copper belly laughing all the way through the show.'

Cactus was not in the least bit surprised to learn that the police recording of Kev's show was inaudible. 'Yes, the police were laughing, but they were in a room of two thousand people who were also laughing. There was so much laughter and distortion on the tape that you really didn't stand a chance of hearing what Kevin was saying, so they had a hard time proving their case.'

Kev was fined a grand total of $1250. Kev, TJ and Cactus walked out of the courtroom to face the barrage of television cameras and newspaper photographers; as the flashbulbs popped, Kev smiled and gave two thumbs up to the press and then turned and whispered in TJ's ear, 'As long as they spell my fuckin' name right.'

Kev's face was splashed all over the front page of the

Courier Mail the next morning. Cactus was thrilled: more shows had to be added to Kev's Queensland tour, all of which were sold out in a matter of hours. 'It was fantastic because it was what Kevin was all about, just being himself, the little rebel kind of guy. We got huge publicity out of it.'

Kev and Cactus have shared many memorable moments on the road together, but the one Cactus remembers most vividly took place in Australia's capital. 'We were playing at the Canberra Labor Club, which was always a pretty rough kinda gig—there were always a lot of roughheads in Canberra—and, as usual, after the show Kev went and signed merchandise, and these bikies were there. They hung around and hung around, and I was looking at the security guys thinking that we needed to get out of there. It wasn't looking good.

'They'd waited their turn patiently, then bought a heap of merchandise, and they wanted Kevin to sign it all. So then they said, "Kev, you've got to come with us—we're having a party in your honour at our club, and there's gonna be girls there and you can have anyone you want, and it'll be great." Kevin's grabbing me, going, "What the fuck . . .?"'

Cactus did her best to persuade the bikies to leave Kev alone, pointing out that he had interviews to do first thing in the morning, but to no avail. 'They literally kidnapped us,' says Cactus. 'They put us in these cars and took us to this bar—it was a bikie bar in Canberra somewhere, and I had no idea where we were. So they're buying us drinks and of course Kevin's the big hero as soon as he walks into the room. I don't think they expected him to do a show, they were happy just to have him "visit".'

Kev and Cactus tried not to look as uncomfortable as they felt. Fortunately, the bikies soon became distracted. 'We were only there for ten or fifteen minutes and a fight broke out,' remembers Cactus. 'Two guys from behind the bar grabbed baseball bats and jumped over the bar and just started smashing into these two bikies who were having fisticuffs. So we saw that this was our opportunity to run for our lives, and we did. We had no idea where we were but we just ran until we found a phone box. I don't remember if we rang the crew or if we rang a taxi, but somehow we got home. It was bloody frightening. Thank God that fight broke out or I don't know what would have happened.'

As much as Kev loves life on the road it can be a tough slog, and at times it can even become life threatening, as Cactus recalls. 'We did a tour of Queensland, this is when we were doing a mixture of theatres and pubs, and we decided the best way to cover out west was to charter our own aircraft. A magician, Phil Cass, was with us as support act, and the pilot doubled as a spotlight operator each night. One day we were flying from Mount Isa to Weipa along the western side of Cape York in the early afternoon, and all of a sudden we all looked up and there was this huge black cloud. This storm had just come up out of nowhere. The pilot kind of freaked out a little bit 'cos it hadn't shown up on his radar either. He couldn't go under it or around it or over it, so we just had to go through this huge black cloud. All of a sudden we could see lightning and all sorts of stuff. I dunno if Kevin was wearing his seatbelt but I wasn't, and we hit this air pocket. I hit the roof and came flying back down onto my seat and screamed my lungs out.

'The pilot was screaming at me to put my fucking seatbelt on, and then lightning hit the plane. It was like in the movies—you know the blue line goes from the wing to the plane? I swear to God I saw that, and I'm digging my fingernails into Kevin's arms. We both really thought we were going to die that day.'

Comedy magician Phil Cass, who cheerfully describes himself as the best in his price range at that time, used to travel wherever he went with three animals that he used in his performance: a duck, a dove and a rabbit. When the plane hit the turbulence, all three animals somehow escaped the confines of their cages and started scurrying madly around the cabin. Phil barely noticed what his animals were up to: he was far too busy processing the thought that he was about to die.

'Well, the thought did cross our minds,' he says. 'You wouldn't be human if you didn't think that. We were totally immersed in cloud and lightning and rain, and it was terrible. It really was frightening. I was sitting in the front beside the pilot, and Kev and Sue are in the back right behind me. I'm a bit of a practical joker, so once things calmed down a bit I turned around and said, "I'm not feeling too good, Kev," and I pretended to throw up. Kev was unbelievably quick to get up out of his seat to get out of the road of the spew. I said, "Just bullshitting you, mate," and he said, "You bastard! That's all I need right now, to be covered in someone *else's* fuckin' spew!" as he sat back down in his seat.'

Somehow the tiny plane made its way safely through the clouds. When they touched down, Kev spat out the duck feather that had landed in his mouth, brushed off all the duck and rabbit shit and then made an announcement. 'Ladies and gentlemen, thank you for flying Buddy Holly Airlines. Would you please place the hostess in the upright position before removing your soiled underwear and placing it in the bin provided. We hope you enjoyed your fright.'

*

Over the years Kevin Bloody Wilson has engaged a number of different tour managers. When he started they were provided by the promoters in the countries or territories he was touring, but Kev changed those rules too. He explains, 'The secret to smooth touring is surrounding yourself with good people. The tour and artist managers mentioned in this book are all great people. I should single out Wally Bishop AKA Sir Walter Fat-Fuck and Jimmy Smith and Mel Bush in the UK as having had a positive impact on my success. The others that aren't mentioned in this book don't rate a fuckin' mention.'

For the last ten years, Kev has employed the same bloke to manage all his global touring commitments. He goes by the name of Hollywood. He's a gentle soul, but not the sort of bloke you'd want to get on the wrong side of.

Peter 'Hollywood' Heeney served twenty-eight years with the Australian military, thirteen months of it in Vietnam. (Kev still insists Hollywood started the Vietnam conflict.) He retired as a major. Way before that he represented Victoria in athletics, and he also played half-back flank for Fitzroy in 1966 as an eighteen year old. Hollywood says, 'I played one season. I had one game, and kicked zero goals. I was lucky to get that game because another player pulled out at the death knock and they pulled me up out of the seconds. I ended up playing about fifteen minutes of football that day—does that make me a superstar?'

Hollywood has also been volunteering for Legacy since 1981, and he was the first person to ever be elected Western Australian state president of Legacy for two consecutive years. Says Hollywood, 'I met Kev at the Vietnam Veterans Motorcycle Club through a mate, PK—they had been mates for many years. He happened to bring Kev along to the club that night just to fuck around, meet the boys and hang out. That's how I met Kev and we hit it off straight away.

'One day out of the blue Kev rang me up and said, "We're going to Bali to do a show. Do you want to come with us?" and I said, "Yeah, righto. What do you want me to do?" "Just look after me." I'm thinking, "Look after him? What does that mean?" So I went to Bali and tagged along for that show, and I've been touring with Kev ever since.'

Standing side of stage during Kev's Bali performance, Hollywood remembers spending the entire show crying with laughter. 'I just remember thinking how funny he was. The audience was predominantly Aussies, Kiwis, Canadians and South Africans, all half tanked and rotten as chops, but they're laughing in the aisles and there's tears streaming down their faces. Actually some of them were rolling on the floor in laughter holding their guts and I thought, "This is fantastic, but what have I got myself into here?"'

When Kev took Hollywood on tour around Australia for the first time he welcomed Hollywood into his road crew with the traditional baptism of fire. Kev explains, 'We were staying at Medina apartments in Flinders Street, Melbourne, and our two Kiwi crew members had flown in the day before us with a suitcase full of duty-free alcohol. By the time we saw them they were totally maggoted. Given that it was a day off we all got on the piss together in the room, but the Kiwis already had a twenty-four-hour head start on us.

'At some stage of the evening I looked around and one of the Kiwis, Captain Zap the sound engineer, had already gone to bed 'cos he was fucked. The other Kiwi, Daz the lighting and vision tech, had gone to bed as well in the other room of their two-bedroom apartment.'

Kev, completely poker-faced, asked Hollywood where Daz and Zap were sleeping. When Hollywood informed Kev that they were asleep in separate bedrooms, Kev put on an even more serious expression. 'I said, "Hollywood, they're fuckin' gay, they're a fuckin' couple, and they are as jealous as shit of each other. If they wake up without each other they'll each think the other one has gone out rooting. I can't afford to have that happen, so I need you to get Daz out of that bed and put him in with Captain Zap, because if you don't, the shit will hit the fan and we won't have a crew for the tour. You have to help me here, Hollywood."

'Holly looked at me and said, "Are you fair dinkum?" I said, "Of course I'm fuckin' fair dinkum!" I'll never forget standing in the room as Hollywood walked past with Daz, full as a bishop's ballbag, slung over his shoulder. Daz was totally unconscious, so Hollywood literally picked him up out of bed, carried him, and gently set him down on the bed next to Captain Zap. I let Hollywood in on the joke the next morning, but from that day forth Daz and Captain Zap have never mentioned it. Ever. Strange, that.'

Ever since this incident, it has been Hollywood's mission to outdo Kev's pranks on the road. He recalls, 'On the last night of one overseas tour, in 2001, we were playing the Cork Opera House in Ireland when Kev sang "Dick'ta-phone", which was the closing song in the show, so I knew I had to get him off stage in a few minutes. Betty is the voice of Operator 42 in the recorded version of that song, and as this was the last night of the entire UK and Ireland tour, and we'd been away for nine weeks, we decided to surprise Kev with a special guest artist.

'We'd arranged it with Betty to come out and sing her part in the song. Kev started into the song, then Betty started singing her lines as she nervously wandered on from the side of the stage with a handheld microphone. Kev shat himself, obviously thinking, "Where the fuck is that singing coming from?" and then the crew and I followed Betty on stage to join them both and the rest of the Cork crowd on the chorus: "Stick that fuckin' phone up your fuckin' arse". Kev loved it. We do those things sometimes just to break up the monotony of being on the road.'

Hollywood's job as tour manager (or tour mangler as Kev calls him) can be a complex one. 'Touring is the ultimate exercise in logistics. It's about getting things to happen in the right place at the right time. So, if things are supposed to happen tomorrow, things are in place for it to happen tomorrow. Like making sure the accommodation and venue are booked. Making sure that the timing is right, if we're supposed to play at eight o'clock I need to make sure that everything is in place to get Kev on stage at the same time it says on the ticket.

'We normally leave the accommodation at ten am every day. So I'm down there at about nine fifteen. I've got the car ready to go, all refuelled, and these days I've got the GPS up and running. In the old days I used to handwrite all my directions.

'The military training helps. You've gotta have things running smoothly, 'cos if they don't you're in the shit. If I turn up in Toronto and we're supposed to be in Glasgow then we've got a lot of problems. Actually, that happened to Kev once before I became his tour manager. He ended up in the wrong town and they had to cancel the show. Kev wasn't very happy.

'Kev and Betty arrive at around ten am, 'cos Kev likes his little sleepies. We normally work it so that we get to the next location by two pm. On the way we stop for something to eat, normally around eleven-thirty.

'In the early days he used to drive in Australia because he knows his way around, but these days I do all the driving, except on the really long trips, like when we drove from London up to Scotland.'

Hollywood has a tour book that he takes on every tour in which he meticulously and religiously notes the details of every town visited and every show played. The notes are later transferred to his laptop, detailing the venue, the crowd numbers, the hotel and even the best places to eat in every town Kev and his crew have visited around the world.

Kev couldn't imagine being on tour without Hollywood. 'I love havin' Holly on the road, he's a bloody good mate and an essential member of our road "family". He makes my job and everybody else's job so much easier. I've worked with tour managers of all ranks from all over the world and he's without a doubt the fuckin' rankest I've ever toured with.'

CHAPTER 18

And the show
goes on

'It's not a real job, it's just a hobby.'

Kevin Bloody Wilson

These days Kev is accompanied on most of his international jaunts by his daughter TJ, who opens many of his shows as Jenny Talia from Australia. Kev explains how TJ's involvement initially came about.

'She happened to look at my website while she was living in Nashville. She said, "Dad, you're doing England, and looking at all these dates you're gonna kill yourself." There were over seventy dates on the tour. She said, "You need a support act." I told her that I'd tried support acts but you can't get them to go away for three months at a time. I said that in a perfect world I'd have a female support act. There was a bit of silence on the other end of the phone, and then she said, "I could do that!"

'At the time she was well on her way to doing good things in Nashville, so I told her she should probably stick with her knitting. She said, "Dad, I've been fuckin' your songs up since I was fourteen. That's my party trick. I drag a couple of your songs out, re-gender them and do them for my girl-friends." I asked her to give me an example and she started singing me her version of "Kev's Courtin' Song".'

Should I suck on first dates?
Will he still love me tomorra?
Should I spit it out,
Or gargle and swallow?
If he still gets it up
Then I'll do my best,
I'll just dim down the lights,
Take out me teeth then gum him to death.

Kev thought it was the best version of the song he'd ever heard, and he immediately made TJ an offer. 'I said, "If you can get ten of those songs together and record them by the time I go out on this UK tour, you can come with me", and so that's exactly what she did.

'When she'd recorded the first album she said, "What'll I call myself?" I said, "Try this: Jenny Talia from Australia." That name stuck right away, although when she's on stage she likes to tell people that she was almost christened Connie Lingus.'

Kev enjoys watching the audience response to Jenny Talia's live shows, and he particularly enjoys it when she rips into an audience member who rubs her up the wrong way. 'One night in Hobart in Tasmania she was doing a song of hers called "Bastard", and she always chooses someone in the audience to direct that song at. This bloke she chose that night wasn't fuckin' cooperating so she stopped the song and said, "What's the matter, mate? Did you wake up on the wrong side of your sister?" I was standing side of stage when she did that and I just fuckin' collapsed laughing.'

TJ has now been all over Australia and the rest of the world with her dad several times, so she knows his daily routine pretty well. 'Dad's gotta walk, wherever he is. He wants to see what he could buy—even if it's just a pie, he loves to shop. His latest thing is Macs. Mum goes to the gig before him and then Dad and I go with Holly. Dad will come to the car and say to Holly, "Hello love, what have you been up to?" and I'm thinking, "You only saw each other three fucking hours ago!" "What have you been up to?" "Well, I went and checked out the venue . . ." It's the same fucking answers every day. It's like *Driving Miss Daisy* meets *Groundhog Day*.

'Then Dad and I go backstage, and these days that involves grabbing his or my laptop and pressing play. It's always country music, which I like too. Right now we're into Graeme Connors' and Harmony James' new albums, our favourites. Instead of saying "Break a leg" he says, "Break an egg", then he might give me a kiss or a hug before I go on, and I can always see him out of the corner of my eye for at least half of my set, usually all of it.'

A comedian knows instantly if they have hit the mark or not, depending on the laugh each gag gets—or doesn't get. That can be terrific or terrifying, depending on your outlook. When TJ supports her dad as Jenny Talia, it's a little bit of both. 'We love nothing more than going somewhere I haven't played before and the announcer says, "Ladies and gentle-men, please welcome . . . Jenny Talia from Australia," and there's silence. That's his favourite thing. He always laughs and says, "I know at what point in what song they're gonna be yours." I used to try to rush to get to that bit, because it was always such an uncomfortable gap for me, but now I really enjoy taking my time to get to that spot.'

TJ likes to return the favour, and watches her dad's entire set from the wings almost every night. 'Everything I've heard of Dad's has been live. I might have listened to parts of some songs I did backing vocals on, but that was just Dad going, "Here it is, this is what you sound like." I've never really sat around with my girlfriends and listened to his stuff. I'd sit around and listen to Rod Stewart or Cindi Lauper. I wasn't embarrassed, but I just never did it.'

Touring all over the planet with her dad means that TJ has spent plenty of time observing his behaviour on the road. Sometimes she wonders if decades of touring have finally started to take their toll on him. 'He took me on a fuckin' flower drive when we were on tour near Carnarvon in Western Australia. "Have you seen the flowers?" "Yeah . . ." "Come on, get in the car." "Tell me you're not taking me to look at fucking flowers, Dad." And then when we got there we got out of the car. "Aren't they beautiful?" "They were beautiful when we drove past them twenty minutes ago." "I'll take your photo." "I'm good, thanks . . ."

'We were driving from Port Hedland to Karratha, one of those fantastic drives where there's mostly nothing but flat ground. I'm sitting in the back seat and Dad said, "Look at that, it's beautiful, isn't it?" Mum replied, "There's nothing out there! It's flat and it's brown!" and Dad points out the window and goes, "This is *Australia*!" Then Mum comes out with, "I think you're looking at the world through rose-coloured dentures."'

When he finishes a tour Kev generally likes to spend his time off pretty close to home. The exceptions to this rule are the trips he and Betty make to Chicago to spend time with TJ and her family—husband Diamond and their two daughters.

'Until recently touring was all the travel he needed,' says TJ. 'And while he loves it, when he returns home after a tour he rarely gets on a plane to go somewhere, he's probably already been there. He'll drive up to Lancelin and that's it. Yet he has no hesitation getting on a plane and flying to the other side of the world just to see his grandkids, and that says something. As he always says, family first, second and third.'

As any live performer will tell you, some gigs are harder to get through than others, but you can't pull the plug on a gig at short notice, and the show must go on regardless of a performer's personal circumstances.

On the day his father died, Kev was booked to do a show in Manjimup, around three hundred kilometres south of Perth. Only about two hundred people had bought tickets in advance, so this wasn't exactly a big gig by Kevin Bloody Wilson standards, but there was no way Kev was going to let his fans down. As he says, 'If I'd sat on my arse in Perth and done nothing I'd have just been wallowing. Fuck that.' It was fitting, given that the instinct to put in a great performance, regardless of the circumstances, was something Kev inherited from his father in the first place.

Kev's sister Maureen had phoned him the previous day and told him that their father wasn't going to last much longer. On the morning of the Manjimup concert Kev put in a call to his sister and asked how his father was doing.

'Listen,' said Maureen, as she held the phone up for Kev

to hear what was going on. Cecil was propped up in bed singing a song to his great-grandkids. It was a familiar song, a children's lullaby, the same one Kev had learned as a kid from his father and the same song Kev had sang to Travis and TJ when they were little.

> *Chingy Lingy Ling Ching*
> *Choo Ching Chow Chow*
> *Me Lubby Liddle Girlie*
> *Closs Da Sea*
> *She Was Velly Love*
> *Not Much Finer*
> *Makey Feelie Velly Sickie*
> *Poor Chi Nee.*

Kev smiled as he listened to his father's final farewell down the phone. 'He came back for an encore, right before he died.'

By this time both of Kev's parents had been in full-time care for several years. Cecil was there because, as Kev so delicately puts it, 'he was really fuckin' old', while Hazel was suffering the debilitating effects of Alzheimer's disease. Says Kev, 'Mum was in maximum security. She'd wander and forget things, and she'd introduce me to the other inmates as her brother. I just had to be patient with her and play along.'

Hazel had never seen a Kevin Bloody Wilson show; Kev's brother Terry would often try to convince Hazel to come along, but she would always sit with Betty at the merchandise stand during the show. Terry explains, 'The old man always used to come to the shows if they were in his area, but not the old girl. That old Catholic guilt thing again.'

Kev still wanted his mother to see at least one of his concerts before she followed Cecil upstairs to the Mates Star, so he flew Hazel to London and made sure she had the best seat in the house for one of the biggest shows of his entire career, his milestone performance at the legendary London Palladium. On the night of the concert, Terry had the unenviable task of convincing Hazel to leave her hotel room. 'It was my job to get her to the London Palladium. I had spent two weeks trying to convince her that he had a different type of act now where he wasn't swearing. I lied. I had to.

'I was working on her and working on her, and the day before the London Palladium I said to her, "Are you coming to the concert, Mum?" and she said, "No." I asked her why and she said she didn't like the swearing. I said, "You are the most ungrateful person I have ever met in my life. Here he is, he's brought you here specifically to go to the London Palladium concert, and you're not gonna go. It's another pinnacle for him and he just wants you there. You are an ungrateful, ungrateful woman." So I told Kev she wasn't going, and he sort of accepted that, and then the next day she says to him she *is* going. You could have knocked me over with a feather.

'They put us in the royal box—of course when people were coming in they automatically looked up to the royal box. She asked, "Why are all the people looking up here?" and I said, "They think you're the Queen, 'cos with your grey hair, and from a distance, you do bear a slight resemblance to the Queen. Just give them the wave." So she did and the audience went berserk. She huddled back down in her seat and said, "I don't think I'd better do that again."'

This was one of the proudest moments of Kev's life, and as he stepped onto the stage he looked towards the royal box and gave his mother a big wave. Hazel was sipping on complimentary sherry, being waited on hand and foot as Kev delivered one of his most memorable shows ever. In typical Kevin Bloody Wilson fashion, he did not tone down his act one bit for the benefit of his mother.

Terry enjoyed watching Hazel's reaction to Kev's performance. 'She thoroughly enjoyed the show. She just couldn't get over it: "How does he remember all that stuff?" It really ended up being a highlight of her life too.'

After the show Hazel gave Kev a hug backstage. He recalls, 'I said to her, "There you go, Mum, that's what I do," and she said, "Dennis, you're a very funny man." Then she gave me a fuckin' backhander and said, "But you still swear too much!" Just as well she didn't have her old ironing cord on her, or else I would have copped a floggin' with that as well.

'Mum did have a sense of humour but you didn't get to see that when we were kids 'cos she was too busy being a mum. She was more the disciplinarian. But one of the nicest things that happened out of her dementia was that I did get to see my mother, through her illness, as a cheeky little kid again.'

'Mum'd had Alzheimer's disease for a fair few years when I remember we took her out for a family dinner at a Chinese restaurant in Lismore. Mum was sitting there opposite me and I must have been talking to one of my brothers when I felt this clunk on the side of my head. It was one of those plastic serviette holders. She'd thrown it at me, and I looked across at this woman who hadn't spoken for about three years at that point, and she gave me this big wicked grin.

'She'd picked all the winegum lollies out of the little bowl on the table and pushed them into her mouth, and as I looked at her the grin gave way to this big gummy childlike smile. Then she went back to nowhere, straight back into oblivion. That's when I realised that Alzheimer's wasn't all bad, because for a few precious seconds at least I got to see my mother as a little girl. It was a very special moment.'

Kev was at the tail end of a UK tour when the news came through of Hazel's passing. TJ was on that tour with Kev and Betty, and she learned a thing or two about comedic timing that day. 'We'd just completed our last concert in Ireland, and Dad was pretty upset even though we all knew it was coming. When we got on the tour bus to go to the airport and home, he accidentally bumped into me as he was getting on. I said, "Don't be so pushy! Just because you're a fuckin' orphan you think you should get on the fuckin' bus first, do you?" I remember when I said it I thought, "I might have just pushed it a little bit too far. That joke might have been funny next week. Comedy is timing. Am I too early?"'

Fortunately, Kev laughed; once she knew she had the all-clear, TJ offered the follow-up: 'OK, everybody with parents get on first! Orphans, go with Dad to the back of the bus, thank you!'

In among the laughter and the inevitable tears on that bus ride, Kev's overwhelming emotion was one of relief. 'I only saw the good in it. Her suffering was over at long last, and the timing was great 'cos we were on our way home anyway. So we flew straight home to Perth, ditched our winter clothes and went straight to Lismore for Mum's funeral.'

Kev sang the same song at Hazel's funeral that he'd sung at Cecil's years before: called 'There's Gotta Be Someone Out There', it's as close to a gospel song as Kev has ever written.

There's Gotta Be Someone Out There

There's gotta be someone out there lookin' on
Lookin' on from out there seein' how we're getting' on
There's a power we don't understand
Helping us along
There's gotta be someone out there lookin' on.

Find some time alone, just lay back, look up at the stars
And try and see the scheme of things
Much bigger scheme than ours
Could we be so naïve to think we've come this far
    alone?
There's gotta be someone out there lookin' on.

Feel a gentle summer breeze or Mother Nature wild
Feel someone's breath upon your skin
Or hold a newborn child
Then no matter where on earth you live
No matter who your god
You know there's gotta be someone out there lookin'
    on.

'I consider myself the luckiest bloke in the world 'cause I get to travel the world with my very best friend in the world—my wife Betty.'.... Kev.

KEV'S FLASH FRIENDS

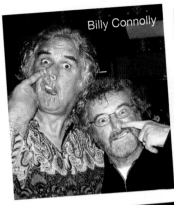
Billy Connolly

Kenny Rogers

John Farnham

John Laws

Cyndi Lauper

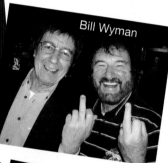
Bill Wyman

Tammy Wynette

Normie Rowe and PK

Brooks and Dunn

Garth Brooks

Adam Harvey

Charlie Pride

Dolly Parton

Elton John

Alice Cooper

Paul Simon

Suzi Quatro

Chubby Brown

Joe Cocker

Gordon Parsons and Slim Dusty

Hale & Pace

Phil Everly

Leo Sayer

Dwight Yoakam

Merle Haggard

Maton Guitars head luthier and master craftsman Andy Allen with just some of the custom guitars he's created for Kev.

Travis helping Andy to assemble his dad's 'Family Man' baritone guitar. Travis also designed the family vine for the pearl inlay, as seen right.

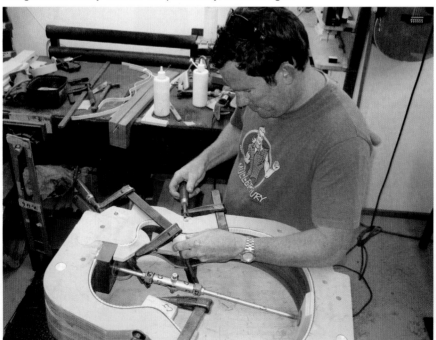

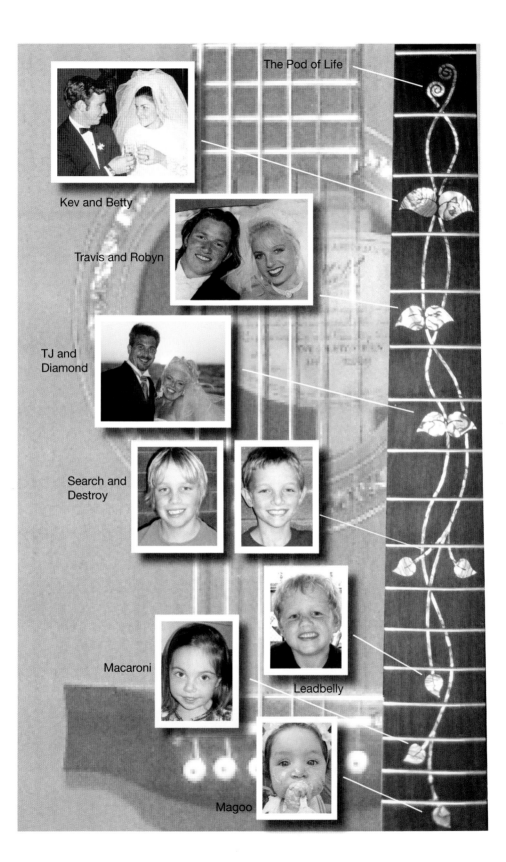

The Pod of Life

Kev and Betty

Travis and Robyn

TJ and Diamond

Search and Destroy

Macaroni

Leadbelly

Magoo

Talented cartoonist and graphic designer Greg Taylor helped establish the Kev cartoon character. Greg has designed all of Kev's albums, DVD covers and merchandise for the last 20 years.

The 'MAKE-A-WISH Kev Klassic', held annually, is now considered one of the most successful corporate golf days in Western Australia.

KEVIN BLOODY WILSON'S

GREATEST TITS!

HELPING PREVENT GLOBAL BORING!

KEV HEADS...

...AND THEIR INK

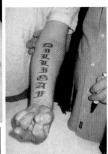

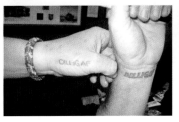

Travis used his talent as a musician to finance himself through flight school and to supplement his income as a bush pilot in Kalgoorlie and Broome. Persistence and hard work paid off securing him a career with Qantas. He still finds time to produce and play on all his father's albums.

Like her father, TJ underwent a couple of name changes. From 'TJ Dennis', the country singer, to 'Jenny Talia from Australia', an outrageous female version of Kev. She now tours the world with her dad as his support act and 'retirement fund'!

WHAT HAPPENS ON THE ROAD....

SHOULD'VE STAYED ON THE ROAD....

CHAPTER 19

Takin' it to the world

'After what they did to our relatives on the First Fleet, the Poms deserve me.'

Kevin Bloody Wilson

Even back in the mid eighties, when Kevin Bloody Wilson's career first began to take off in Australia, he always had the idea in the back of his mind that he should take his show overseas. Cactus for one was never in any doubt that Kev's act would translate internationally. 'I think we knew from the beginning that it could be taken around the world. When I was working with Kevin we had so much demand in Australia that we were working really hard to meet that demand, and to try to give Kevin some time off to record and some time off to recover and then we were back out on the road again. And then he took it to New Zealand.'

New Zealand was the logical place for Kev to test his international appeal for the first time. It's overseas, but only just, and the Kiwis have an almost identical sense of humour to the Aussies. Kev's been going back on a regular basis ever since. Kev's first New Zealand tour was managed by Ian Magan at Pacific Entertainment, and Kev and 'Big-hand Magan' have since forged a strong and lasting friendship. Says Kev, 'I do all the sheep-fucking references. I tell the exact same stories to the Kiwis as I would to an Aussie crowd. Kiwis and Aussies are like twin brothers, they fight all the time but they'd kill for each other if they had to.'

Another part of the planet where the locals seem to appreciate the humour of Kevin Bloody Wilson is Canada, but as most Kev fans are already aware there is a certain word you can't say in Canada, apparently. Says Kev, 'When we were organising our first tour into Canada we had to apply for a work visa from the Canadian government, which they issued without a problem. Shortly after, my office got a call from the Australian embassy in Canada. They wanted me to know, off the record, that as a live performer you are not allowed to say the word "cunt" on stage in Canada. So I immediately wrote a song called "You Can't Say Cunt in Canada" and I opened the shows with it over there. And guess what, contrary to what the Australian embassy had said, it turns out you can. The crowd fuckin' loved it, and they kept requesting that I sing it again. All night you could hear them from all over the theatre yellin', "Cunt! Cunt! Cunt!" I *think* they were requestin' the song. Either way, it became the opening number for the entire Canadian tour.'

The man who helped transform Kev's thinking about the scale of his tours was one of the world's greatest-ever comedians, and a performer Kev had always idolised. Kev recalls their meeting. 'Cactus was touring Billy Connolly around Australia, and when he was in Perth I was invited backstage and then to a party at Observation Rise, as it was called in the late eighties, at Scarborough Beach. Billy said, "I've heard a lot about you," and I said, "Well, I'll get some cassettes for you."'

Kev suspected that those cassettes would slowly make their way to the bottom of Billy Connolly's suitcase, where they would be crushed to pieces by the time Billy arrived home from his tour. As it turns out, Kev had underestimated Billy's generosity of spirit.

'At the end of his tour we caught up again in Perth and by then he had listened to the stuff. He told me he thought it was very funny and he said, "Have you thought about England?" and I said, "Yes, I have," and he said, "I know some people over there I can put you in touch with," and he did. Promoters, publicists and, most importantly, his UK tour manager, Malcolm Kingsnorth.'

The timing was perfect. Kevin Bloody Wilson was ripe and ready to have a serious crack at the UK market, and Billy Connolly was busy making a movie. That meant his tour manager, Malcolm, was available to work with Kev.

'Malcom did my first tour, and subsequent tours as well, and Billy gave me all his production equipment. So that's your PA system, lights, microphones, mixing desks, trucks, the whole lot. My first tour over there was about forty-seven dates, I believe, and Billy Connolly basically paid for it by lending me all that gear.'

Billy also had a few important lessons for Kev when it came to the economics of touring. At one point Kev had sixteen people on the road with him, including a full five-piece band, and it was making a serious dent in the profit margin. Billy suggested to Kev that he could still pull off a great live show without having to fork out for a full band. 'He sat me down backstage one night and he said, "They're not paying to see a band, they're paying to see you. If you don't have a band you can save yourself nine wages each week—five band members and four road crew. Plus you won't have to lug the band's gear around or hire it when you get there." He said I was better off doing it the way he does, just getting up there and doing it by myself.

'A few years ago Billy and I did a show together at the Oxford Apollo when Malcolm Kingsnorth died, and all the people he'd tour managed over the years got together and did a big show to help his wife, Mary, with the mortgage and all that sort of stuff. It was Billy Connolly, myself and Bjorn Again.'

Many Australians would be surprised to learn just how big a live act Kevin Bloody Wilson has become in the United Kingdom, where he plays to capacity crowds in all of the major theatres from Inverness in Scotland to Brighton on the south coast of England. Perhaps it's got something to do with colonial humour, but for whatever reason the poms seem to really 'get' Kev.

'The whole concept of the bawdy ballad comes from England in the first place. Sometimes I have to explain the Australiana, like "root" and "chook" and that sort of stuff. The people who come to the shows have usually got the albums by then anyway, 'cos they're available all over the UK now, so they kinda know what they're in for, and if they don't, fuck 'em. Also, I explain some of the words in the songs in the liner notes of the albums, so in "Livin' Next Door to Alan" the words "burnt-out blue FJ" are highlighted and at the bottom of the page there's an explanation.'

As well as his regular trips around the UK, New Zealand and Canada, Kev also occasionally visits places like South

Africa and Bali, and any other part of the planet where the natives aren't too easily offended.

Now that he's in his sixties, it stands to reason that Kev would be eyeing off retirement from touring in the not-too-distant future. 'I love touring, but once I get to about sixty-five years of age I won't do full tours, just individual concerts. If I still feel as enthused about it as I do now then I'm more than happy to keep doing it. I was talking to Billy Connolly about that very same thing. Billy said people were asking him, "When are you going to retire?" and he said to them, "Did they ask Picasso that?" He's right. You don't retire as an artist, that's who you are. You can retire from touring, but you can't retire from being an artist.'

For her part, TJ can't see her dad retiring any time soon. 'He might not tour as much, or tour for as long, but at the end of the day he's Kev, and Kev is all about getting out there and entertaining people. He and Mum have a pact that if he starts getting all dithery and forgetting the words and he doesn't even know he's doing it, she's gonna tell him that's it. But he's actually getting better as he gets older.'

CHAPTER 20

What Kev does GAF about

'Life ain't no dress rehearsal, it's the real deal. So enjoy the show.'
Kevin Bloody Wilson

For Kev's sixtieth birthday, in February 2007, Betty, Travis and TJ presented him with a unique, custom baritone guitar made by Kev's mate Andy Allen at Maton Guitars. Andy says, 'Up until then I had only ever made one other baritone guitar. That was for American rock legend John Fogarty, but in my entire time as a luthier I've never built a guitar with so much love and respect as went into the making of Kev's "family man".'

Travis took time out of his busy schedule with Qantas to assist Andy with the construction and also design the Bryant family tree which appears on the pearl inlay on the neck of the guitar. Andy was impressed by Travis's involvement. 'He's a bloody amazing bloke: he handpicked each piece of shell for the neck and body, helped me put it all together, then buggered off and flew a bloody jumbo jet to India.'

Kev's birthday bash was one of the greatest parties he has ever thrown, and that's saying something. The guest list not only included Kev's family and friends from all over the world, but also mates from what Kev describes as his 'Dreamtime'—his former lives as an electrician, a music teacher, and even back as far as his schooldays in Sydney.

One of the best things about a Bryant family gathering is that there are always a lot of musicians around. The PA and the instruments are always set up on stage before the party begins, and there's usually an impromptu jam session as soon as a musician spots an unmanned instrument or microphone on stage. Once everyone has had a skinful, it becomes anybody's turn; as Kev says, 'Talent and ability are directly disproportional to the amount of alcohol one's consumed.'

At one point Kev jumped up on stage and sang some old rock and roll tunes with Travis and TJ as part of his backing band. An hour later Kev was up again, this time with his old mates from Bryan Dennis and the Country Club, in their first live appearance since their gigging days in Kalgoorlie more than twenty-five years earlier.

Fairly late in the evening, I asked Kev how it felt looking around the room and seeing so many friends, people from all walks of life, partying together. Admittedly, Kev was slurring his words by then, but this is what I believe he attempted to say: 'These people have stayed in my life through thick and thin, and they're all people who are comfortable with each other, warts and all. I'm a lucky man, Gav . . . I'm a fuckin' lucky man . . .'

Before the guests arrived, Kev had strategically placed a wishing well from the Make-A-Wish Foundation at the entrance to the venue. 'We got the bastards when they were sober on the way in and got 'em again when they were pissed on the way out.' The party invitations had also asked guests to donate money to the Make-A-Wish Foundation in lieu of a gift.

As Shelly Budd from the Mandurah-Rockingham branch of the Make-A-Wish Foundation explains, over the years Kev has become known to a special group of children and their families as the Hairy Fairy. Says Shelly, 'Eight years ago, on behalf of Make-A-Wish Australia, I called to see if Kev would be interested in being a special guest at a golf day being held to raise money for local Wish children. He didn't even hesitate. He came, he saw, he conquered, and so the Make-A-Wish Kev Klassic corporate golf day was born. Not only have we had success with this event, but Kevin has backed up a couple of these days with a concert the night before with all proceeds to our charity. He has also become the face of our national Swear Can Campaign.

'So many wishes have been granted because of Kevin's outstanding generosity, but I think the most poignant moment of Kev's relationship with Make-A-Wish came at the 2008 Make-A-Wish Kev Klassic.'

'Wish child Ben was, at the time, thirteen years old and suffering from advanced cystic fibrosis. Being a muso, we knew that Kevin would appreciate this particular wish: Ben's greatest desire was to own a Gibson Les Paul Custom Black Beauty guitar, a rare and legendary item, as designed for the one and only Jimmy Page, one of Ben's idols. Kev amazed us all on the day: when presenting the wish he also extended an invitation to Ben to visit his recording studio and perhaps make a demo CD. Ben was thrilled, his parents were ecstatic, and we were in tears.

'I am so happy to have Kevin involved with our charity.

He has helped us raise our profile tremendously, and has granted countless wishes to seriously ill children who so desperately need a little magic in their lives. Kevin is a truly amazing human being, one that I am proud to call a friend.'

Deep down, Kevin Bloody Wilson is a bit of a soft cock, according to his daughter TJ. 'By soft cock, I mean he has a marshmallow inside. But Dad's big heart hasn't always attracted the best people, and he's had his fair share of arse-holes try to take him for a ride. I'm happy to say his inner circle is pretty fuckhead-free these days but he still, for the most part, just can't say no. For example: "Wow, Kev, that's a great boat. Man, I'd love to have a boat like that one day . . ." So of course Dad says, 'Well here, you take it. I'll get another one." What the fuck, right? You name it, he's given it—cars, boats, TVs and wads of money not even he keeps track of—and occasionally not to the most worthy recipients. But it's this part of his character that I'm probably most proud of too. To those he loves, he'll do anything for you, *anything*.

'The kids he meets through Make-A-Wish turn him into a big sookie-sookie-la-la, but nothing makes him happier than making those kids happy. Whatever it takes. Like I said, he really is a big old soft cock. And you can tell him I said that.'

Kev's soft-cock side has also been exposed by Betty, who made a rare media appearance in an episode of Andrew Denton's *Enough Rope* on ABC TV in which Kev was being interviewed. Betty answered Andrew's questions from her seat in the audience, next to Travis. After asking Betty how she and Kev had first met, Denton raised the subject of Kev's attitude to women.

Andrew Denton: . . . [A] lot of Kevin's music is about,
    you know, women are sheilas and good sorts and
    they're good for a root or a head job and that's
    about it.
Betty Bryant: True, true.
Andrew Denton: Was he a romantic?
Betty Bryant: I'm going to ruin his reputation here I
    know, but yes he is actually. He buys me flowers
    and all of those things. So he is a bit . . .
Kevin Bloody Wilson: You really are fucking up my
    reputation . . .

For many years Kev has had an affinity with Bali, the
place and its people, and like a lot of Western Australians
Kev had been a frequent visitor to the Sari Club, where
the Bali bombings occurred in October 2002. That same
weekend, through a flood of tears, Kev was on the phone
to his mates around Perth, working behind the scenes to
organise a free show to not only raise money for the victims
and their families, but to try to raise their spirits a bit as
well.

A couple of weeks later at the legendary old Raffles
Hotel, a place where Kev had played many a great show
over the years, he gave one of his biggest and best free shows
ever. Kev asked me to introduce him, and the response from
the crowd at the moment he walked on stage was one of the
loudest sounds I have ever heard.

Kev was in ripping form that night and no punters ap-
preciated it more than the guys in the front row, the survivors
from the Kingsley footy club. They'd just lost seven of their
own, so no doubt it would have been difficult, perhaps even

frightening, for those boys to be in a bar jam-packed with people so soon after the horror they had witnessed in the Sari Club in Bali a few weeks earlier. Yet by the end of the night everyone was laughing again for the first time in a while, and when Kev struck the opening chord to 'Livin' Next Door to Alan' the Raffles crowd roared as one. Somehow Kev had made the world a fun place to be again for people who had lost sight of that for a while.

During a triumphant 'homecoming' tour of Kalgoorlie in 2005, Kev took some time out to visit the local correctional facility, something he does quite often in places all over the world, often surprising the inmates with a visit on one of his days off. Kev's philosophy on doing prison shows is pretty simple. 'Just because someone is in prison it doesn't mean they're a bad person. With the exception of rock spiders and rapists, quite often they're good people who have been pushed to the wall and fucked up along the way, and unlike heaps of their mates, myself included, who might have done the same things, these unlucky bastards got caught. I reckon they deserve to be entertained once in a while as much as the next bloke.

'The funniest one I ever did was at this same jail in Kalgoorlie a few years back. I did a show for the boys and they were having a ball, then the fucking preacher, the jail reverend or whatever he's called himself—he wasn't even a proper priest, just some fucking dickhead who saw himself as the apprentice Pope—anyway, he saw me entertaining the troops in there and he came up to me and said, "Have you ever thought about putting that good work to God's use?" I looked him in the eye and said, "Have you thought of cuttin' back on jackin' off?" Oblivious to the intended put-down, he actually said, "No, but I believe you have a talent for engaging people, and you should be using that to do God's work." What a fuckin' chronic masturbator! Where do these fuckin' idiots come from?

'I was talking to the superintendent of the jail afterwards and he said, "Did you enjoy your day?" and I said, "I fuckin' loved it, mate, thank you very much." He said, "The boys loved it too," then, "Did anybody upset you?" He was obviously thinking of the inmates. I said, "Nobody upset me, but the biggest fucktard I've met all day was that fuckin' preacher!" He knew exactly what I meant. I don't tend to suffer them God-bothering cunts all that well.'

In 2005 Kev had a mate in this prison who he hadn't seen for a few years, an old drinking buddy from his days living in Kalgoorlie who, the story goes, came home early from work one day and found his wife in bed with his so-called best mate. He did what some would argue many people would do in that situation. 'He stabbed the bastard. He's been in prison ever since.'

The guy's eyes light up when he sees Kev walk through the gates, and Kev wanders straight over to him, gives him a warm hug, and sits down to have a chat. The other prisoners, predominantly Aboriginal, are sitting in small groups on the grassy area inside the prison compound, most of them suspicously eyeing off the little bearded guy with the guitar. After catching up with his mate Kev goes up to one group, introduces himself quietly, then sits down with his guitar and starts singing.

Some of the prisoners start laughing and singing along, some are overcome with what appears to be shyness at receiving Kev's attention, and some look completely unmoved. Kev keeps singing and playing regardless, and not just his own songs—he also plays tunes by Hank Williams, Charley Pride,

Slim Dusty and even a couple of Johnny Cash's gospel songs. Then he thanks the guys and shuffles on to the next group, again introducing himself before playing a few songs.

An hour later Kev is in the mess hall playing 'Hey Santa Claus' and the groups have merged into one. By now he's won them all over: the entire prison, including the men and women who work there, are all laughing and clapping and singing along. Once again Kev has worked his magic, and he wraps up the show, thanks everyone, and gives his mate another hug before he leaves.

Kev spends a significant amount of time on the road each year, and wherever he is he does his best to stay connected to his close mates. These days he's more likely to phone a mate to help him pass the time as he's driving between gigs, but before the invention of mobile phones Kev used to write to his loved ones on a regular basis. Wayne 'Jock' Pride still has a postcard that Kev sent to him in the late eighties from a tour of the Northern Territory. 'It's got a big tree and about half a dozen or so Aboriginal kids sitting up in the branches of the tree. He wrote on it, "Hey Jock, they grow on fuckin' trees out here!"'

On the day of Wayne's sixtieth birthday, ten thousand dollars worth of guitars and musical equipment was stolen from his Perth home. He was in a state of high anxiety when Kev rang him from the UK to wish him a happy birthday. 'He said, "G'day, Jock, happy birthday," and I said, "Happy bullshit!" He asked me what was wrong and I told him, so when he got back from his tour I went to visit him and he said, "I've got something for you," and he got out a beautiful brand-new Maton guitar. "This is for you, Jock." I said, "I can't take that," and he said, "No, it's yours." That's the way he operates.'

Kev is notoriously generous to his friends, and sometimes even to strangers. In 2007 Kev went with his family
to Fiji as part of his sixtieth birthday celebrations. Like
most people who have been to Fiji, Kev fell in love with
the people, the food and the traditional music that can
be heard almost everywhere you go. It's a beautiful
music with sweet harmonies usually played on acoustic
guitars and ukuleles, and Kev immediately responded to
the music's straightforward warmth. 'It's got the same
honesty as country music, but in this case the country just
happens to be Fiji. My brother Terry and I even went to
a Sunday morning church service to listen to their choirs
. . . Fuckin' beautiful!'

Kev was sitting with Betty enjoying the band at his hotel
one night when he took a closer look at one of the guitars
being used on stage. To his amazement, he noticed that there
was no machine-head—or winder—for the A string. As a
brave attempt to keep the thing even moderately in tune the
string had been tightly wound around the neck of the guitar.
Kev then noticed that one of the other guitars had a string
missing altogether, but the guy playing it was smiling and
playing on regardless.

At the end of the song Kev walked up to the band and
thanked them for their beautiful music. One of the musicians
asked Kev if he played, and then offered him his guitar. The
first thing Kev noticed when he strummed the old Fijian's
guitar was that the top E string had a knot tied in it. 'My
finger hit the knot and I thought, "What the fuck was that?"
All of their instruments were absolutely fuckin' shithouse,
and I just couldn't believe that they were still smiling and
making this great music with these piece-of-shit instruments.
You couldn't help but admire that.'

As soon as Kev returned to Perth he bought two brand-new guitars, a ukulele and a big box of guitar strings, tuners, machine-heads and anything else he could think of that the band might one day need to care for their instruments. Then he threw in a couple of handfuls of Kevin Bloody Wilson guitar picks and posted it all off with a handwritten note that said, 'Thank you for the beautiful music. Here are some gifts to help you to continue making it.'

Since the early days of Kevin Bloody Wilson, Kev has done shows for Aussie troops stationed all over the world. In June 2008 Kev and daughter TJ were part of a select group of entertainers who made the trip to Timor to entertain our troops.

In the weeks leading up to this visit the story broke that Australian actress and TV personality Tania Zaetta had been falsely accused of having inappropriate relations with three Australian servicemen while she was entertaining the troops overseas. These claims were swiftly revealed to be nothing more than a fantasy, and the Australian Defence Force quite rightly issued an apology to Ms Zaetta. Still, this story gave Kev his tongue in cheek opening line for the troops in Timor.

'OK, hands up, which one of you cunts *didn't* fuck Tania?'

Kev and TJ are in the middle of their tour of duty when they call me from what Kev describes as the middle of the Timorese outback. TJ is the first person on the phone, and she sounds suitably full of adrenaline. 'Dad and I have been parachuting out of Blackhawks and driving tanks and blowin' up shit and all sorts of stuff. We have done on average three shows a day since we got here last week, and after every one of those shows we get back on a Blackhawk and they drop us somewhere else.

'We go wherever the Aussie boys and the New Zealand boys are, that's where they drop us with a couple of guitars. Sometimes there's a few hundred blokes there and they've got a sound system and a stage and everything set up; other times it's just us sitting around on crates or boxes or whatever playing for ten blokes.'

TJ had no hesitation in flying over from Chicago for this trip. 'Dad and I both put our hands up. We reckon if we can set aside time every year to do something like this, it's really worth it. It's just an amazing life experience and the blokes over here appreciate it so much, and obviously because they're Aussies and Kiwis their sense of humour is fairly well intact. We've taught the locals some new words, too.'

Our time for this phone call to the middle of nowhere is limited, and it's now time for TJ to hand over the phone. She reminds me that she really is a chip off the old block with her closing remarks. 'Hang on, Gav, I'll get Dad for you. He's really been missing you, Gav. He's got a picture of you on his bunk bed and he's drawn camouflage pants on you and everything.'

Seconds later Kev is on the phone, and he sounds like he is enjoying his adventures in Timor just as much as TJ. 'I think we've spent more time in helicopters than we've spent on stage. It's just an amazing experience to be dropped into these places that you can only get to by helicopter, and our troops are out there working their butts off, so it's a fabulous thing to watch, and a fabulous thing to be a part of.

'There's no drinking allowed over here, and there's no rooting going on. I'm told though you're allowed to have sex as often as you like but only with yourself, so I'm lovin' it. I've been battin' well above my average. I've been slappin' me dick like it owes me money. The army have even given me a new rank now. I'm Major Jism.

'It's not about us. It's about the troops. We're only here for a week, but they're here for six months at a time, so they're doing it hard but you'd never recognise that. They're all happy and laughing and you wouldn't believe how strong the camaraderie is.'

The army need their phone back. I only have time for one more question, so I ask Kev which songs seem to be getting a good response from the troops while he's been doing these shows.

'There's one song they all seem to like because they can relate to it, called "Fuck Ya Guts Out". It's a love song.'

Click.

Here's a taste of the chorus:

I'm gonna fuck ya guts out
And I'm never gonna stop
Not even when I see your kidneys
Wrapped around me cock
'Cos I'll just whip it in
And whip it out and wipe it on your frock
I'm gonna fuck ya guts out
And I'm never gonna stop.

After completing their Tour de Force, and with TJ now back in Chicago with her family, I caught up with Kev and his tour manager Hollywood in his Perth home. While Kev's secretary Skye organised lunch and another carton of beer, Hollywood proceeded to tell me one of the many funny incidents that took place in East Timor. It seems that on this particular day, the entertainment crew of approximately twelve, including Kev and TJ, had finally arrived back at their Dili HQ around ten pm (2200 hours army speak) after completing a fairly full-on and intense day that had started at seven thirty (0730 hours army speak) that morning.

According to Hollywood, 'This sweat-soaked, raggedy-arsed mob were totally focused on hitting the showers and fartsack, but the two army officers in charge of this motley crew insisted on the customary debriefing of the day's events and briefing on their next day's adventure. Now, Kev is one of the most astute blokes I know and has the unique ability to instantly gauge people. These two officers, a lieutenant colonel and a major, had accompanied us on the flight from Sydney. After getting to know them on the plane, Kev had already established that while they were both good blokes, they hated each other's guts. By the time we had landed in Dili he had nicknamed them Colonel Gomer and Major Pyle.

'So here we were with our assigned armed military security standing around outside the mess in the still-sweltering tropical night with these two lovebirds trying to outwank each other.' According to Kev and Hollywood, the ensuing conversation went something like this:

Gomer: Tomorrow morning we'll assemble at 0630.
Pyle: Shouldn't that be 0700, sir?
Gomer: Who changed it?
Pyle: You did, sir.
Gomer: When?
Pyle: This morning, sir.
Gomer: Didn't.

Pyle: Did, sir.
Gomer: Didn't.
Pyle: Did, sir.

As Hollywood watched the conversation between Gomer and Pyle unfold, he noticed that Kev appeared to be getting ready to fire a missile of his own. 'Not only were they pissing us all off by cutting into our precious and long-awaited downtime, but you could see that our military escorts were embarrassed by their officers' childlike behaviour. I glanced at Kev, he was shaking his bowed head from side to side, and I thought, "Fuck! He's loading one up—officers or not, these two blokes are about to cop it!"

'Kev lifted his head as he raised his right arm in the air. Gomer responded, "Yes, Kev?" and Kev casually asked, "With respect, sirs, do either of you cunts know what you're fuckin doin'?" With that the team was quickly dismissed as Kev and I were escorted back to our quarters under a barrage of backslaps, "thank yous" and "good onya, mates."

'In environments like these rumour and gossip spread like wildfire, and over breakfast the next morning, which incidentally was served at 0745, that's 7.45 am civvy time, Kev and I were bombarded by a constant stream of both soldiers and officers seeking a heads-up on what had occurred the previous night.'

Having made such a lasting impression on our troops in East Timor, Kev is planning his next trip for the troops and he wants to visit our boys and girls in Afghanistan. Hollywood explains, 'We are in touch with the British Armed Forces Entertainment Unit, and we're trying to combine with them to do a tour of Afghanistan that would include shows for both the Aussies and the British Forces.'

CHAPTER 21

The kid Kev

'Growin' old is mandatory, growin' up is optional.'
Kevin Bloody Wilson

Kevin Bloody Wilson is a dog person through and through, and these days he's got a chocolate labrador called Chucka, short for Chucka Browneye. Chucka is a pretty mellow dog, as was his former playmate, the late great Skoota. Skoota was a golden labrador, and a clever one at that. Says Kev, 'I taught Skoota how to bark on command using eye contact. I'd just get him into a sitting position and look him in the eye, and he'd bark at me until I stopped looking at him.'

Once Kev and Skoota had refined their act, Kev tried it out on Travis and Robyn's twin sons, known as Search and Destroy. The boys were five years old at the time, and thoroughly impressed. 'I had 'em convinced that Skoota knew maths. "Hey Skoota, what's five minus three?" and then I'd look away from Skoota after two barks. "Now let's try two plus two?" After four barks I would discreetly look away. Search and Destroy were in awe of Skoota.'

Kev's favourite birthday party trick was to sit Skoota on a chair and make him sing, using the same technique.

Family: Happy birthday . . .
Skoota: Woof! Woof!
Family: Happy birthday . . .
Skoota: Woof! Woof!
Family: Happy birthday . . .
Skoota: Woof! Woof! Woof!
Family: Happy birthday . . .
Skoota: Woof! Woof!

'I remember one day showing my mate Normie Rowe how Skoota could add and subtract and sing "Happy Birthday". As expected, he was suitably impressed. I then decided to take it to the next level.'

Kev: You reckon *that's* good, Rowie? Just listen to this.
He even knows one of yours! Ready, Skoot?

Kev then led Skoota in a chorus of 'Que Sera Sera'.

Skoota: Woof!
Kev: Que-a-a sera . . .
Skoota: Woof! Woof!
Kev: Sera . . .
Skoota: Woof! Woof!
Kev: Whatever will be will be . . .
Skoota: Woof! Woof!

'By now Normie's mouth had dropped fully open and his eyes were poking out of his head like fuckin' golf balls. "How the hell did you teach him to do that?" I went on to explain that the hardest part was to teach ole Skoot to read music, after that it was easy. Until Normie reads this book he's probably convinced that I'm Australia's, if not the world's, most fuckin' amazing dog whisperer.'

Skoota had his true moment of infamy in the summer of 2002. Kev had left Skoota's lead at his holiday home in Lancelin, and on arriving back in Perth he took Skoota for a walk along the beach in front of the family home. This is the same beach Kev has christened 'Kev's melon patch' due to the large number of topless women who adorn his view during the warm and seemingly endless Perth summers.

'After walking and splashing about together, I happened to look up and I could see that about a hundred metres further up the beach the fuckin' dog catcher had parked his van on the side of the road and was checkin' us out through his fuckin' binoculars. I figured he must've been watching us, 'cos it was winter and there were no melons on the beach. Skoota wasn't bothering anybody or even shitting anywhere but, sure enough, this big, tall, fat, bald-headed pommy cunt came walking towards us, and as he got closer I could see he was almost salivating and smiling the sort of smile that says, "I've gotcha, cunts."'

Here's how the conversation went:

Dog catcher: I know who you are and where you live.
Kev: Do ya? Good on ya, mate.
Dog catcher: Yes, sir, and I just seen you walking your dog without a lead, so I'm going to have to book you.
Kev: Fair enough, mate.
Dog catcher: Can I have your name and address, please, sir.
Kev: Hang on a minute, the first thing you said to me was: 'I know who you are and where you live!'

Dog catcher: I'm sorry, sir, but you have to tell me who
    you are and where you live.
Kev: No I fuckin' don't. You already know.
Dog catcher: Sir, can I please just have your full
    name and address?
Kev (glancing at Skoota): Whaddya reckon, Skoot?
Skoota: Woof! Woof! Woof!
Kev: Skoota, don't call him that. That's rude.
Dog catcher: What did he just call me?
Kev: He called you a stupid old cunt.
Dog catcher: I can book you for that too, Mr Wilson.
Kev: Hang on! It wasn't me. I didn't say a word. My
    fuckin' dog did. So see ya later, mate, and don't
    forget to post your silly little form. Come on, Skoot.
Dog catcher: Wilson! If you don't stop and tell me who
    you are I'll get the police involved.
Kev: Look mate, just fill out your silly little form and
    post the fuckin' thing to me. By the way, do your
    grandkids know what you do for a livin'?

Kev and Skoota headed for home, and Kev forgot all
about their confrontation with the dog catcher until twenty
minutes later. Kev was feeding Skoota when he heard the
doorbell ring at the entrance to his home. He went to investi-
gate and saw a police patrol car parked in his driveway, and
a couple of cops standing outside his garage. Both of them
broke into broad grins when they saw Kev walking towards
them holding a freshly opened can of beer in one hand and
an empty can of Pal dog food in the other.

Cop #1: Bloody hell, Kev, they told me it was you,
    what happened?

Kev: Whaddya fuckin' mean, what happened?

Cop #1: We got a report that you assaulted a ranger.

Kev: Fuckin' ranger? D'you mean the fuckin' dog catcher? Well, we may have *insulted* him, but we didn't *assault* him.

Cop #2: Who's we?

Kev: Me and me dog Skoota.

Cop #2: Can you tell us what happened?

Kev started running the officers through the events of the morning, but midway through the story he decided that he needed some backup. He called Skoota, sat him up on a plastic chair, borrowed a torch from one of the officers and shone it in Skoota's eyes, and began interrogating him.

Kev: Is Skoota Bloody Wilson your full name?

Skoota: Woof!

Kev: Did you have a run-in with the dog catcher today?

Skoota: Woof!

Kev: Did you call him a nasty name?

Skoota: Woof!

Kev: What did you call the cunt, Skoot?

Skoota: Woof! Woof! Woof!

Kev (to the cops): Are you blokes writin' this down?

The two policemen were still wiping tears of laughter from their eyes when they left half an hour later clutching signed copies of Kev's latest CD, having witnessed the funniest and most intimate Kevin Bloody Wilson / Skoota Bloody Wilson concert ever. Two weeks later Kev got a fine in the mail for two hundred and forty dollars. He still considers it the best two hund-red and forty dollars he has ever spent in pursuit of a laugh.

Kev is the kind of bloke who would do just about anything for a belly laugh, for example the April Fool's Day prank he once played on the unsuspecting residents of Kalgoorlie. It happened about fifteen years after Kev moved from Kalgoorlie to Perth.

As with every city, as you drive into Kalgoorlie there's a sign welcoming visitors. Kev had an idea for what he would like to see under the sign that says, 'Welcome to the city of Kalgoorlie/Boulder', so he went ahead and got a new sign made up. With the blessing of the mayor, Kev put his April Fool's Day prank into effect during a daytrip from Perth.

'Travis was doing his private pilot's licence at the time, so he flew me up there from Perth on one of his training flights. We gathered at the sign welcoming people into town, stuck up the new sign with Blu-Tack, and had photos taken with it. Then we removed it, stowed it back in the aircraft and pissed off back to Perth.'

When the 1 April edition of *The Kalgoorlie Miner* hit the streets, the front page carried a photograph of Kev standing under his new version of the sign.

WELCOME TO THE CITY OF KALGOORLIE/BOULDER
HOME OF KEVIN BLOODY WILSON AND HEAPS MORE
JUST LIKE HIM

'Below the photo was the news that the town had installed the sign to honour one of Kalgoorlie's most infamous residents, and the story also said they were going to issue a further honour by changing the name of Wilson Street to Kevin Bloody Wilson Street. Then it said, "More on page 7," and when you turned to page seven it said: "*The Kalgoorlie Miner* and Kevin Bloody Wilson wish all of our readers a happy April Fool's Day."'

Kev was belly laughing all morning, fielding one call after another from his mates in Kalgoorlie as he watched the waves roll in at Sorrento.

When it comes to things Kev does GAF about, his grandkids are right at the top of the list. Travis and Robyn have three boys: the twins, Search and Destroy, and the youngest, called Leadbelly by his pop. In Chicago, TJ and Diamond have two girls, known as Mrs Macaroni and Mrs Magoo. Says Kev, 'The girls call me *Parpy* with their American accents. They sound like midget Chicago gangsters. "Yo Parpy, how ya doin?"'

Being the fiercely patriotic bloke he is, Kev always has the Australian flag flying in his front yard. Whenever the grandkids come to stay, there is a ceremony Kev insists on carrying out right after breakfast every morning. 'First, we all line up in the kitchen. We pick a leader, and the leader has to march us, left-right left-right, out to the flagpole. We take it in turns. Sometimes we get Nanna to be the leader, sometimes it's me, but it's usually one of the kids.

'We all stand on the balcony in a line, raise our right hands to our foreheads in salute, and together we say, "Australia, you FFFFFFFFFairdinkum beauty!" as we slap our right hands to our sides to end the salute. It's just a silly little ritual we have, but we all love it. TJ's kids have been known to do it in America when they see an Australian flag.'

The same creativity that has spawned Kevin Bloody Wilson's albums and live shows is also put to use for the benefit of his grandkids, and Kev's own sense of childlike adventure goes into overdrive. 'I write pirate books for them, and they're good adventure stories because we played these adventures out together before the books were written.'

The adventures that form the basis for these books are three-day extravaganzas, all meticulously planned by Kev. The first one, for his two eldest grandkids, began at the holiday home in Lancelin and resulted in a pirate book Kev gave Search and Destroy for their fifth birthday. It's called *The Adventures of Deaf Captain Bungeye and His Two Buccaneers, Lefty and Righty.*

First, Kev drew up detailed maps for Search and Destroy, then took them with their little brother Leadbelly out to the island off the coast of Lancelin, where they met some 'real pirates' (Kev's mates from the Lancelin, Pirates footy club, all dressed up and in character), who gave them more clues, and when the kids eventually worked their way through the clues and figured out that the treasure was buried on the beach in front of Big Mick's Ale House—the local pub—everybody ran along the beach with plastic shovels to go and find it.

A few years later Kev put on a similar adventure for Mrs Macaroni and Mrs Magoo, who were still telling their mum all about it long after they returned home to Chicago, as TJ recalls. 'The kids were so excited. They were getting clues to go all over Perth, then they ended up back at Mum and Dad's house digging up Mum's new landscaped front garden to find a big wooden treasure box full of beads and crap jewellery and dollar-shop stuff. Dad was going to buy pirate and princess costumes for the girls to wear while they were on their treasure hunt but he forgot the costumes this time around so he improvised with a bunch of black DILLIGAF T-shirts that he cut up. The girls were wearing

DILLIGAF dresses and DILLIGAF bandanas. His American grandchildren in Kevin Bloody Wilson DILLIGAF attire? That would have made Dad proud.'

Kev is as proud of the pirate books he's written for his grandkids as he is any of his songs, although unlike his songs the books are G-rated. Well, mostly.

'*The Adventures of Deaf Captain Bungeye and His Two Buccaneers, Lefty and Righty* made interesting reading for the adults as well—for example, when they're in their little rowboat and they lose the oar, the line is "You can never find a good oar when you need one." I like the idea that they'll be able to come back to those books when they're thirty-five and appreciate them in a whole new way.

'The line that Search and Destroy liked in their pirate book was, "This weather is crap"—to a five year old, crap is such a great word. They actually learned to sight-read the book, as five year olds, and they'd only just started school so it was pretty good 'cos it probably helped them to learn how to read, although that was never the intention.'

Kev also wrote a book based on Mrs Macaroni and Mrs Magoo's adventure. *Macaroni & Magoo, the Fair Dinkum Fairy Princesses* was a big hit with the girls, and their mum loves it too. She explains, 'The book was chock full of Aussie slang, so on returning to America the girls took their copies to school for show and tell to spread the Aussie culture. They were a huge hit. Dad could totally be a children's author if he chose to. They will tell anyone that their Poppy is the funniest, best *Parpy* in the universe, and he's famous, 'cos he writes *books*!'

As well as organising adventures for his grandkids, Kev also loves throwing a party for his mates. Whether it's a get-together on a Friday afternoon in DILLIGAF HQ—Kev's bar in his Perth home—a spontaneous backstage bash after one of his live shows or an extravagant production complete with fireworks, like Kev's legendary sixtieth birthday party, this is a man who loves being around the people he loves.

Hosting a party for himself is one thing, but what really gets Kev excited is planning a party for someone in his family. Betty's sixtieth, for example, was a lavish Gangsters and Molls–themed affair, with fireworks on the beach supplied by Kev's good mate Mr Bling, a beautifully produced photo retrospective of Betty's life (compiled by TJ and using many of the photos featured in this book), and a performance by one of Betty's favourite singers, Kev's old mate Normie Rowe. Later in the evening a long and loud jam session kicked off.

However, the party to end all parties was the special Aussie wedding celebration Kev arranged for TJ and her husband, who Kev nicknamed Diamond. Kev shows off his exceptional diplomatic skills as he explains, 'TJ married a sepo, and sepo is an Australian World War II slang term. It's short for septic tank, which is rhyming slang for yank. But no, it still means septic tank 'cos mostly they're full of shit. But Diamond's a great bloke, TJ chose well.'

TJ recalls the lead-up to her and Diamond's actual wedding, which took place in 2002 in the groom's hometown of Chicago. 'I was thirty, and as far as I was concerned I was never getting married anyway. I didn't have visions of white frocks and bridesmaids or whatever. Diamond told me he'd love it if I wore white, so that was my compromise for him. I'd always imagined myself in some sort of punky red thing, but I wore white. I pretended I was saving myself for him.'

She may have worn white, but TJ didn't get too carried away with what she considered to be the less important aspects of planning her US wedding. 'I spent a hundred and fifty bucks on the wedding dress but the band cost ten grand. Priorities, you know?'

Kev and Betty flew over for the big day, but unfortunately Travis, who at this point had not even met Diamond in the flesh, couldn't make it. He had just started his pilot training with Qantas and couldn't get the time off. By Kevin Bloody Wilson standards, TJ and Diamond's Chicago nuptials were a fairly conventional affair, even though they were held in a hotel and not in a church. Both Kev and Betty gave TJ away and, as mums do, Betty cried all the way down the aisle.

A few of TJ's Australian and English friends jetted in for the big day, and they were joined by many friends she had made during her time living in Nashville. By all accounts the food was great, the band were worth every cent, and the guests had a terrific time. Two days after their Chicago wedding TJ and Diamond flew to Perth for an Aussie family get-together to welcome Diamond into his new Aussie family.

Although Kev had told the couple it would be just 'a little Aussie barbecue at the house', TJ had started to suspect there was something going on. 'Dad asked me if I would wear my white dress so my Nanna Pascoe could see it, and then Mum started talking about flowers. I told them to do whatever they wanted to do but not to go spending a shitload of money 'cos I knew from our Chicago wedding that it's all just a big blur anyway. Then Dad said, "I've got a little thing lined up," and straight away I'm like, "No! Whatever it is, you can't do it!" He said, "I told your mum and she said it's OK," and I relaxed a little bit because I knew Mum wouldn't let it be done if it was too overthe top.'

Kev hadn't been completley honest. 'I dunno if I was

exactly lying, I was just omitting some of the truth. I hadn't checked anything with Betty. I couldn't. I wanted it to be a surprise for her as well.'

TJ and Diamond flew into Perth on a Sunday, and hit the town that night for their respective hen's and buck's nights. For TJ, her hen's night was a great chance to reacquaint herself with her Aussie mates. Diamond's buck's night turned out to be a somewhat socially awkward affair, thanks in no small part to his new father-in-law. To this day, none of the men who were at that buck's night are prepared to talk about it, but here's an account from TJ of what allegedly took place.

'Diamond had never met Travis, and of course Dad got a really classy stripper who did a vegetable act. Diamond's thinking, "That's hard enough when you're around your own mates, but I'm very aware that all these people are meeting me for the first time." He wasn't worried about me 'cos he knows I don't give a shit, but he was terrified of fucking up in front of Travis. He didn't want to be looking at a stripper going, "She's hot!" and have my brother go, "Fuck you, pal, you just married my sister!" Diamond said it was very uncomfortable for him, but I'm sure it was fine for Trav. The hens and the bucks met up later on and Travis rocks up with a pocketful of vegetables, and right away I knew exactly where they were from.'

Two days later, still nursing his first proper Aussie hangover, Diamond was indoctrinated into the family in the most Australian way Kev could dream up. When he saw what unfolded that day, Diamond must have wondered what on earth he'd got himself into.

Longtime family friend Ray Green was roped in to run through the exact same vows Diamond and TJ had taken in

Chicago, and he played his part brilliantly. TJ had no idea what was coming next.

'Ray Green did the normal vows and then he said, "OK, Diamond! We've got that out of the way, now we're gonna do the Australian version! Would you please put this on." Then Ray, Diamond's dad and my dad and Travis all put on these outrageously colourful Mambo shirts.'

Diamond and TJ's Aussie vows were one hundred per cent pure Kev.

'TJ, if Diamond came home pissed as a fart, would you go into your grocery money and give him the last twenty bucks to pay for his taxi when he got home?'

'Diamond, would you give TJ your last Tim Tam?'

'TJ, if Diamond came home drunk and tapped you on the arse and said, "How 'bout it?", would you or wouldn't you?'

After each of the vows, rather than the usual 'I do', the response was a resounding, 'Bloody oath!'

Diamond found the experience a bit bamboozling, but TJ was having the time of her life. Little did she know that her dad had planned a much bigger surprise.

Midway through the Aussie vows, Ray Green suddenly stopped mid-sentence. He acted curiously nervous as he addressed the crowd. Kev did his best to stifle a grin as his old mate Ray stuck to the script Kev had written for this occasion.

'I'm not very good at this,' said Ray. 'I choked when Kev asked me to do it, but I agreed to do it as a mate. I have to be honest with you all, I don't think I'm really the most quali-fied person here for this job. Is there another, more qualified matchmaker here who can take over for me?'

And with that, the theme to the eighties Australian TV dating show *Perfect Match* filled the backyard. The congregation broke into spontaneous applause as former *Perfect Match* host Greg Evans strode down the red carpet. TJ couldn't believe her eyes.

'Greg Evans starts walking towards us, and I was whispering to Diamond, trying to let him know what was going on. I explained that *Perfect Match* was kind of the Australian version of *Love Connection*. I said, "This guy is like the Australian Chuck Woolery. He's huge over here."'

Greg Evans and Kevin Bloody Wilson already had a bit of history together. Greg had been an ardent Kev fan for many years before meeting him in person for the first time, as he recalls. 'I was working at 3AK, a talkback radio station in Melbourne doing the afternoon program, and my producer asked me if I would like to do an interview with Kevin Bloody Wilson because he was in town. I thought he wouldn't be able to put two words together without swearing, and my producer said she'd been assured by some bloke called Hollywood that he doesn't swear during interviews.

'The afternoon arrived and my producer said, "Kevin Bloody Wilson's here," and I looked out through the studio window and I saw this little bloke with curly hair and a beard, and I thought he looked like a nice guy. He bounced into the studio and he was just delightful. He was very amiable, pleasant, well-mannered and gracious. Butter wouldn't have melted in his mouth. We had a fantastic interview and we got on like a house on fire right from that particular moment, and we have been friends ever since.

'Every time I had the opportunity to go and see a Kev show I went, and at one of those shows my wife and I went backstage and Kev said to me, "My wife's a big fan of yours," and I said, "Jesus, really?" and he said, "Yeah, Betty and my daughter TJ used to watch *Perfect Match* every night, and they used to piss 'emselves laughing." He said Betty and TJ used to watch *Perfect Match* with a towel over the TV and they listened to everything that was said and then they'd both pick a number. Then they'd pull the towel off the telly and see who got the ugly one.

'So he said, "The reason I mentioned all this is that my daughter TJ is getting married. We're having a repeat service and reception at my home in Perth for all of her Australian friends. Would you consider, as a big favour to me, coming across to Perth and conducting the ceremony?" And I said, "Kev, it would be my bloody pleasure!"'

At the time Greg Evans was not a registered marriage celebrant, but given that TJ and Diamond had already been legally married in the United States he didn't need to be. 'I was smuggled in, and put up at Hollywood's place with my wife Sue, and then we went and saw the house, saw where the ceremony was going to be, but I had to be completely hidden. He wanted to surprise everyone, and they were well and truly surprised. Kev was delighted too, and the fake reverend himself, Ray Green, just stood there and had a bit of a chuckle.'

In typical Kevin Bloody Wilson style, he had gone out of his way to ensure that the big reveal would be as theatrical as possible. The big moment turned out to be every bit as memorable for Greg Evans as it was for the other guests. 'The look on TJ's face is something that I will never forget. She looked as though she had swallowed a baby grand piano sideways, fair dinkum. Kev had pulled it off, he had surprised not only his daughter and her new husband, but every single friend and family member who attended.'

TJ had already figured out that her dad was up to something, but this was beyond her wildest imaginings. 'We all went fuckin' nuts when Greg Evans showed up, and then Ray said, "Ladies and gentlemen, if you would all take your positions . . ." and we looked around and over a hundred people had put on bloody fishing hats with *TJ and Diamond: Perfect Match* embroidered on them. I just remember looking at all my girlfriends who had been to the hairdressers all morning going, "Arse-hole!" But then my mates who came from the bush, places like Collie and Kalgoorlie and Newman, they were all like, "Yeah! Right on, TJ! Fuckin' rippa!"'

Greg Evans took over and led them through the vows, much to the delight of the assembled guests. When the ceremony ended, says Greg, 'I got to kiss the bride, and then the mother of the bride came up and I got to kiss her as well, so we pulled it off you might say. And consequently that rolled straight into the reception, and I got to meet a lot of Kev's friends and we kicked on well and truly into the night with a beautiful wedding reception.'

As is usually the case with Kev's family gatherings, the instruments had been set up in a corner of the yard and the reception soon descended into a raucous jam session. The bride sang, the groom played blues harp, and the bride's brother played guitar. Travis smiled and surveyed the crowd as he played, still reeling from the surprise his dad had managed to pull off so perfectly. 'Dad didn't tell me about the Greg Evans thing in advance. It was just the best. It was just such a cool wedding, and Greg Evans was a really cool bloke to talk to as well. Dad just loves seeing his plans come off like that. He gets a genuine thrill out of it.'

Greg Evans's surprise appearance at TJ and Diamond's Aussie wedding celebration not only helped to further cement Kev and Greg's friendship, it was also the start of a new vocational direction for Greg. 'When I was standing there looking into TJ's eyes at that ceremony, something hit me like a bolt of lightning. It was the look in her eyes, and I felt this wonderful sense of being in the right spot at the right time. To be there at that warm and intimate moment of their life, to be a part of it, that's what being a marriage celebrant means to me.

'During the reception Kev said to me, "Mate, you're a natural at that, you should do more of it," and I said, "I've never thought of it." He said, "It's a natural follow-on to *Perfect Match*. Everyone in Australia loved ya doing *Perfect Match*, why wouldn't they want ya to marry 'em?" It made so much sense, and I thought, "Well, I might do that when I'm seventy."

'Then one day I was sitting next to someone at a function and I asked him what he did. The man's name was Dally Messenger III, and Dally told me he taught marriage celebrants. I said, "I'm gonna do that when I'm seventy," and he said, "No, you should do it now." Kev's words were ringing out in my ears, so I went and I did a course with Dally Messenger III in Melbourne, graduated and became a marriage celebrant.

'It's gone gangbusters. I'm getting emails from all over Australia and I cannot keep up with the amount of ceremonies I'm asked to do. So Kevin has not only touched my life but he's influenced my career as well.'

Kev loves being involved in planning a party for his friends, even when the circumstances behind the event are tragic, as Wayne Pride recalls. 'Martin Jenner came out to Australia in '89. He had been Cliff Richard's guitar player after Hank Marvin, and we all became friends with Martin. He was a great guitarist, in fact, he worked with Kev for four years managing and engineering his studios.

'Martin got very ill, he got cancer, and we knew he didn't have much chance but we tried to help him. Kev and I were the ones who virtually lived with him for the last eighteen months of his life. Martin wanted Kev to be the funeral director, in other words, take over all the arrangements for his funeral. Kev took me to lunch one day and he said, "Listen, Jock, I'm going away on tour in two weeks' time. I'm going to be gone for three months and Martin might not be here when I get back. Will you please be the funeral director for me?"'

Martin Jenner passed away while Kev was on that tour. His wake was held at Kev's offices and was overseen by Wayne Pride. Says Wayne, 'Martin loved Tim Tams. I used to take them every day to the hospital for him, so we had a big silver plate chock-a-block full of Tim Tams and we all got a Tim Tam as we entered the wake. Kev rang up on the day because he couldn't be there, and he spoke to almost every guest. It was sad, but Kev knew how to make us all feel good, even on such a sad day.'

CHAPTER 22

Disgraceland

'"Don't count the days, make the days count."I wish I had said that.'
Kevin Bloody Wilson

Whenever Kevin Bloody Wilson gets some time off he likes to head north from Perth to his beachside holiday shack in Lancelin, ninety minutes' drive away. Kev and Betty call it Disgraceland.

'Disgraceland is our retreat,' explains Kev. 'The phones are switched off and I like to get my mates together of a Friday arvo, get them drunk and pinch all their funny material.'

Lancelin is still a true Aussie country town in every sense of the word, and the Kev you see at Disgraceland is the most relaxed Kev you could ever hope to spend time with. This is also the place where songwriting inspiration is most likely to hit, as I found out when I spent a weekend there with Kev.

I am sitting on the front porch admiring the view when Kev suggests we jump on pushbikes and go for a ride around town. Kev and Betty both have pushbikes that they leave at Lancelin for this very purpose, and with Betty spending the day down in Perth I borrow her bike. (No streamers hanging from the handlebars—it is not, thankfully, *that* much of a girl's bike.) We ride around the corner for breakfast and discuss all sorts of random stuff over our bacon and egg rolls, like how Willie Nelson plays behind the beat, according to Kev.

'I went to see Willie Nelson live once and I spent the entire show sitting on the edge of my seat going, "Come on Willie, for fuck's sake, catch up!"'

Another topic that comes up over breakfast—and it's one that Kev talks about a lot—is his grandkids.

'An amazing thing happened on the weekend. Travis's young bloke, the one we call Destroy, he plays clarinet, and he's now into guitar and piano too. He's like Travis was, which is like I was. "Show me something else, Pop!" So I'd show him something and he'd spend the next half hour banging away on his little Maton guitar, then he'd come up again—"Can you show me something else?"

'Travis was trying to teach him the chords and timing for "Long Way to the Top", and being a clarinet player Destroy said, "Can you write it for me in tablature, Dad?" and Travis says, "Nope!" It's like Chet Atkins always used to say, it's OK to read music as long as it doesn't get in the way of your picking.'

Back on our bikes, and up the road we go to visit a couple of Kev's mates. Kev's brother Terry happens to drop in while we are there, and asks Kev what he got up to the night before. Kev replies, 'Me and Gav sat up drinking last night,' to which Terry shoots back, 'When are you gonna fucking grow up? Dad would be turning in his urn if he knew the sort of shit you get up to.'

Kev is club patron and one of the sponsors of the local Aussie rules team, the Lancelin Pirates, and they have a game today. After dropping off the bikes we drive to an oval on the southern side of town and grab a parking spot on the same side of the oval as the other Pirates supporters.

This is a real country footy game, the kind where you sound your car horn every time your side kicks a goal. And the Pirates kick plenty. Kev keeps asking me to sound his car horn whenever the Pirates score. There's a dog running around in the goal square for almost the entire game, and as people recognise Kev a crowd starts gathering around us. I mention to one of them how funny I think it is that this dog has been running around on the field.

'Yeah, that's the fuckin' umpire's dog . . .'

Gotta love a country footy game.

Kev tends to attract a crowd wherever he goes, especially in Lancelin where he is by far their most famous semi-regular resident and where everyone seems to know him personally. Most people are completely relaxed around Kev but there's one young guy at the footy wearing a very well worn Kevin Bloody Wilson T-shirt, and he starts visibly shaking when Kev notices his shirt, sticks his hand out and says g'day to him. 'Fuckin' awesome' are the only two words the lad can muster before he disappears back into the crowd. A lot of celebrities would not be so accommodating on a day off, and I asked Kev if he ever feels like just going, 'Not today, mate, fuck off.'

Kev looks slightly offended by my question. 'Never. It's not all that convenient sometimes but then it's not hard to shake somebody's hand and say g'day, is it?

'I remember one time I was takin' a piss at the footy and the bloke next to me at the urinal asked for an autograph so I told him, "You've got two choices, you can hold me cock while I find me pen or I'll piss me initials on your leg."'

The Lancelin Pirates have a resounding victory, and now it's time for their team song. I can't recall all of the words, but it's got a very memorable last couple of lines.

> *We're the Lancelin Pirates,*
> *And ya's can all go and get fucked.*

After the presentation ceremony, most of the crowd stick around for a beer and a sausage sandwich. Everyone is having a great time, right up until the moment a paddy wagon starts rolling down the hill towards us. Kev and I watch in amazement as two policemen (one of whom Kev would refer to as a Dickless Tracey) walk into the middle of the group and start asking people questions. After a couple of minutes the officers walk up to one of the opposition supporters and ask him to follow them to the paddy wagon and empty his pockets; they then frisk him in full view of the rest of the crowd, before throwing him in the paddy wagon.

Everyone has gone from relaxed and happy to edgy and disappointed—except for Kev, who can't help himself. A devilish grin spreads across his face and he starts singing.

> *'The local chef's a poofter*
> *The local doc's a drunk*
> *The local priest likes little boys' bums*
> *And the local cop's a cunt.'*

Kev turns to what's left of the crowd and goes for the big finish: *'What did I say?'*

The braver members of the crowd join in the chorus at full voice: 'The local cop's a cunt!'

Perhaps not surprisingly, with the cops standing about ten feet away, only a dozen or so of the locals felt like joining Kev in this singalong, but those that did, sang with vigor. Dickless Tracey and her male partner looked towards Kev and his choir, smiled and shook their heads, then, still smiling, departed with their prisoner in the paddy wagon.

A few hours later I'm part of a crew of Kev's mates hanging out on the verandah at Disgraceland watching the sun disappear into the ocean. It does so in its usual spectacular fashion as Kev makes sure everyone has a beer.

While Kev heads to the fridge I pick up a guitar he's left leaning against the wall—it's the one he calls Roadkill—and attempt to play Jimi Hendrix's 'Little Wing'. Kev returns with the beers and takes his guitar back out of my hands. 'Hey, Gav, how long have you been playing guitar ... roughly?'

By the time I get Kev's joke he's already sitting down with Roadkill and strumming away. 'Had an idea for a song.'

Kev moves forward in his seat and retunes his guitar. Nobody else even appears to notice what he's up to; they're used to seeing Kev in songwriting mode.

'Common sense ain't that common any more
Seems common sense is past tense
Just like the dinosaur
Political correctness has got a lot to answer for
'Cos common sense ain't that common any more.'

A few hours later the guys have stumbled home and Kev starts looking for his best songwriting pencil, the one with the eraser at the end. He picks up his guitar again, strums a few chords, then puts it back down and goes hunting for food. He finds a big bag of mixed lollies that Betty has left in one of the kitchen cupboards; it's as if he has just found a giant gold nugget buried in his backyard. Chewing on a red snake, Kev mumbles, 'I love that woman.'

Kev sits back down at the kitchen table and proceeds to write the next verse, stopping occasionally either to use his eraser or to grab another lolly. I sit drinking my beer in silence as Kev scribbles furiously all over the piece of paper in front of him. Once in a while he stops writing, grins to himself, and grabs another lolly. Eventually I tell Kev I'm going to call it a night.

'Righto then, goodnight … fuckin' piker.'

The next morning I awake to the smell of bacon and eggs. This can only mean one thing: Betty has arrived at Disgraceland. I head out to the kitchen, where Betty greets me with a big smile and a hot coffee, then I amble out onto the balcony to stare at the coast as I slowly wake up out of the haze created by the previous day's activities.

A few minutes later Kev emerges and squints at the sun. He gives Betty a kiss and a hug and grabs Roadkill. He looks excited. 'I finished that song, Gav. Whaddya think of this?'

Common Sense Ain't That Common Any More

Common sense ain't that common any more
Seems common sense is just past tense
Just like the dinosaur
Political correctness has got a lot to answer for
'Cos common sense ain't that common any more.

Political correctness, what a crock of shit
If it's political it ain't correct
Those two words don't fuckin' fit
Nor do military intelligence

Friendly fire or holy war
'Cos common sense ain't that common any more.

Words made up by academic fuckwits
Hidin' out in little fart-filled rooms
Throwin' random words together
'Cos they've got fuck-all else to do.
Starts out as yuppie jargon
Ends up fuckin' law
Common sense ain't that common any more.

Common sense ain't that common any more
Seems common sense is just past tense
Just like the dinosaur
Political correctness has got a lot to answer for
'Cos common sense ain't that common any more.

Words like illegal immigrant
Is that a fucked-up double or what?
If you're an immigrant, 'G'day and welcome'
If you're illegal, 'Fuck off!'
And who's them low-life toe-rags
Letting them sneak through our back door?
Common sense ain't that common any more.

'N 'racist!' There's one overused word
That's laced with toxic venom
Spat out by every do-gooder and minority group
When you don't agree with 'em
Mate . . . this is Australia
One size fits all
But common sense ain't that common any more.

Common sense ain't that common any more
Seems common sense is just past tense
Just like the dinosaur
Political correctness has got a lot to answer for
'Cos common sense ain't that common any more.

'Petty crime', there's no such thing
Some poor bastard's left to pay
Here's two words that just might work:
'Rattan cane'.
We don't need a fuckin' police service
Bring back the police force
'Cos common sense ain't that common any more.

So all you soft-cock politicians
Try gettin' your head around this
You're fuckin' up a great country
And we're sick of that PC shit
Try using a bit more common sense
That's what we're paying you for
'Cos common sense ain't that common any more.

(Repeat chorus as Betty serves breakfast.)

Just like me at Disgraceland, Kev's friends and family continue to be blown away by the speed with which he can turn a raw idea into a song. During her days traveling around Australia as Kev's tour manager, Sue 'Cactus' Maloney witnessed the birth of many of Kev's most famous songs. 'You'd be in the car driving somewhere and you'd see a funny road sign or something comes on the radio or you're just talking and something funny happens and then the next day he comes back and says, "Listen to this," and half a song is done.'

Another mate who has seen Kev's songwriting process in action on more than one occasion is Wayne 'Jock' Pride. Says Wayne, 'I'd be driving in my car or I'd be at home and I'd get a phone call and he'd say, "Listen to this, Jock," and he'd sing something he'd just written. As usual I'd think, "How's that gonna work?" but they all ended up being little gems. Someone will say something and it will hit a chord with him and he'll put it in the memory bank. Then he'll go home and straight away he'll write a song out of a phrase someone said to him, some funny line, or just something that brings back a memory to him, and he'll do that in no time at all.'

Kev can pull songwriting inspiration from just about any situation, good or bad. Unfortunately for General Motors Holden, they found themselves on the wrong end of Kev's songwriting pencil in 2003 when they dragged their feet delivering the new Commodore Kev had ordered. Kev recalls, 'They told me they'd have my new car ready in three weeks and it took three fuckin' months. All they had to do was change the factory model's interior to blue leather as opposed to grey leather, everything else was fine. It was a standard fitting for them, it wasn't even like blue was a colour they had to make specially.'

Kev vented his frustration with a reworked version of 'Hey Santa Claus'.

Hey GMH

Little while back I got thinking; don't use the ute much any more

Should retire the old girl gracefully, I'd look beaut in a
    new Commodore
They told me it'd take three weeks, three weeks, pig's
    fuckin' arse
'Cos as soon as I signed the dotted line, the fuckin'
    bullshit started.

Hey GMH you cunts, where's me fuckin' car?
You told me it'd take three weeks, it's been three fuckin'
    months so far
I could've crocheted a fuckin' Commodore by the time
    you cunts got started
GMH you cunts, where's me fuckin' car?

If I'd wanted to listen to bullshit I would've played one
    of me own CDs
And I could've fertilised the fuckin' Nullarbor with the
    crap you fed to me
And as far as fuckin' excuses, mate, I'm a married
    drunk
I tell lies for a livin', so don't practise on me ya cunts.

Hey GMH you cunts, where's me fuckin' car?
You told me it'd take three weeks, it's been three fuckin'
    months so far
I could've crocheted a fuckin' Commodore by the time
    you cunts got started
GMH you cunts, where's me fuckin' car?

Next time I come to see you, I'm gonna bring me
    mongrel kids
And let'm loose in your fuckin' showroom while I drink

ya fuckin' piss
And when the cops come 'n round up my mob and sling
us out the fuckin' door
I'll go and do what I should've done, I'll go and buy a
fuckin' Ford.

Not happy mate.

Hey GMH you cunts, where's me fuckin' car?
You told me it'd take three weeks, it's been three fuckin'
months so far
I could've crocheted a fuckin' Commodore by the time
you cunts got off your arse
GMH you cunts, where's me fuckin' car?

Kev wrote 'Hey GMH' on a Friday night and recorded it in his home studio over the weekend. On the Monday he stormed into his Holden dealership with a CD copy of the song and threw it on his dealer's desk. He said, 'I want you to listen to this song, and if you cunts don't deliver my car by this Friday I'm taking this song and I'm gonna give it to the people at Ford.'

Kev took delivery of his new Commodore the next afternoon.

CHAPTER 23

Ups and downs and demons

'The first time I smoked dope I was thirty-five, and two years later I was Kevin Bloody Wilson. Coincidence? I don't remember . . .'

Kevin Bloody Wilson

Kevin Bloody Wilson has had his fair share of ups and downs. He has occasionally battled depression, and he freely admits that smoking dope hasn't helped him in that respect. He says, 'I eventually worked out that marijuana is a very toxic thing if you do too much of it, so I don't smoke the stuff at all any more. Don't worry, I already smoked my fair fuckin' share of the shit over the years, believe me, but I'm finished with it now. I would never judge anyone else who likes a choof, fuckin' good on 'em, but for me it just became really obvious that it wasn't making me happy.'

Even before he gave it up Kev rarely smoked dope on the road—as with his beer cans filled with Coke, he likes to be as sharp as possible for each live show. The same cannot be said for Kev's crews over the years as Kev's tour manager, Hollywood, recalls. 'After the show we'd go back to the hotel and be in what we called the roadies' sauna. You couldn't see anybody for the marijuana smoke. I've never had a cigarette in my life, let alone marijuana, and of course just inhaling it would make me as high as a kite.'

Kev's brother Terry used to be astounded by how much wacky weed Kev was able to put away himself, and how much of it he gave away to his mates. 'When he had people coming over he used to roll them all up in advance. I used to tell people that going around to his place was like running into a Rothmans rep, he'd always have a pocketful of his special cigarettes to give you. He always had half a dozen in his pocket, so he'd light up one and you'd be expected to light one up too. I used to say to him, "Why don't you just have a bong? It's a better way to smoke it instead of rolling them up all the time." I mean, he'd go through an ounce in a week, easy. At one stage, my kids nicknamed him Kevin Bloody Marley.'

Indeed, at the height of his dope-smoking days, Kev could churn through a bag of buds faster than Bob Marley. Betty doesn't mince her words when she talks about Kev's marijuana consumption. 'I hate the stuff, to be honest. Being a sportsperson, the idea of smoking anything doesn't sit well with me. Back in the early days he'd share a joint with his brother, but then he started rolling his own with tobacco, and of course as an ex-smoker he became addicted to tobacco again. Then he started smoking it a lot and just lost all of his motivation, and I hated seeing him like that because that's not who he is, he's always been so motivated. Frankly, he became useless when he was smoking dope.'

Marijuana and decision-making are sometimes not the best of friends. It was during the height of Kev's purple haze period that he stopped touring and recording for a couple of years after being distracted, as pot smokers tend to be, by something new and shiny: the Internet.

When Kevin Bloody Wilson launched his first website in 1993 it was still considered something of a geek novelty by most people. 'Back then it was really only for the nerds, and we used to get emails from the nerds all the time saying, *Please remove this commercial site off the Internet. The Internet is not designed for commercial enterprise.*'

Kev was way ahead of the pack when it came to this new technology, but like a lot of early adopters he ended up getting carried away.

During the nineties lots of people with simple but clever ideas made their fortune by designing and running a successful website, and then selling it to some other sucker for millions of dollars. If you had even a half decent idea attracting investors wasn't too hard, and soon every entrepreneur in town wanted a piece of the action. The bubble finally burst with the worldwide tech crash in 2000, but Kev's own personal tech crash happened a couple of years before that when he came up with his own clever idea.

Worldwide FM was to be a network of online radio stations designed for specific businesses to use in their work areas or retail spaces. The audio feed would run that company's commercials, and the music would be picked to suit the company's demographic. All of the music would be stored on servers at Kev's studios and streamed directly into stores via the world wide web. Brilliant, right?

It certainly seemed like a pretty decent idea to Kev, who invested heavily in this new venture. 'I personally chose the names of all the radio stations, like Golf FM, Footy FM, we even had West Coast Eagles FM and McDonald's FM. First we researched the company, then we went to them and told them that this is the music that suited their specific demographic and they could be playing it in their store or workplace.' He'd seen his own website generate quite a lot of cash, so he saw no reason why Worldwide FM wouldn't work too. At the time Kev knew or had heard of plenty of people who were enjoying initial success with their own online ventures, and he wanted to get in on the action. 'In retrospect I saw every one of them do their arse. Every one of them.' He'd hoped to see his money turn into much more money. Instead, within eighteen months Kev saw everything almost turn to dust.

It may have been a great idea that was years ahead of its time, but Worldwide FM was always going to be a tough sell. One of the fundamental problems entrepreneurs such as Kev faced in the late nineties was that most of the ideas were designed with broadband in mind, and most people were still using dial-up Internet. 'We were at the cutting edge of technology, but like a lot of people at that time we got so close to the edge that we fell off a cliff. A very tall cliff.'

And while Kev was spending the vast majority of his time in his office doing whatever he could think of to make his little dot.com profitable, he wasn't spending any of his time writing new songs or touring. He was also smoking more pot than ever before. The situation was not only harming Kev's career, it was also having a drastic effect on his mental health.

'I just couldn't face going downstairs to the office 'cos it was just too fuckin' hard. One of the worst days was when the accountant rang and said, "You're going to have to close it down, you can't keep pouring money into it." I was in a depressive heap, a spent force, full-on fully fucked.'

The empire Kevin Bloody Wilson had built from nothing

in the early eighties seemed to be turning right back into nothing as he finally gave up on his dot.com dream and put WWFM into voluntary liquidation. It was either that, or he'd have faced the prospect of losing his home.

Kev then got to work on putting together what he considered to be his comeback tour. The punters weren't even aware that he'd been away; they showed up in droves, laughed their arses off, and before long Kev's Internet debts were erased and forgotten about. Kev went back to focusing on and maintaining just his own website—'Only this time it was in a fresh and revitalised smoke-free zone.'

If you haven't been to kevinbloodywilson.com you should put down this book and take a look right now. It's grown to be a bloody great website, and it's also the hub of Kev's business. Kev's fans love it, and Kev loves using it to communicate directly with his fans.

As Kev says, 'The three things that drive the Internet, as most people who use it are aware, are, in order, sex, music and comedy. My site has all of that.' Log on at any time and you are guaranteed to see, at the very least, breasts. It's all part of the service Kev provides, to his fans and to himself. 'It's the women themselves who send in some extremely candid photos of themselves. That's one of the joys of this hobby. Of a morning I wake up and go into my office, and I log on to the Internet and there we have some naked ladies, some funny stories and people telling me how fuckin' wonderful I am—not a bad way to start the day.'

The Internet has also proved to be a useful vehicle for Kev to share brand-new songs with his fans. He writes so many that he sometimes ends up with a few spares he can share for free. In 2003 Kev wrote a lament for Aussie cricketing legend and notorious pants-man Shane Warne. It was called 'The Shane Warne Song', and the lyrics contained some timely advice for Shane.

The Shane Warne Song

A cricketing legend, all-Australian boy
A real blokes' bloke 'n we all loved him for it
But he's gotta zipper problem
'N it's affecting his game.
So Warnie, put your wanger away.

Warne put your wanger away
That pecker's gonna get you into trouble one day
You stick to the cricket, I'll do the rootin' for Australia
Warnie, put your wanger away ... maaate
Warnie, put your wanger away.

Caught out drinking 'n smokin' 'n drugs ... maaate
I'll take care of alla that, you just get on with the game
And keep it in the crease where it's supposed to be
And give them 'dirty bird' numbers to me mates and me.
Maaate!
They asked five hundred sheilas if they'd sleep with you,
    Shane
But over seventy-five per cent of 'em said, 'Never again.'
So take a tip from Russell Crowe and do what he asks
And stick that fuckin' phone up ya fuckin' arse.

So keep your cock in its box is what I'm tryin' to say
And stay away from pommy sheilas like that Paula
    Yates
She started the trend now it seems to be catchin'
Poms fuckin' the Aussies and keepin' the Ashes.

Kev posted the song for free on his website and within days tens of thousands of fans had downloaded it.

'I didn't think when I wrote the song that it would make the next album because I thought the whole Warnie sex scandal thing would blow over, so to speak, but it didn't. Warnie kept on fuckin' 'em quicker than they could pull 'em out from underneath him. I thought Warney's escapades would be a one-off, but he turned out to be a serial shagger, so I finally stuck the song on an album.'

Kev's not a guy who spends a lot of time dwelling on his past failures. During one of the many interviews I conducted with Kev for this book, I asked him if he regretted doing so much of his dough on his little Internet venture back in the nineties. He looked me right in the eye for a couple of seconds, a deadly serious expression lurking under his beard, as he carefully considered his answer.

'Honestly, Gav? DILLIGAF.'

As you'll have noticed, this is an expression Kev uses a lot. It helps to remind Kev not to take the world or himself too seriously. For Kev, DILLIGAF is more than an acronym, it's a lifestyle. As Kev metioned in the foreword, Betty even got him a DILLIGAF tattoo on his left wrist for his sixty-third birthday.

'People often ask if it hurt. Fucked if I know, I passed out. I was gonna get the entire "Do I look like I give a fuck" tattooed on my donger, but at my age, even on a good day, all you would be able to read is DILL.'

Before we decided to name this book *DILLIGAF*, I originally thought it should be called *Kevin Bloody Wilson for Dummies* (an idea that was quickly dropped for obvious legal reasons). Kev originally wanted to call it *Cock on the Block,* because that's exactly how he feels about his life. As he explains, 'cock on the block' is 'a fairly well used Australian expression that indicates that you are prepared to back yourself, your ideas and your decisions. Greg Taylor, a good mate of mine and the talented graphic artist and cartoonist responsible for all of my album covers and posters, even drew a mock-up cover for the book featuring his unique cartoon caricature of me dressed in a butcher's apron with a shit-eating grin on my face and wielding a meat cleaver over the extended neck of a soon-to-be-dispatched rooster.'

Fan or not, you have to admit there is a certain amount of bravery involved in standing on stage and doing the kind of material that Kev does. Figuratively speaking, Kev does indeed put his cock on the block every time he performs. Kev knows damn well that he's going to push people's buttons every time he does a gig—and he is also well aware that if he didn't push those buttons there wouldn't even *be* a gig in the first place.

In interviews, Kev often gets asked if he perceives himself as a racist, and his standard response is usually something along the lines of, 'It's comedy, you fuckwit! What makes something racist is malice, and there is absolutely zero malice in what I do. It's parody, pure and simple, and the Indigenous crowds get that. Hitler was a racist. I'm a fuckin' comedian for fuck's sake.

'As a young bloke in Kalgoorlie one of my best mates was a bloke called Nigel Prior—he's still a great mate. At one stage Nige and I played in a band together. Nigel was born on a cattle station just outside of Alice Springs. He told me that his tribal name was Nunga-nunga-stein, half Aboriginal and half Jewish. He claims that his family ran a whole chain of empty stores. That's fuckin' funny shit. The best Aboriginal jokes I've ever heard, I got from Nigel. Fuckin' legend. While he now lives in Adelaide with his second wife, Jen, his stories are always included in my shows. The audiences love them and have elevated Nigel to fuckin' legendary status.'

Nigel, Fuckin' Legend

Nige and I been mates all our lives
Even played in the same band
Best gig we ever got was at a country pub
One Easter long weekend
But better than that, the wives were invited
And we all had double rooms
Bit a quality time for the boys and the brides
Like a second honeymoon.

So we set up the band while the girls got settled
While we done a final sound check
Then we ran upstairs for a peck and a promise
Then we ran back down again
'Cos the pub was pumpin' and the band kicked arse
So me and Nige got on the piss
With a guaranteed root waitin' upstairs
Life don't get better than this.

Then after the gig we had a few more beers
And we played a few rounds of pool
We were both pretty pissed when we give it a miss
I lost twenty, Nige beat me by two.
Then he said, 'Kev, I'll make you a bet
Double or nothin' will do

I'll bet you that twenty when we get upstairs
That I get more roots than you.'

So we both stumbled upstairs and then shook hands
And wished each other good luck
Knowin' full well that the competition's on
And tomorrow we'd be tallyin' fucks.
I could hardly wait to get the key in the door
'Cos the missus was waitin' there too
Spread out on the bed in a negligee:
'Come here, Rambo, I've been waitin' for you.'

Well, number one was fun for the missus 'n me
Got up to stuff we hadn't done in years
So I marked it on the wall with a piece of chalk
That I found behind me ear.
Then I must've dozed off 'cos when I looked at the
    clock
By the bed it said a quarter past two
So I give her a nudge 'n said, 'You awake, love?'
… No response … thank you … number two!

I must've rolled off drunk 'cos when I woke up
I woke up with a huge piss-horn
But before I could go the missus had him by the throat:
'Rambo want some more?'
So she dragged me to the shower, took another half
    hour
But I didn't mind at all
Lay back on the bed, thought, 'Good onya, Kev'
As I marked a third stroke on the wall.

I was layin' back again, a contented man
Just thinkin' about my good luck
With the missus whisperin' in me ear,
'Rambo want another fuck?'
When all hell broke loose, there was bangin' and
    smashin'
And you'd never guess who crashed through the door
Pumped full of Viagra, frothin' at the mouth,
Dick dribblin' all over the floor.

He left a snail trail as he crawled to me bed
And looked up at the marks I'd made
Then he shook me hand and gave me a hug
And a big ole 'Maaaaaaaaaate!'
Then he stood up straight, dick danglin' in my face
And saluted to the lines I drew
'Fuckin' hell, Kevin, a hundred and eleven,
You beat me by two!'

Even those who Kev offends have to admit that he is an equal opportunity offender. 'I sometimes get accused of being homophobic too, but again humour is all about contrast and whether it's poofs or Aborigines or poms, Muslims, Catholic or whatever, it's always set within a humorous scenario. Have these politically correct types ever noticed that I take the piss out of myself as well? Actually, the youngest of my two adopted brothers was gay. I'd left home by the time he was a teenager, and my brother Terry and I had spotted from a very early age that he was gay, but that's cool. We didn't treat Stephen any differently because of it. We still took the piss out of him at every opportunity. As he did with us.

'My brother Stephen died of AIDS in 1990. He was only twenty-eight, which—like Stephen himself—was a bit of a bummer. It must run in the family or something, 'cos I get outback AIDS all the time—Alcohol Induced Dizzy Spells.'

Is there *anything* that's off limits?

'But Gav, that's what humour is all about. Orson Welles said, "Humour is tragedy given time." It's about contrast and laughing at shit you shouldn't be laughin' at. That's where proper belly laughs come from. Australians have a unique and irreverent sense of humour that probably stems from our convict ancestry, by makin' humour out of a bad situation. When things fuck up in the world, the rest of the world goes into mourning. Not us; we rip open a can of piss and start makin' up fuckin' jokes about it. For instance, how many text messages did you get when Michael Jackson fell off the perch? And how many did you forward on to your friends? We all did. When the Boxing Day tsunami hit, I got a text message from a mate tellin' me that the Bells Classic surf competition in Victoria had been won by an Indonesian on a wardrobe.'

Just because you paid for a ticket to a Kevin Bloody Wilson concert that doesn't necessarily mean you got the joke, as Hollywood has discovered over his ten years as Kev's tour manager. He says, 'I've had about three occasions in the last ten years where people have stood up and walked out in the middle of one of Kev's shows. They've gone up to the venue management on their way out the door and said, "He's a racist pig, I'm out of here!" We don't even bother telling Kev when that happens; three out of hundreds of thousands is not worth telling him about—not that he'd give a fuck anyway. As far as we're concerned they should have known what to expect, so why the fuck did they come to the show in the first place? Kev's whole act is very obviously tongue in cheek so really nobody should be taking it too seriously. There's no malice at all.'

I ask Kev's brother Terry if he thinks Kev is a racist, and there is a three-second pause as he carefully considers his answer.

'No, I honestly don't think he is. I mean, he's no more racist than anybody else, and at least he can joke about it. The real racists can't even joke about it. And when you think about it, a song like "Livin' Next Door to Alan", who is that song really taking the piss out of? Look at the words. The Aborigines in that song are a hell of a lot smarter than Bondy. Alan Bond had everything but the Aborigines had everything he had and even better, so they're doing all right out of it in that song.'

What about TJ, aka Jenny Talia from Australia? As a performer who says some fairly controversial things herself, where does she stand on the issue of racism as it pertains to her father?

'The idea of being thought of as a racist doesn't bother him at all. He knows he's not. That's another one he files under DILLIGAF. I don't think he is, but he says a lot of stuff that could be construed as racist, sexist, homophobic, all of that. But he's a comedian, so he's going to take whatever that is and use it. So if you push in front of him in the line at the shops and you've got a burka on, then you're gonna be that fuckin' Muslim sheila that pushed in front of him at Woolies. And if you're three hundred kilos and you do the same thing, you're gonna be the big fat fuckin' moll that pushed in front of him. There's always going to be a description of some sort.

'You're thinking it, and he's saying it, and there's a little pang of guilt from laughing at it. But there's always going to be people who are mortified by what he says, but really that all came from calling Santa a cunt twenty-five years ago. There was such shock value to that song when it came out, and some people have just never gotten over it.'

On stage, Kevin Bloody Wilson does not care who he offends, but off stage Kev lives by a slightly different set of rules: simple common sense.

'If Betty and I are going out to a nice restaurant one night and they had a piano player in the corner and the mood was just right for a romantic dinner and then he started into one of my songs, I'd be the first bloke to go and have a chat to him about it, because it's inappropriate for the situation.'

I asked Kev if his kids used to look at him strangely when he told them not to swear at home, considering what their dad did for a living.

'I didn't swear around the kids when they were little. Again, it comes back to common sense with swearing. If I gave them any instructions at all on it, I would have told them to be careful where they use it. Tammy reckons we used to have a swear jar at home and every time she said "fuck" she got to take a dollar out. She tells people she had her first car when she was twelve. That's not quite true ... she was nine.'

CHAPTER 24

Mates and fans

'I love Kev. My favourite is "Livin' Next Door to Alan".'
Paul Hogan

Kev enjoys connecting with his fans and goes out of his way to do it as often as he can, but who or what is a typical Kevin Bloody Wilson fan? Is there even such a thing? Just who are these people who fill concert halls and theatres worldwide and have propelled his CD and DVD sales to almost four million units globally?

Over the years I have been mates with Kev I have been to many shows all over Australia, and two things have become abundantly clear: he never performs the same show twice, and there is no such thing as a typical Kevin Bloody Wilson fan. For a start, the usual age demographics simply don't seem to apply; Kev fans are aged anywhere between eight and eighty. (He does however apply a self-imposed over-eighteens rule for his live concerts.)

Betty points out that it is now a nightly occurrence to find three generations of the same family coming to his concerts.

'It's not just the menfolk of the family either. I've seen situations where you've got the grandma, the daughter and the granddaughter all jockeying for front-row seats alongside bikies, accountants, blue-collar workers and career professionals. They all love him and they all totally get what he does.'

Although Kev's humour may be considered fairly blokey, just over forty per cent of the fans who buy tickets to the gigs are female. It would seem fair then to suggest that maybe—at least figuratively speaking—there is a little bit of Kev in all of us.

There is also no such thing as a typical Kev venue, as he seems to glide seamlessly from the most prestigious world theatres to the remotest outback pubs. He loves the contrast, and to him the size of the venue matters little. 'Some venues hold more mates than others, but all audiences are equally important. You know what they say, Gav, "Size really doesn't matter".'

Kev is constantly surprised to find out about some of his more famous fans. Back in the days when flash new cars still had cassette players in them, legendary Australian media magnate Kerry Packer was said to rarely have anything other than a Kevin Bloody Wilson cassette in his car.

In December 2006, when Australia was in the process of reclaiming the Ashes, about half of the Aussie cricket team came directly from that day's play at the WACA to see Kev's show at the Burswood Theatre in Perth. (For the record, our boys went on to beat England five–nil in that Ashes series.)

Kev has famous fans from all walks of life, but there is one English fan that Kev was particularly surprised and delighted to find out about. He remembers, 'We were in a place called Usk in Wales on our second or third UK tour. At the end of the night I noticed that there were about six or seven blokes in suits that hung back after I'd finished doing the signing. I'd picked them as coppers. I was right. I thought, "Surely they're not gonna arrest me?" One of them came over to me and told me he was a Kiwi working with the special branch in the UK. He said to me, "I heard your stuff for the first time about three weeks ago. I was moving the boss's car and the first thing I heard when I started it were the words 'Stick that fuckin' phone up your fuckin' arse'." He said he thought it sounded like a Kiwi or an Aussie so he rummaged through the glovebox and there were two cassettes, both Kevin Bloody Wilson albums. He then went on to reveal, "You might be surprised to learn that my boss is the Prince of Wales, Prince Charles," and the other special branch officers who were with him confirmed it. It made sense to me because I knew that Charles and Billy Connolly were good mates. They used to fax jokes to each other a lot.

When Australian sports teams head overseas a Kevin Bloody Wilson album is often packed as a ready piece of Australiana for when the homesickness kicks in. Aussie tennis star and renowned larrikin Lleyton Hewitt was involved in a Kevin Bloody Wilson–related incident that threatened to wreck his career before it even started.

Lleyton first became exposed to Kevin Bloody Wilson's music when he was on tour in Holland as part of the Aussie under-fourteen squad. One of the other up-and-coming young players at the time was Nathan Healy, who later became Lleyton's coach. The boys apparently played Kev's tapes as party starters in their dressing rooms and hotel rooms after the matches. A couple of years later Lleyton

Hewitt and Nathan Healy were orange boys at White City, where Australia ended up beating France three–nil in a Davis Cup tie. A corporate evening was organised for the sponsors of the team and, following the tradition established by Aussie tennis elders John Newcombe and Tony Roach, the orange boys were asked to get on stage and sing a song to entertain the sponsors.

Lleyton was fifteen; Nathan was sixteen. Without checking their song choice with anyone they both strode up to the microphone and tore straight into Kevin Bloody Wilson's 'Dick'taphone', much to the chagrin of the Australian tennis officials in the room. To Lleyton and Nathan's credit, at first they had the presence of mind to adjust Kev's lyrics slightly, singing, 'Well, you can stick that bloody phone up your bloody arse.'

At least some of the sponsors looked like they were getting the joke, so Lleyton and Nathan relaxed into their performance. Actually, they relaxed a little too much. By the time they got to the second chorus they forgot all about taming down the lyrics, and sang the original version: 'Well, you can stick that fuckin' phone up your fuckin' arse.' Legend has it that at the end of the song, those who hadn't passed out stood up and applauded.

When Kev heard this story it immediately elevated Lleyton and Nathan to legend status in his mind, and he's remained in contact with our Davis Cup squads ever since. The team even came up with a nickname for Kev: they call him Australia's tennis court jester.

Another of Kev's mates from the world of tennis is Patrick Rafter, who once famously said, 'Kevin Bloody Wilson albums to Aussies are like American Express cards to Americans: you never leave home without one.'

Todd Woodbridge is another former Aussie tennis ace who calls himself a Kev fan. One night, after Kev had performed at a Davis Cup team function, Todd came up and asked him to sign a CD. Kev recalls, 'He said to me, "I've already got this album, I'm on your mailing list. But could you sign this for my neighbour in Florida, 'cos he won't give me my copy back." I said, "Who's your neighbour?" and he said, "Tiger Woods. Fair dinkum, Kev, he loves it. He won't give my copy back." So I signed it and said to Todd, "You tell Tiger he fuckin' owes me!" A matter of months later I was at the Davis Cup in Melbourne and Todd spotted me sitting with the rest of the Australian supporters. He came up to me and said, "I've got something for you," and it was a golf glove signed by Tiger. How's that? My very own autograph from, as it turns out, the world's most infamous intercourse champion. I wouldn't mind betting there's five different kinds of fuckin' DNA on that glove. I also find it hard to work out why the Americans are so worked up over a few little indiscretions. Poor ole Tige, all he did was root a few sheilas on the side and forgot to tell his missus about it. That's the sort of quality I *look for* in my mates.'

Kevin Bloody Wilson fans are scattered all over the globe, and sometimes even under it. In late April and early May 2006 just about everyone in Australia was transfixed by the plight of Tasmanian gold miners Brant Webb and Todd Russell, who were trapped almost a kilometre underground for fourteen days after a massive rock fall took place in the Beaconsfield mine they were working in. Tragically, their mate and coworker Larry Knight didn't make it.

During those two weeks, as the rescue crew worked their way through the wall of solid rock to save the miners, they managed to get a small pipe through to the tiny steel cage that had become Brant and Todd's makeshift residence. The pipe was used to get food and medical supplies down to the boys to sustain them while they waited to be rescued.

Almost every media outlet in Australia was stationed in Beaconsfield for a couple of weeks while the drama played out. Veteran reporter Richard Carleton, who was covering the story for the Australian *60 Minutes* program, had a fatal heart attack at the mine site shortly after interviewing the mine's manager.

Voice communication had been established fairly early on between the rescue crew and the trapped miners, and one of the first things Brant and Todd asked for to keep their spirits up was an iPod with some Foo Fighters and Kevin Bloody Wilson music on it. The request was very quickly fulfilled, and as soon as Kev found out he had a couple of fans deep below the Beaconsfield earth he sent them a handwritten note: 'ARE YOU CUNTS AWARE THAT YOU KILLED RICHARD CARLETON?' Kev went on to explain how, as average Australians, we were all thinking of them, and asked if he could catch up with them for a beer and a bit of a chat once they got back to the surface and things settled down.

Brant and Todd's plight had particular significance for Kev; as an ex-miner himself, Kev has mentioned to me on more than one occasion that being trapped underground is one of his greatest fears. He was delighted to see them successfully rescued; he was also pleased when, in the days immediately after the rescue—at a time when just about everyone in the Australia media was throwing vast quantities of cash at Brant and Todd in return for an interview—Brant took the time to leave a message on Kev's answering machine: 'Yeah, listen, Brant Webb here. I'd like to thank Kev and everyone there for your letter of support.

It was just great. And we'd like to thank you for all the gear you sent us. I'm sure we've had hours of laughing, and that's about what we need at this stage. So listen, thanks a lot from Brant and the family and hopefully we'll see you soon. Catch ya later.'

Kev and Todd Russell have since caught up for a beer, on several occasions, on both sides of the continent. Whenever they sit down together, there is a particular aspect of Todd's story that always fascinates Kev. 'I still can't believe Todd didn't have a shit for the whole time he was down there. I'm glad I was out of range of the poor bastard when he squeezed that first turd out. The back pressure on that one would've killed a fuckin' rhino.'

Another famous Aussie who is proud to call himself a Kev fan is the Screaming Jets' lead singer Dave Gleeson. Like most people, he will never forget the first time he heard Kev's music.

'I was a bit of a late bloomer, I guess. It must have been about 1986 and I was up in Forster on the New South Wales coast for holidays. I had this mate whose father used to let us hang out in his caravan and drink beer and stuff, and we listened to the outrageous lyrics of Kevin Bloody Wilson and we laughed and laughed. I mean, "Santa Claus you cunt, where's me fuckin' bike"—that lyric just speaks volumes to me.'

The Screaming Jets scored their first big hit in 1991 with 'Better' from the album *All for One*. If you listen to track ten on that album, Kevin Bloody Wilson's influence on the Screaming Jets suddenly becomes very obvious. The song in question is called 'F.R.C. (Fat Rich Cunts)', and the crowd goes ape whenever they play it live. Says Dave, 'Prior to the Screaming Jets putting out "Fat Rich Cunts", as far as I knew there was only one other person who had used the word "cunt" in a song, and said it with such vim and vigour, and that was Kevin Bloody Wilson. There was so much trouble from the record company over "Fat Rich Cunts" and I just fuckin' stood by it. The song, really, in the grand scheme of things, probably didn't need the chant of people singing "Fat rich cunts" in the middle of it, but nobody was going to tell me we couldn't have cunts in that song.'

Kev's also helped a lot of other musicians. While working in Musgroves Music store during his early days in Kalgoorlie, Kev met and befriended fellow musician and 'eastern stater' Peter Dee. Peter and his friend Kim Baker had just crossed the Nullarbor from Melbourne and decided to drop anchor in Kalgoorlie. After washing off, and washing down, the dust, they headed stright to the local music store to get a fix on the live gig scene in the area. After talking and jamming with them both in the store, Kev made a few phone calls and secured them their first job. That same night, Peter and Kim started as the resident band at the notorious 'starting stalls' brothel in Kalgoorlie's infamous Hay Street.

Peter Dee was a natural comedian, and after watching one of his hilarious performances at a shared gig at the Boulder Town Hall, Kev asked Peter, 'How do you get the balls to get up there and do that sorta stuff?' Peter remembers, 'Kev asking me that. I just wish I could fucking remember what it was that I told him.'

'Pete and I share a lot in common,' Kev says, 'except Pete's a great guitarist, a fantastic vocalist and the funniest bastard on the planet. When I grow up I wanna be just like him.'

*

When Kev won his ARIA in 1987 for *Kev's Back (The Return of the Yobbo)*, it was presented to him by Elton John with the words 'My mother loves you!' Elton was not kidding, as Kev's (and Elton's) former tour manager Sue 'Cactus' Maloney reveals.

'It was '86 when Elton's tour with the Melbourne Symphony Orchestra happened and Elton's mother, Sheila, was in Sydney. She decided that she wanted to go and see Kevin Bloody Wilson's show, 'cos Kevin's tapes and CDs had kinda gone through the band and the crew and everybody. So one night when Kevin was doing a show at the Balmain Leagues Club, I took Sheila and about five other people from Elton's entourage via limo and we turned up at Kevin's show. Sheila laughed like crazy. She absolutely loved it. They stayed the whole show, and Kevin didn't know they were there until the end of the night. Then Kevin came back to the Sebel Townhouse after his gig and there was a big party with Elton and everybody and Kevin was treated like royalty when he walked into the bar with Elton's mum on his arm.'

When you go on the road with someone, especially if you can stand doing it with them more than once, there's a good chance you'll end up mates for life. Of all the touring artists Cactus has been involved with over the years, she counts Kev as one of the best mates she has ever made in the business. Says Cactus, 'When you literally live with somebody for two years on the road then you just become extraordinary friends, and there was nothing any more than friendship in our relationship, he was just an amazing friend. We would go to museums and the art gallery and all these fantastic things while we were on tour. He was never one to sit in his hotel room and watch TV. We were always busy. It was just fun, it really was. He's an extraordinary mate to have. We've been friends for over twenty years and we'll always be good friends.'

Australia's most prominent radio presenter and talkback host, John Laws, was also a closeted Kevin Bloody Wilson fan—that is, until Kev awarded him a guernsey in the only Kev song ever to be given radio airplay. Kev explains, 'We always listened to Lawsy in the car when we were touring Australia 'cos you could hear his program all over the country, fuckin' everywhere. I remember writing the song. It was written on a Thursday night, and with the help of Travis doing all the technical shit and playing all the instruments, we recorded and mixed it on the Friday and had a CD copy of it sitting on Lawsy's desk first thing the following Monday.'

Hello John

Hello John? ... Hello Lawsy?
Hello John, is that you?
Mate you've no idea how hard it is
Tryin' to get through.
Am I on the air? Fuckin' hell!
Oops, sorry John ... didn't know
I'll try not to say fuck again, all right?
Hello? ... Hello?

Hello John?

Hello John? ... Hello Lawsy?
G'day John, is that you?
Mate I'm calling from a payphone

'N look I didn't mean to be rude before
An I'm sorry I said 'fuck', all right?
Made a prick of meself I know
So I rang to say fuckin' sorry, mate.
Hello? ... Hello?

Hello John ... Lawsy!
Fuckin' hell, what're they doin?
Fuckin' phone keeps cuttin' out
When I'm tryin' to talk to you
'N I'm runnin' out of fuckin' change
'N just wanna say hello
'N some cunt keeps on cuttin' me off
Aw fuck! ... Hello! ... Hello!

Hello John? ... Fuckin' hell, mate
Cunts cut me off again
'N just wanna have a fuckin' chat
'N put my two bobs worth in
'N them cunts keep fuckin' cuttin' me off
While I'm talkin' on the phone
Useless fuckin' poofta bastards
Ohhhh fuck! ... Hello!

Hello Lawsy ... Lawsy fuck ya
Oh fuck, I give up
You can stick ya fuckin' radio show
'N who gives a fuck
Ya pompous prick
'N fuck ya radio show
Hello? ... Hello?
Lawsy ...

Maaaaaaate!
Lawsy? … John … John? … Lawsy
Pick up the fuckin' phone
Get one of them handmaidens to pick up the fuckin'
*   phone*
For Christ's sake then, give us fuckin' Derryn Hinch's
*   number*
DERRYN … I wanna fuckin' talk to Derryn Hinch
I've gone right off you, ya cunt
Give us fuckin' Hinchie's number
You don't wanna fuckin' talk to me
Fuckin' Hinchie needs a mate at the moment.

John Laws played the song three times on his program that Monday morning, and wrote to Kev to tell him 'Hello John' was the funniest song he'd ever heard in his entire radio career.

Kev is also a friend of Australia's country music community. He's been known to show up in Tamworth during the January Country Music Festival, which Kev calls 'schoolies week for hillbillies', to enjoy other people's shows and to play a few packed-out gigs of his own. Kev is, in his own quiet way, part of the fabric of the Australian country music scene. Kev likes this association, and I put it to Travis that his father might have a secret desire to be taken much more seriously as a songwriter.

'Mate, you are so on the money there. Dad's got all the accolades for being a comedian, and certainly he is probably one of the funniest comedians this country has ever seen, but being a songwriter and a musician has always been important to him.'

On one of his recent UK tours, when Jenny Talia was a little too pregnant to be his support act, Kev invited velvet-voiced Aussie country star Adam Harvey along. Kev and Adam have been mates since even before Adam first recorded. Kev says, 'I'd never met a young bloke with such a unique voice coupled with a passion and expansive knowledge on country music. Adam and I share that keen sense of country music history, and we also have a mutual love of Guinness.

'That was a great tour. The crowds absolutely loved Adam, and on one of our nights off in Killarney in Ireland we got on the piss together and cowrote a song called "Genie in the Bottle".'

The song, with its memorable chorus—'The genie in the bottom of a Jim Beam bottle made me do what I didn't wanna do'—was a number one hit on the Australian country music charts for seven weeks. Travis cites this as an example of his dad broadening his musical horizons as he approaches the latter stages of his touring career.

'He's starting to really get there as a songwriter now. He's also had songs on Slim Dusty's albums, but you have to wonder if he could go out and be a serious songwriter. I don't think anyone in Australia would be able to take him very seriously if he tried to record that stuff himself, because everyone already knows him as Kev.'

So does this make Kev a prisoner of his own success? Has his ability to write funny words killed off his chances of ever being considered a serious songwriter? Not according to Travis.

'There are other ways of doing it, especially in the songwriting vein. He's a great songwriter, a great storyteller, and he's proved that he can be a credible songwriter for other people. I think he's only just tapping into that now and he's probably going to go a long way with that too.'

Kev and Billy Connolly have remained friends since they first met each other in Perth in the late eighties. Whenever the two of them find themselves in the same town they usually catch up. Says Kev, 'He's a lovely bloke. Not what you'd expect. He's a non-drinking, non-smoking (except for the occasional cigar) vegetarian who spends most of his time in the kitchen. He loves it. He's not the drunken loudmouth Scottish Yid people might perceive him to be.

'I went to dinner with Billy once and with him being so instantly recognisable he was getting people coming up to him at our table the whole night. He said to me, "You're so lucky, Kev. You've got all this success and you can still walk down the street and not be bothered. I can't do that because of the television and the movies." He told me he thought I've got the perfect balance, and he's bloody well right. You imagine what would happen if Billy walked in here now.'

Kev and I were sitting in a Sizzlers restaurant in Perth's northern suburbs when we had that particular conversation, and I could imagine just how nuts the place would have gone if Billy Connolly had walked in and ambled up to the salad bar. But that's not to say Kev wasn't getting his fair share of attention from among the Sizzler patrons. I could tell that the middle-aged ladies two tables over had recognised Kev but they didn't approach our table, opting instead to talk behind their hands and point whenever they thought Kev wasn't looking in their direction. On his way to the toilet Kev must have noticed them out of the corner of his eye, because on his way back he went out of his way to stop at their table and initiate a chat with them. He says, 'I always love saying g'day to people, whether they know me or not. I just really love talking to people.'

I mention to Kev that I reckon anyone who wants to be famous for the sake of being famous needs to hear that Billy Connolly story in order to understand just how uncomfortable being famous can be.

Kev nods. 'TJ said something similar as well. "I don't want to be famous, I just want to be good at what I do." Unfortunately she's in an industry where if you are good at what you do you also end up with a high profile.

'As a toddler, TJ once said, "Dad, when I grow up I'm gonna be a singer, I'm gonna call myself TJ Dennis, and I'm gonna buy you a helicopter." Two out of three ain't bad, but I'm still waiting for the fuckin' helicopter.'

Another good mate of Kev's who also proudly calls himself a fan is multimedia personality and marriage celebrant Greg Evans. Says Greg, 'I like his song "GMH You Cunts". I mean, he's tapped into everybody that has ever had a promise from a car salesman that hasn't come through. The lyrics are so hilarious and so close to home. But the thing is, he's such a lovely bloke, that's what appeals to me also, to think that this wonderful entertainer and world-class performer can be such a beautiful person, and he really is a very gentle soul.

'Kev will walk into my home while he's in Melbourne doing concerts and the first thing he goes for is the family photos. He always asks after my kids. "How's Jodi, what's she doing? How's Jason, still enjoying being a country vet? How's he going?" He goes through all the family photos and takes a great interest, genuinely, in what my family are all doing. He's one of the most genuine, loyal blokes I've ever met in my life, but what appeals to me about Kev from a musical point of view is that you can always put his songs on and hear them over and over again and laugh and laugh and laugh.'

As you'll have noticed throughout this book, once Kev gets to know you chances are you will be given a nickname. Wayne Pride has been mates with Kev for almost half a century and knows him as well as anyone, but he still has no idea why Kev calls him Jock.

'Nobody else in the world but him calls me Jock. I'm not Scottish—I'm a fifth-generation Australian—but he calls me Jock. If he sends me a new CD he signs it, *To Jock*. I've never asked him. I haven't got a clue why I'm Jock, but as far as I'm concerned, I'm Jock. You ask him.'

I took Wayne's advice and asked Kev why he calls Wayne Jock, and furthermore, does he have a nickname for me that I should know about?

'I dunno why I call him Jock. No fuckin' idea. Everybody around me gets a nickname. You've always been "Gavvy Love". Whenever I'm talking about you to Betty and the kids it's always Gavvy Love. I hope you don't mind—not that I give a fuck. DILLIGAF.'

Wayne Pride is fine with Kev calling him by his assumed name, but he sometimes finds it difficult to know how to return the favour.

'I know him as Bryan, though in company I call him Kev, but I find it very hard to call him Kev because he's my mate. Kevin Bloody Wilson exists, but all I know is this kid called Bryan who was on stage in 1964. I've known him for nearly fifty years, and we've never had a cross word in our lives, ever. He's just my mate.'

Kev is into his sixties now and he has recalibrated his life considerably, but more than a few people I spoke to for this book have seen Kev go off his nana once or twice. I'm pleased to say that I am yet to see Kev in full flight, but our friendship has had its ups and downs.

This book had already been through several different authors before I had a crack at it. One guy walked away from it because the stress of writing a biography got the better of him, and I believe Kev's longtime mate Bruce Tuffin had a heart attack after drafting a few chapters. Then it somehow landed in my lap, and after a few months of research and planning I eventually realised how much work I had in front of me, and I freaked right out. After sitting at my computer and sweating for a while I went to Kev and told him that I really didn't have a clue how to write his book, and that he should give the job to a more experienced writer. I felt like I'd totally let him down, but as it turns out Kev could not have been cooler about it. I still remember what he said: 'No fuckin' worries, Gav. Thanks for being honest with me, mate.'

Over the next couple of years Kev continued to make albums and tour, and I had my job on the radio and did a writing course in my spare time. Kev knew I was doing the course and patiently waited until I had completed it before he approached me again. 'So, do you wanna have another crack at this fuckin' book or what?'

So began the process of writing the bulk of this book. I still had no idea what I was doing, but I just used some of Kev's own advice and jumped in and had a go anyway. For the next three years I worked part-time on telling Kev's amazing life story—and then we had a bust-up.

I'm not going to get into the specifics of what that dispute was about, but suffice it to say I walked away from the project at the end of 2008 and suggested to Kev that he should finish his own fucking book, or words to that effect.

A day or so later, an email arrived in my inbox from a Dennis Bryant. The subject heading was 'Please Read'. And right there, in huge letters at the top of Kev's email, were six words that go a long way to explaining what sort of bloke Kevin Bloody Wilson truly is.

'I FUCKED UP AND I'M SORRY.'

For the record, Kev did not 'fuck up'. The whole thing was just a simple misunderstanding, really. But how could I not be impressed by his willingness not only to apologise, but to do whatever he could to make things better? I could tell that this was a man who really did GAF. Straight away I emailed Kev back, accepted his apology without reservation, and explained that I still thought he was totally capable of finishing the book himself.

Another year went by before we sat down for lunch at Hillary's Boat Harbour in Perth and he asked me, yet again, if I wanted to finish writing this book with him. So, for the third and final time, I got back to work on telling Kev's story. Kev told me that the reason he wanted me to write the rest of his book was because he still thought I was the best guy for the job, but I think it runs a little deeper than that. Kevin Bloody Wilson is a fiercely loyal man, and once he's on your side he stays there forever no matter what.

From my point of view, Kevin Bloody Wilson is a one-of-a-kind world-class entertainer, a greatly underrated poet, a naturally funny bugger, and a loving family man. But above and beyond all of that, Kev is a good mate to have. Kev's brother Terry agrees. 'He's a very giving person. He does a lot of stuff for people who are down on their luck that you never hear about. He's funny, he's talented, and he could have turned that talent in any direction, but comedy is what he decided on and he's good at it. But he's not just a brother; he's a mate.'

When I asked him who is his best mate in the world, Kev didn't hesitate for a moment. 'Betty is my best mate, without a doubt. Jesus Gav, you ought to know that, you've tasted her cookin'. You allow your mates, and hopefully they'll allow you, a ten per cent faultline, but in Betty's case, she's allowed me a fifty per cent faultline.

'We just have so much in common and the older you get the more you have in common, 'cos you have this shared history of everything, and daily that shared history keeps getting bigger and better. We've been through it all together. The good, the bad and the total fuckin' desperation you feel when you can't change the situation. But with time and a positive attitude you can swing things around. Betty and I are living proof of that. We both realise how lucky we are to have salvaged our marriage and to have made it this far together. Yeah, we're real good mates ... fuckin' *real* good mates.'

Kev's professional life, like his home life, is also perched comfortably on the winner's podium. He has become a fair-dinkum Australian icon. Without traditional media support, all of Kevin Bloody Wilson's albums and DVDs have achieved gold sales status worldwide, with many reaching platinum, and one, *Kev's Back,* awarded an amazing quadruple platinum. He's been listed in *Who's Who,* his entire body of work has been preserved for future generations with the National Film and Sound Archive in Canberra, and he is now one of the most sought-after speakers and motivators for sporting and corporate Australia. His unique story is as remarkable as it is inspirational, as funny as it is sensitive, and as positive as it is motivational.

Retirement doesn't seem to be on Kev's radar at all at this stage ('I retired twenty-five years ago'), with commitments to touring, writing, recording, and even a voiceover for a feature-length animated movie called *Little Johnny: The Movie* which is currently in production. Kev plays himself. But, as he says, 'If the wheels fell off all of this tomorrow, I'd be happy to go back to where it all started, just fuckin' around with my mates at barbecues and piss-ups in Kalgoorlie.'

Kevin Bloody Wilson is a guy who spends a significant amount of his time with his tongue firmly wedged in his cheek, but not when he says this: 'I finally get it, and I'm livin' it now. Family is first, second and third, and everything else that comes in the wake of that has just been a fuckin' bonus.'

It seems ironic that twenty-five years ago, Kevin Bloody Wilson was being arrested for performing his songs in public, yet on 26 January 2010 he was officially nominated for Australian of the Year for doing exactly the same thing. No, he didn't win the coveted gong, but in the words of a much-loved Australian comedy legend, 'DILLIGAF.'

Kev's discography

All of Kevin Bloody Wilson's recordings and DVD's are available on www.kevinbloodywilson.com and iTunes

ALBUMS

Your average Australian Yobbo (1985)
Sunday morning
I gave up wanking
Cum chin mi gurflen
Arr fuck (The instrumental)
Country bumpkin
That fuckin' cats back
Stack the fridge
Ailments of the eighties
Wow, did I get whacked!
The festival of life

Kev's Back (1985)
The last lager waltz
That's what he really said
Kev's courtin' song
Breathe through my ears
Mick the master farter
Living next door to Alan
The pubic hair song
It was over (Kev's lament)
Dick'taphone
Hey Santa Claus

Born Again Piss Tank (1987)
Born again piss tank
Kev's love song (Dinkum 'bout ya darlin')
Supa mega fugly
Manuel the bandito
I knew the bride (When she used to be a moll)
Fair & just
Anytime at all
The kid (He swears a little bit)
Dick on her mind
Rootin' in the back of the ute

My Australian Roots (1989)
You oughta see me (When I'm pissed)
Double decker dog
The great Roberto
Me dicks on the dole
The featherbrain championship
The first six rows
Ollie & Olga
You can never find one
'Flowers'
The builder
Amazing grass

Let's Call Him... Kev! (1991)
Me dick (Just dialed your number)
Festival of farts
Big fat bum
The potato song
The perfect ten

Bali belly song
Jack can't get up
This ones for you
Rockin' & rootin'

(The ode to) Huey & Billy

Let Loose Live in London (1993)
I gave up wanking
Kalgoorlie
Bungee jumping
Happy tobacco
Electricty
Swearing
The builder
Guitars/nigel
Bali belly song
Nashville
Tears n' snot
Don't touch your sister
Hospitals
Poofters
The kid (he swears abit)
Mick the master farter
Leprosy
Religion
The festival of life

CD 2
My Grandfathers cock
American humour
Politicians
Manuel the bandito

Living next door to Alan
That fuckin' cats back
'Hey, Cheryl'
Kev's courtin' song
Diesel dykes
Dick'taphone
Hey, Santa Claus

Kev's Kristmas (1996)
Hey Santa Claus
Kristmas without snow
He only comes once a year
Ho ho fucking ho
Santa's fuckin' roadies
Kristmas on the piss
Tatoo of Santa
Roo dog
Santa was stoned
Grandad's finger
Amazing grass
What about poor old Santa Claus

The Worst of Kevin Bloody Wilson (1997)
The last lager waltz
The pubic hair song
Living next door to Alan
Festival of life
It was over (Kev's lament)
Hey Santa Claus
Kev's courtin' song
Born again piss tank
That fuckin' cats back

Dick'taphone
Bali belly song

Kalgoorlie Love Songs (1998)
She's the sorta sheila
Do ya fuck on first dates? (Kev's courtin' song)
Darlin', I'm so horny
She's a good'n
Grandad's got a bone
Sheila, you were there
It was over (Kev's lament)
Hello John (The John Laws song)
Take it like a man
Five-second foreplay
Caring understanding nineties type
Fuck ya gut's out

The Second Kumin of Kev (2001)
The local
Kev's wedding waltz
The apprentice
Ol' langs iron
Chucka brown-eye for Australia
More tea vicar
Pussy tricks
Don't touch your sister (A Tasmanian love song)
Don't be a bunny
Nigel krap
Out of bounds

Let Loose Live in the Outback (2002)
She's the sorta sheila

P.C. free zone
The local
Outback education
Banjo country
She's a good'n
Grandad's got a bone
The apprentice
Fuckin' ferals
Take it like a man
DILLIGAF
Pussy tricks
Nigel fuckin' legend: decompositions
Missing you
Kev's courtin' song
You can't say cunt in Canada
Australian anthems
The browneye medley
My Grandfathers cock (live in London)
Absolute cunt of a day (live in Nashville)

20 Years of Kev Double CD (2004)
I gave up wanking
Festival of life
Kev's courtin' song
Mick the master farter
The pubic hair song
Hey Santa Claus
Dick'taphone
It was over
Manuel the bandito
The kid (he swears a bit)
Supa mega fugly

Double decker dog
The featherbrain championship
Ollie and olga
The builder
Me dick (just dialed your number)
She's the sorta sheila
Hello John (beeped version)
Grandad's got a bone
The local

Bonus Live CD
Bali belly song
That fuckin' cats back
She's a good'n
Nigel talkabout
DILLIGAF
Can't say cunt in Canada
Absolute cunt of a day
New Christmas song
The browneye medley
Living next door to Alan—complete with Talkabout
Bonus track—Root'n in the back of the ute—tribute by Dave
Gleeson and the Stilsons

DILLIGAF (2006)
DILLIGAF
His cocks got ribs
Missin' the missus
The truckie's kid
The house of the rising flood (live)
Nothing funnier than a fart
The Shane Warne song

Missing you
Hey GM
Nigel, fuckin' legend
Disgraceland

Excess All Areas (2010)
Nigel and Wilma
Old home videos
Bring back the biff
Butter face
You can't call me Kev anymore
Nana never farted
The cougar song
Common cense
Me beer's cut off
Readin' me my wrongs

DVDS AND VIDEOS

Let Loose Live in Ireland DVD (2003)
Let Loose Live In Ireland was recorded at the Vicar St Theatre in Dublin at the completion of a sixty date tour over nearly four months throughout the UK, Wales, Scotland, Canada and Ireland. This performance sees Kev take his unique brand of Australiana to the world, performing sell-out concerts as part of the DILLIGAF World Tour. It features a catalogue of self-penned bawdy ballads that translate to every English-speaking country in the world. In addition to the performance, we see another side of Kev and the hectic and comical aspects of touring the world, with performances in such places as Nash-ville and Bali, where his legion of fans converge for a party

like no other. Also included are bonus film clips from Kev, as well as a special on stage performance from Kev's support act on the tour, Jenny Talia from Australia. After twenty years at the top, Kev has deservedly achieved Legendary status—there is no stopping this true Aussie Icon, who continues to delight fans from all corners of the globe!

Kevin Bloody WIlson 3 DVD Box Set (2006)
Three of your old favourites previously unreleased on DVD, this box set is over five hours of sidesplitting entertainment! The three DVDs cover the past two decades of live performances with Kev *Live and Uncensored* and *Let Loose Live In London* being recorded live in the hallowed halls of London's Her Majesty's Theatre. In *Kalgoorlie Live* Kevin returns to his home town for a history making concert that shunts 'Kev Kultcha' directly into the orbit of the new millennium.
DVD 1—*Live And Uncensored*
DVD 2—*Let Loose Live In London*
DVD 3 —*Kalgoorlie Live Songs*

Let Loose Live in London (DVD box set and video)
I gave up wanking
Kalgoorlie
Bungee jumping
Happy tobacco
Electricity
Swearing
The builder
Guitars/Nigel
Bali belly song
Americans
Politicians

Don't touch your sister
Hospitals
Poofters
The kid (He swears a bit)
Mick the master farter
Leprosy
Religion
The festival of life
My grandfathers cock
Kev's courtin' song

ENCORE
Dick'taphone (The telecom song)
Hey Santa Claus

Kalgoorlie Live Songs (DVD box set and video)
She's the sorta sheila
Grandads got a bone
Darlin' I'm so horny
Living next door to Alan
She's a good'n (The goatfucker song)
Chucka browneye for Australia
Santa was stoned
Ho ho fucking ho
Take it like a man
Fuck ya guts out
Roo dog
Hey Santa claus
5 second foreplay
Do ya fuck on first dates (Kev's courtin' song)
Hello John (The John Laws song)

Live And Uncensored (DVD box set)
The last lager waltz
It was over
Supermegafugly
Ollie & Olga
Livin' next door to Alan
Dick'taphone
Stack the fridge
Kev's courtin' song
Manuel the bandito
That fuckin' cat's back
Hey Santa Claus

Karaoke Kev DVD (2007)
Hey Santa Claus
It was over
I gave up wanking
Stack the fridge
The Shane Warne song
Manuel the bandito
Take it like a man
Missing you
DILLIGAF
Kev's courtin' song

Let Loose Live Back Home DVD (2007)
(Filmed at the Burswood Casino Perth, Western Australia, in
December 2006)
It'll be right on the night
DILLIGAF
It was over
The Shane Warne song

His cocks got ribs
Stack the fridge
The boodjyu dance
Nothings funnier than a fart
Missing you
Parody pisstake
Nigel fucking legend
The house of the rising flood
Observations of England
Hollywood
Sheila, you were there
Kristmas kompliation
Dicktaphone

Kev urges you to support the Make-A-Wish Foundation in your community.

Jenny Talia's discography

All of Jenny Talia's recordings are available on www.jenny-talia.com and itunes

Jenny Talia from Australia (2003)
Pamela Lee
The bastard song
Things in hidden spaces
(I don't do) Déjà Vu
It was over
The blonde song
These boobs
Trashville wankers
Take it like a man
How can I be under you

Tunnel Vision (2004)
Nice girls
Grocery shopping blues
Says-a-me Steve
Chocolates better than sex
Jenny's courtin' song
Hey lady
Fuckwit
Oh Donald
Christmas list
10 things
Tunnel vision dance track

Without Adult Supervision (2007)
Cameltoe
Hey Mum
David Beckham
Supa-face 2000
No more bush
Wax song (wax off)
Horses hoof
Fuck for a living
Boys think with their dicks
Shitty day
They beat me

The Blonde Leading the Blonde (2009)
Dumb, dumb, dumb
Fuck it
Not going to give you...
Hillbilly love machine
Facebook
Sarah Palin
New Christmas song
Billy the kids
I want a new set of tits for Christmas
Silent night
The bastard song (recorded Live in Auckland, New Zealand)